"Carlos Warter is a first-rate storyteller. *Recovery of the Sacred* is a compelling personal adventure and an accelerated course in the Perennial Philosophy, with a celebrated cast of characters."

Marilyn Ferguson
publisher of Mind/Body *and author of* The Aquarian Conspiracy

"Now that all us baby boomers are opening up at mid-life to our own spirituality, it's great to have travelogues—like this one by Dr. Carlos Warter—to help us understand where we have been, and where we are going. I have enjoyed reading this account of his own inner explorations."

Dr. Raymond Moody
author of Life After Life
and Reunions: Visionary Encounters with Departed Loved Ones

"I have known Dr. Carlos Warter for many years, as a deeply spiritual person, physician and healer. His presentations for our organization have been dynamic, inspiring and charged with the energy of soul awareness. The stories from Warter's life take people beyond their ordinary state of awareness to a realm where they can establish contact with their very essence."

Willis W Harman
President
Institute of Noetic Sciences

"*Recovery of the Sacred* is a poignant and charming account of one man's journey along the road of self-discovery and fulfillment. My hope is that the very young of all ages may find in Carlos Warter's story the nudge that is needed to heed the inner voice that quietly points the way to satisfaction with life's journey."

Edgar D. Mitchell, Sc.D.
astronaut and founder
Institute of Noetic Sciences

"In this remarkable book, Dr. Warter not only describes the spiritual hunger of modern times, but describes how he sought for and obtained the nurturance he needed to fill this void in his life. Drawing upon his own experiences, Dr. Warter describes the role played by meditation, mental imagery, spiritual teachers, and journeys to sacred sites in his own quest for understanding."

Stanley Krippner, Ph.D.
co-author of Personal Mythology *and* Spritual Dimensions of Healing

RECOVERY OF THE SACRED

Lessons in Soul Awareness

Carlos Warter, M.D., Ph.D.

Health Communications, Inc.
Deerfield Beach, Florida

Library of Congress Cataloging-in-Publication Data

Warter, Carlos
        Recovery of the sacred: lessons in soul awareness/Carlos
Warter.
            p. cm.
        ISBN 1-55874-313-8 (pbk.): $9.95
        1. Shamanism. 2. Warter, Carlos. 3. Shamans—Biography.
4. New Age movement. I Title.
BF1611. W35 1994
291.4'092—dc20
[B]

Publisher: Health Communications. Inc.
            3201 S.W. 15th Street
            Deerfield Beach, Florida 33442-8190
Cover Design by Andrea Perrine Brower

I dedicate this book with love to
David-Gabriel, Charles and Alexandra
whose presence in my life is a constant rekindling
of my reverence for life;
to my beloved wife Carolina whose existence has brought
harmony to my sense of mission;
to my parents and the parents of their parents
whose connection to a lineage has allowed me
to transcend its forms;
to all my teachers who have cleared
that which is superfluous and left untouched the essential;
and to all readers embarked on their own path
of spiritual autonomy at this most auspicious
time of planetary transformation.

Contents

Acknowledgments

Events happen as a confluence involving a time, a place and a people: these three rivers meet and become one. The happenings in this book, from my birth to the manifestation of my soul identity, are a result of this interaction.

My deep acknowledgment goes first to the Creator of Time and to Time itself: to that element which allowed me to explore the universe outside of ordinary chronological sequences. These occasions of temporal exploration, like perennial openings into a cosmic sabbath, have permitted me to learn about and master the dimension of time. From youth onward, I have been able to utilize doorways which open to travel and wisdom beyond the chronological barriers that so often enslave humankind.

I give thanks to the Cosmic Mother and to Gaia, the earth mother, for the blessing and inspiration of our planet and its cornucopia of beauty. I have visited many places that are filled with the presence of the sacred: my native Chile, with its glorious Andes Mountains and beaches caressed by the Pacific Ocean; the heights of Machu Picchu in Peru and Tiahuanaco in Bolivia; the entrances to the rain forest in Colombia and Venezuela; the rhythmical echoes of Brazil; the extensions of Argentina. From early on in my life, I received and gave fruits of soul awareness in all of these countries.

As I traveled away from my South American homeland, I experienced a host of locations fragrant with the spirit: the majesty of the

Atlas Mountains in Morocco; the strength of Gibraltar; the cathedrals anchoring vortexes of energy throughout Europe; the profoundness of Egypt and Israel; the depth of the different regions of Bharat, India; and the majestic nature of the United States contained in Yosemite, the Grand Canyon, Montauk, Mt. Shasta and Sedona. To all these places which are organs and members of Gaia, I give my acknowledgment and gratitude.

I also give my thanks to the people and other life-forms who have enabled me to feel connected and secure in this dimensional life. There are many people besides the ones who I expressly dedicate these pages to that have made valuable contributions to the manifestation of this book.

I began to find my teachers early in life, and I have spent a great many pages in this book describing their specific influences on me and my attainment of soul awareness. In this book of spiritual adventure, some of my teachers have been fictionalized; only a handful have maintained their real identity. Nevertheless, I hereby wish to acknowledge three groups of people: those Masters of the Past who blessed me with their influence, the team of participants that shaped the book and those who are my friends. They have all allowed my work to fulfill its intention as a story that serves the reader and contributes to greater enlightenment on our planet.

In the first category, there are many people I want to mention. Mr. Alejandro Tarrago, headmaster of the Kent School where I spent my teenage years, gave me full encouragement and empowered my self-esteem. Dr. Hernan Alessandri was my guide professor in medical school and a professor of Internal Medicine in Chile. He was a man who, being a son and a brother of heads of state, knew the whereabouts of policymaking. He was the dean of my medical school, introduced high-tech medicine in Chile and essentially created modern medicine in the country, but he never forgot the importance of the heart and the true element of soul in his teaching and profession. Helena Hoffman, M.D. is a courageous spiritual psychiatrist and disciple of C. G. Jung. Her esoteric influences and practical therapeutic teachings showed me, at an early stage, the importance of psycho-spiritual integration in professional work. These three taught me the importance of intuition, human love, compassion, respect and ethical responsibility. These qualities allowed me to embark on a journey that was balanced by ethics as a central pivot. They also helped me recognize that management, information, technology and knowledge only have meaning if there are ethical standards and a valuable final product that benefits the self and others. They were living examples of the true meaning of vocation of service.

During my basic sciences courses at university, Humberto Maturana opened my mind to realms of research which led to a non-conventional perception of human physiology.

It was the trust of Pablo Neruda which sent me on a literary adventure in my early years. His assistance gave me the means of expressing "scientia and conscientia"—what we would call a balance of the hemispheres today—in a literary or poetic form.

I had the honor of sitting in the presence of Alan Watts, R. Buckminster Fuller and Norman Cousins at different stages in my life. The three masters of profound compassion and love, creative thinking and wisdom opened my horizons to other dimensions of consciousness.

Others I have learned from and need to mention: Idries Shah, both through his writings and guiding presence; Claudio Naranjo M.D., through his innovative and exploratory charisma; Janet Lederman at Esalen Institute; Mrs. and Mr. Jim Simkin, my female and male shaman friends; Moshe Feldendrais; Lama Thartang Tulku Rimpoche; Prem Pal Singh Rawat; Rabbi Cook-ha Cohen. Still others entered my life after the period related in this book: Darshan Singh, the teachings of Mother Teresa, Tentzin Giatso HH The XIV Dalai Lama, Sai Baba, Mohammed Afzaluddin Nizami. There are also those contemporary saints and sages who validated the introduction of divine elements into the healing process, taking physicians beyond the Hippocratic Oath to the service of humankind with sympathy and a true feeling for the sacredness in life.

Carl Rogers, the late psychologist, Dr. Rodrigo Carazo, the former President of Costa Rica and founder of the United Nations University for Peace, and Luis Alberto Machado, the former Minister for the Development of Human Intelligence, have all been boosters to my own research and pursuits through their trust in Peace and Human Development, my foundation for world peace. Currently I am aided by Akio Matsumura, the Director of the Global Forum of Spiritual and Political Leaders for Human Survival, Willis Harman, President of The Institute of Noetic Sciences, and Louise Hay, author of *You Can Heal Your Life*, whose hopeful visions for humankind's future are more than inspiring.

My parents at their last stage in life before transcending this world and my beloved companion, wife and mother of my three gracious children deserve my gratitude and full acknowledgment. There are many others that include the thousands of women and men, patients and students who have taught me variations on the many ways to recover the sacred in our lives.

In the second group, those who have shaped this book, there is Leroy Foster and his wife Dianne, who captured a vision upon my descent from Mt. Shasta just a year ago and who introduced me to Gary Seidler, vice president at Health Communications. Gary's loving and professional support, coupled with that of president Peter Vegso, established a relationship of sacred brotherhood. Their empowerment; the astute vision of Barbara Nichols; the editorial attention and insight of Matthew Diener; and the supportive editing, rewriting and polishing of my ideas and principles by Mark Salzwedel, Christine Belleris and Erica Orloff have brought to the reader's hands this book which we intend to be a valuable contribution to the highest good of all concerned. I would also like to thank Kim Weiss for her insightful comments and her skill at getting the word out on this book.

The third group I wish to thank are my many friends. The world of friendship is the web in which our closer communal life flourishes and prospers. There have been many individuals with whom I have grown over the years. Here are some I wish to honor, asking for forgiveness from those whom my memory has not brought to the forefront. You all reside in my heart.

Among the many friends that have been my companions, confidants and compadres are: M. Morgheinstern; R. Kane; R. Biaze; R. Landman; R. Sann; J. Baier; E. Mandelbaum; T. Barros-Ortiz; G. Alcaino; J. Garcia-Huidobro; C. Yaluff; F. Klohn; E. Holz; A. Nevai;

J. and N. Sweet; R. and K. LaChance; H. Trayles; B. Blum; V. Tarasiuk; F. Dibella; O. Rigonat; M.L. Maggi; I. Hertzriken; D. Amon; J. and I. Dodero; C. Kaman; M and S. Lehyt; M.T. Baeza; C. Mugaburu; P. Orellana; P. Quiroz; E. Weber; E., C. and K. Rosemberg; A. Ancarola; R. Aron; H. Ali; M. Ali; M. Seligman; D. Curtis; N.L. Meyerhoff; L. Mosquera; I. Tipping; D. Aliaga; I. Krausz; C.L. Abalo; J. and E. Kasner; R. Szekely; P. Pusso; E. Ordonez; M. Moreno; G. Ebner; L. Baumel; I. Katz; E. Cohn; V. Shnitzer; R. Peters; C. Bennet; R. Rojas; M. Belochi; M. Ferez; K. Singh; M. Bolivar; S. Shapiro; J. Ortuzar; Hnas. Casteres; S. Subotnik; C. Moss; A. and M.C. Costabile; R. Davis; S. and S. Boorstein; A. and E. Jaimovich; C. Wilson; S. Krippner; T. Cole-Whitaker; H. Cass.

I ask of you, a reader who felt inspired by some conscious or super-conscious motive to pick up this book, to journey with me through this spiritual adventure and integrate for yourself the elements that are transferable to your own life, making this a work of personal and global value.

Carlos Warter, M.D., Ph.D.

Prologue

We live in a time of great spiritual hunger, but within each of us is the means of ending this famine. People around the world are beginning to sense the presence of a seed inside them. This seed has long been ignored by psychology, sociology and the medical profession. Without the guidance of these fields, men and women are forced to search for its proper care: how to water it, fertilize it and make sure it receives enough light. Some look to ancient wisdom, some to religious traditions, some to modern science. Regardless of the path individuals take, all want the same thing. Each wants his seed to mature into the fruit that will feed all of mankind: the fruit of the spirit, the soul.

In our present time, most human experience does not include the sacred and the secular in combination. We tend to separate the two, giving each a place to reside that is completely unconnected with the other. And as our world shrinks and speeds by at an ever-quickening pace, we seem to have moved all things having to do with the contemplative nature of the soul far away from us. We view altered states of consciousness, states in which we can perceive an existence beyond our own, as signs of illness or psychosis. We view ancient mystical traditions that talk of living a life of spiritual pursuits in combination with service to our fellow man as so much superstition. Doctors who promote spiritual psychology as a means of radical self-transformation, and the use of prayer as a means of healing the body, are viewed with suspicion or viewed as dangerous to their patients and themselves. This is a strange development from an historical perspective because in the past humankind has always joined the mind, body and spirit in harmony and mutual support.

But all of this is beginning to change. A new spiritual consciousness is entering the planet, one that connects all of us. We see this manifesting in many ways. Businesspeople are reevaluating what they want in life, and are finding that their families are more important than their careers. There is a movement in progress in this country that involves people acting with kindness towards others for no other reason than the connection that exists between all people. Bestseller lists are full of books on the human soul, angels, near-death experiences and the importance of virtues. We are realizing that all mankind came from the same traditions, and all our religions developed from these shared traditions. Current science is also a part of this change. The development of quantum theory in the past 25 years has led physicists to view the world and the universe as an organic whole, not a fragmented reality. It is the realization of these numerous connections that is bringing mankind forward into a time of spiritual awakening.

Even though the book you hold in your hands is my personal journey, it is intended to touch on bigger events: the big story that encompasses my little story. My hope is that you will connect with my intent in writing this book, that you will experience an awareness of your sacred self and use this awareness to proceed on your own journey. There is an emerging culture of peace on our planet, one that will forgive the errors of the past and allow each individual to live the life that was intended for him. I hope this book can be your guide to this future, a future world where we are all part of the loving family of man.

Perhaps you feel an unexplained longing in your heart. Maybe a voice inside you echoes with a quiet uneasiness or a deeper sense of desperation. Listen to that voice. In the still hours before dawn or in the darkness before you fall asleep, pay attention to your longing, uneasiness or desperation. You may be hearing a call to change. When I teach workshops around the world, that is the most frightening thing I tell people. Your life is going to change. And when it does you will probably never be able to return to your old ways, your old life. And it's possible your friends won't recognize you as the same person they used to know.

Sometimes people approach me after their hearts' longing has been whispering to them for a while; it could be weeks, months, years. They can no longer turn a deaf ear to the call. By that time, they have often figured out specifically where their lives need change.

"I need to be more self-assured," a successful businesswoman in her mid-thirties tells me. She projects independence and power to the rest of the world. However, she confides that, despite her stellar job performance and the constant reassurances from her coworkers that she's doing fine, she thinks her skills aren't as sharp as those of her colleagues. She feels she's just faking it, and nervously waits for the day she'll be "found out." Sometimes she's convinced her world would unravel if her husband wasn't so attentive and understanding.

"I need a closer, more intimate relationship," a man in his forties states. He gets along fine with each of his lovers until some point a few months or years into the relationship. Then, typically, the fighting starts or the distance grows between the two of them, and he realizes that his partner wasn't right for him somehow. He senses there is someone out there to share his life with who will complement his personality and love him without smothering him. Why hasn't he met her yet?

"I need a more fulfilling job," a woman in her mid-twenties says to me. Her current job provides her with money, praise, respect and even a sense of community. But the work no longer challenges her and, worse, she has started feeling that her job is not important or meaningful. She believes there's a job out there somewhere that will excite her and make her feel she's making a significant contribution to the world. Unfortunately, she has no idea what kind of work that would be.

Others feel they are merely surviving and want to live their lives actively. Some say they are surrounded with possessions that bring them no joy and are toying with the idea of giving up everything and starting over. Older people may be letting the aging process affect not just their bodies but also their inner vitality, and they want to reconnect with the young man or young woman they used to be.

My experiences have taught me that these various needs, goals and longings have a common solution. All people need to connect with a timeless, unchanging, essential part of themselves. Until they do, the call to change echoes in their minds. They need to feel that life is sacred, including every plant, rock, animal and other person in the world. They, and perhaps you, need to go through a process sometimes called individuation: they need to stop doing what everybody else is doing and become comfortable sticking out in a crowd.

Even if your differentness brings you fame, like some popular musician or radical reforming politician, you still risk being called strange or even crazy. We as a society rarely support the different individuals among us, even though that is exactly what each of us needs to become. People often hope that if they aren't too different, maybe they will just be labeled eccentric and their differentness will be tolerated.

So following your heart carries a cost. When you become an individual and go beyond or outside of what others expect of you, you may find few people understand you. You may not be able to plan your life as far in advance as you would like to. But you may start to think of the call of the heart as a grand adventure, and your life as a journey, not a destination.

And although the changes you undergo will bring wonderful new things into your life, you may have to let go of some cherished, familiar things that no longer serve you. You won't necessarily have to give up your job, but you might. You won't necessarily have to leave your marriage or other committed relationship, but you might. You won't necessarily have to relocate or change your religious affiliation, but you might.

These changes do not signify moving from a bad way of life to a good one. The lifestyle you feel stuck in at this point in time may be just what someone else needs and dreams about. Caring for your sacredness does not imply your sacredness is ill. It does not mean curing it or making it better. Instead, it signifies a shift in focus. You begin recognizing that you are the soul, and that this soul, when nourished, allows you to live a more harmonized life than you could ever achieve through your usual problem-solving methods.

In the two hundred years following the industrial revolution, men and women forgot the soul and the sacred, believing them theoretically or philosophically confined to old books, churches and temples. But we are now entering a time when the information in those sources is generally available to the masses, no longer restricted to the few scholars or holy men with access.

Occurring in the last fifty years, this change represents an acceleration in our time-space continuum. Our explorations of the natural world, especially in quantum physics, have come to the same universal enigmas once solely the domain of religion. Quantum physicists have demonstrated that some facts are created simply by faith and belief. If we expect a particle of light to act like a wave it does; if we expect a wave of light to act like a particle it does. If we expect it to act like a point it will accommodate this idea. How? The observer created the reality. In essence, observing the world necessarily changes our perceptions of it.

This new quantum era is ushering in a new awareness. Many are calling it a spiritualization of culture. The old comfort zones of the last century's lifestyles have been challenged, creating a new search for the meaning and purpose in our lives and bringing about a more honest, authentic and real way of living.

In each spiritual tradition I have studied, this era for humanity has been subtly announced. There are elements that show us we are in the midst of this shift: synchronicity and coincidences; the intensity of the general energy flow of life; fast turnover of ideas and feelings; national and international boundaries shifting at an accelerated rate; and a global economy that links the financial state of the world on an instantaneous level. You may even sense the world is on the brink of great change. The so-called information superhighway overflows with opportunity and excitement. We are now in the genesis of this era, yet we have not found all the means to comprehend it. The entire population of this arising culture, the entire population of our transforming world, has one vital task: recovering the essential sacredness of life.

During this time of change, we need to be cautious not to exclusively identify with one banner or another, but to comprehend that the longing for consciousness and the re-acknowledgment of the soul belongs to many different traditions. It is our birthright as conscious human beings.

Every individual has had, probably on more than one occasion, a deep awareness of his or her soul identity. There are as many paths to access this awareness, however, as there are individuals on the planet. Laughter, prayer, meditation, music, poetry, lovemaking, the birth of a child, the passing of a loved one, a victory in sports, a defeat or success on the battlefield, or any of the experiences we tend to call "crises" are doorways to some life-transforming experiences.

When these events occur, we embark in search of our individual truth. That search must not end in a new, superficial identity. Instead of grasping at the first established tradition that intrigues us or seems to meet most of our needs, we need to recognize and follow our own path completely. That recognition fully involves the heart.

Therefore, a spiritual adventure like the one in this book does not have formal guidelines. It is the undercurrent of the mystery of life that guides us and gives us the correct timing for our actions. Thus we need to learn patience, an important element in the larger context or "big story" of our existence. In the "small story"—that of our daily ego, frustrations, hopes, successes and failures—we are chasing after an elusive sense of permanence. We are subjected to anxieties and conditioned by time. And we never find the true meaning of our lives with this focus. Yet this side of life does serve as a spiritual exercise for entering into the "big story," wherein love, light, timelessness and wholeness is our destiny. Then we learn to live our daily life with greater harmony and peace.

I became a psychiatrist, but I felt that recognizing a patient's soul and focusing attention and energy there produced better results than drugs or other treatments. I studied the philosophies and healing techniques of many different traditions, including Sufism, shamanism, Buddhism, yoga, kabbalistic Judaism and a variety of psychological approaches. I traveled the world from my native Chile to the deserts of Morocco, to the ruins of Macchu Pichu in Peru and to teachers in Europe and North America. I have tried to include some of the more important teachings and techniques I learned along the way, so that you too may learn to connect with your soul and gain the meaning and purpose in life that is uniquely yours.

I offer my story in the hope that others also reach this new understanding. I don't want to crystallize this perception into a theory exemplifying a new way of intuitively living life. Instead of the current mode of separate thinking we need to shift to whole-system thinking, and instead of external authority we need to awaken the inner knowing, the inner wisdom and the inner authority that is the destiny of each and every one of us.

This book is about essence. Essence is what our human existence is really all about. We are the first people in human history to be able to manifest the essential self into action. I am calling people to recognize their essence: to become part of a renaissance in which the psyche is unlocked and the human soul is breached so that the internal and the external become one. I believe that this era is the renaissance of renaissances. Essence is not about self-improvement or personal development. Essence is not just a state of mind. It is our very depth manifesting as an image before the mind's eye. Essence is so real it transcends symbols or language. It is what's guiding us all the time. It is that inner voice we hear in the stillness. It is the love of life remembering its source.

The recovery of the sacred takes us from the state of yearning that is born of false identification with our third dimensional everyday living, to our rebirth when we reidentify with the landscape of our soul. In a very real way, I became a midwife of the soul for my patients, my acquaintances and, above all, for myself. The reintroduction of the soul in our life means planting our roots in heaven and seeing our third dimensional small story as mere circumstance.

Developmental psychology is melancholic because it stays far from divine possibilities. Recovery of the sacred is the expansion, in love, from our roots in heaven to our manifestation in life. With this approach, I see healing taking place in a different way, a way that allows both the possibilities of human evolution and the rights and obligations that our people and our societies must embrace in order to become a society of souls. These rights and obligations include debts to parents and ancestors of humanity, to the ancient explorers of spiritual traditions of wisdom, to the natural order and to various levels of divine agencies without which human existence would not be possible.

Listen to your heart. Heed the call to change. And prepare to look at the world as a newborn does, with wonder and excitement. My story contains coincidences and happenings some might term miracles. Perhaps. Or perhaps they are merely our birthright once we set our course for a soulful adventure.

The Healing Journey: Awakening to the Sacred

1

As an only child, I grew up in the company of adults with no one my own age to play with. But I was never bored because, like many children, I had a friend no one else could see. Adults sometimes call these friends imaginary, but most children will tell you their friend is very real, and I was no exception. I can see him clearly to this day, a tall, glowing being who lived in a corner of my room. My friend visited me frequently, playing with me and also imparting much wisdom to me. Most significant was the vision he shared with me in which I healed people through the laying on of hands. With the scene playing in my mind like a motion picture, he said, "Hold tight to this vision, Carlos, for this is your destiny."

So I determined early in life that I was put on Earth to serve humanity. With a child's ingenuousness I decided I would not be happy until the entire world was also happy. With time, of course, I realized the world was filled with much suffering and hardship, but I swore I would do my best to positively touch the lives of those around me.

When I read about and witnessed the miraculous work of the medical profession, I believed I had found my calling. I would become a healer. Yet I knew that the language of healing encompassed more than just the terminology and practice of medical technology. A sense of purpose, fulfillment and wholeness is found only through an awareness of the sacred. This awareness often stands dormant and forgotten. I sought a new language: an integration of spirituality, healing and theology. I was looking for a language that could reawaken our sense of the sacred and connect us with a deep, timeless energy.

My search began in high school in my native country, Chile. My favorite subjects were history and biology. History interested me because I had visions of the past, which I later realized were past lives; biology intrigued me because of my fascination with life and its processes. Despite my love of learning I sensed a deep chasm between so-called book learning and life experiences.

My country was in the midst of great social and political turmoil at this time, turmoil I could see on a personal level in the faces of my countrymen. What we learned in school was theoretical, and I felt as though we were being indoctrinated with no regard or application to the upheaval and suffering in the streets.

Despite my young years, questions about our purpose on this planet gnawed at me. I wrestled with philosophical explanations of life, death and suffering, and sought answers in the form of mystical explanations or experiences from my teachers. I found inspiration in the writing of the middle ages, most notably in the ideas of St. Francis of Assisi. Despite his privileged upbringing, St. Francis became a messenger of spiritual and social concern to all the world's people, rich and poor alike. I was convinced my native country was worth saving, worth trying to bring to life in my own space and time. The timeless directive inscribed on the oracle at Delphi, "Know thyself," implored me to continue looking for answers.

I began medical school in the sixties. Change was in the air. The Chilean government was now controlled by the Christian Democratic Party which had undertaken a large-scale land reform program. This was also a time when many scientific theories were being tested and questioned. The prevailing idea of the cosmos as an eternal machine running out of steam, heading towards a thermodynamic death, began to be superseded by evolutionary cosmology. Matter, once thought of as a mere thing, was now seen as more of a process. Energy and fields were considered the ultimate principles, more fundamental than matter. I sensed that science was slowly converging from many different disciplines toward a new view, one with unique and profound implications. And of course, I had an inkling that this new view was spiritual in nature. This notion was fueled by the fact that spiritual awareness groups were springing up all over Chile.

During the selection process for medical school in Chile, prospective students were interviewed to find out, among other things, their motives for becoming a doctor. When the question was posed to me, I told the examiner, "I would like to dedicate my life to serving all those in need."

"It sounds like you ought to become a priest then," the examiner replied.

While sitting in my first biology class in medical school a few months later, the professor was discussing the process of evolution from bacteria to plants to animals with ever-increasing complexity. "So where is it all leading?" I asked the professor. "What is the purpose of life?"

"Perhaps you ought to be studying philosophy," he replied, intending to get a laugh out of my fellow students at my expense.

My professor's attempt at a joke did not fall on deaf ears. I took his suggestion seriously and studied philosophy along with my required medical courses. I felt they would broaden my reach as a healer. I devoured the teachings of Martin Heidegger and other existential philosophers. Their concept of the here and now confirmed what I had thought all along: human beings are larger than their physical, biological existence.

The first step to acknowledge the sacred, in my eyes, was an examination of our relationship with animals. All religious traditions are grounded in an awareness of the sacred qualities of plants and animals. Christianity, for instance, associates the dove with the Holy Spirit and evokes images of the eagle carrying the Bible. Somewhere along the way, Western culture's recognition of this sacred relationship with animals fell by the wayside.

Animals were used in school to help us understand biological and physiological processes. Most often, the animals were dead. While the technical term in science for killing an animal is "sacrifice," I didn't feel that any sort of sacred ritual was performed. The animals were not treated with the compassion that should have been accorded living beings. In my eyes, a scientist was a kind of priest and the laboratory was a temple. The treatment of the animals left me somewhat bitter. In one class, for instance, twelve rats were sacrificed. Their livers were extracted, homogenized, blended and centrifuged. The procedure was cold, unfeeling and mechanical.

During my time in medical school I came to realize my calling to heal the whole person—the body, mind and spirit—would not be as easily fulfilled as I had expected: it would not be accomplished simply by becoming a doctor. Priests handled the spirit. Philosophers dealt with the mind. The medical profession, I was coming to know, specialized in the body. We were taught how to treat physical symptoms with technological cures. Any treatment or even speculation outside the physical-technological realm was a mark of unprofessional behavior.

This was not mere speculation on my part either. We were literally taught to ignore the emotional and spiritual well-being of the patient. In medical school my surgery class was introduced to a 27-year-old man with testicular cancer. His 23-year-old wife and his baby were there in the room visiting as our professor explained the man's scheduled surgery. Later, outside the classroom, our professor explained to us that the man was sure to die in a matter of weeks, but the surgical procedure was standard in such cases. I thought it crazy to put the man and his family through the trauma of surgery when it would not substantially increase his comfort or his chances for survival. "Wouldn't it be better to spend our time and resources helping this young man and his wife come to terms with his death?" I asked the surgery professor.

The professor turned to me and a silence came over my fellow classmates as he intoned, "You will never be a good surgeon if you start worrying about the patient's emotional state."

Yet it became clearer to me, as observed patients and how they were treated in the name of healing, that the connection between the physical, spiritual and mental spheres of life was substantial and not to be ignored. I saw patients recover more quickly or more fully when doctors simply explained how treatments worked. Giving patients the power to select from a variety of treatment options seemed to help as much as the treatments themselves. And though many of my fellow students scoffed or made jokes when passing rooms where the patient's bed was surrounded by friends and family members all bowing their heads in prayer, some of the more remarkable recoveries "coincidentally" happened in those rooms. The combined energy of people in prayer, I saw, was a great resource and complement to medical procedures and bore no costs or harmful side effects.

Physicians, accustomed only to working with hard, measurable data and enslaved by scientific cause and effect, were uncertain how to interpret findings that suggested, for instance, that a wife's love and support could reduce her husband's risk of developing heart disease. Most also dismissed cancer cures that appeared to have been passed down on faith.

There was a retired dean and professor of the medical school who visited my ward at the hospital for three of my years there. He caused a stir among some of my fellow students because he lied to his patients. He told a woman with cancer that everyone felt her recovery was very important and they were all praying for her (the doctor himself was an avowed atheist). He told a man with liver failure that he was going to be fine and would feel better soon. In too many of those cases I saw patients outlive their clinical prognoses because of the hope inspired by this man's "white lies."

In my final year of medical school, I was living in Santiago, Chile, with a young woman named Isabella. She was beautiful, with long dark hair that moved with a life of its own when she turned her head, and often fell in front of her beautiful blue eyes. She was tall and her slim, lithe figure was evidence of the many hours she spent at sports and dance. She was also conventional and somewhat shy, and I began to realize that we didn't have much in common. She was an administrative secretary and her life seemed to revolve around getting a high-paying job, making lots of money and accumulating expensive material possessions. I believe she appreciated me more for the potential income I could make as a doctor than for who I really was.

Isabella didn't seem to understand what I meant when I talked of spiritual matters. When I told her I had seen a patient die and wondered what happened to his soul, she told me I shouldn't worry about it. On more than one occasion we discussed breaking up, but we always patched up our disagreements and continued on together. I feared living with Isabella would inevitably lead me to a dull, shallow life based on materialism and what the two of us could acquire, rather than what we could contribute to our relationship or to others. In spite of my fears, I had taken no action to avoid this sort of life. I persisted down the easy route of keeping the status quo.

One day I drove down Avenida Providencia, one of the main thoroughfares in Santiago, with no particular destination in mind. I had been swimming with Isabella and, after dropping her off at our apartment, took off to "be by myself."

Stopped at a red light, I glanced at the blue Fiat next to my car. The beautiful, young blonde woman driving the car glanced over at me. It was a chance moment that would change the course of my life. When I looked into her sparkling green eyes I was immediately and irresistibly attracted to her. My heart, now pounding in my chest, felt as though it were opening and expanding. It was a strange and overwhelming sensation I had never really felt before. In an instant I wanted to follow this woman anywhere and do anything that she asked. I leaned over to open the window, desperate to talk to her, but she looked away. When I finally rolled the window down, I noticed the light had changed and realized she was driving away.

I tried to follow her, but she immediately pulled over and parked her car. While I was strongly attracted to her beauty, there was also a curiosity and familiarity I had never felt for anyone before. Since she hadn't held my gaze, though, I decided she probably wasn't interested in me. That assumption, along with my obligation to Isabella, made me drive past and on toward home.

I attempted to clear my mind of this confusing whirl of thoughts about the woman, but after driving only a few blocks, I circled back to where I saw her park. Though I had managed to eliminate many scattered thoughts and ideas from my mind, one would not go away: I still held the vision of this blonde woman as clearly as a single candle in a darkened room.

I tried to reason with myself. I thought: If I drive down that block again and neither she nor the car is there, I will forget about the whole incident.

As I turned the corner onto the street where the woman had parked, I saw her leaving a nearby building and approaching the car. She was a rather petite woman, but she carried herself with elegance in her stunning dress which I could tell was expensive. I slowed and stopped beside her as she opened her purse to look for her keys. I quickly rolled down the window and searched for a pen and some paper on the seat beside me.

"I realize this must seem very strange," I said. "You are not only the most beautiful woman I have ever seen, but I also feel somehow that we were destined to meet."

She smiled at the compliment and then peered into my car to get a better look at me. "What do you want from me?" she asked.

"I don't want you to think I'm accustomed to meeting women this way," I said.

She shot me a look of disdain. "Don't bother me," she said, turning to open her car door. "I'm married."

A car behind mine was honking for me to stop blocking traffic. "I don't care," I pleaded. "I need to know who you are. I beg you, please let me have your phone number and I will try to explain later."

Reluctantly, she told me her number and quickly got into her car. I drove off toward home and saw in my rearview mirror that she had turned around and headed in the opposite direction. At the next stoplight, I stared at the slip of paper on the seat beside me, checking to make sure I could read the phone number my trembling hand had written. In the excitement of the moment, I realized, I hadn't even asked for her name. I prayed the number she gave me was really hers.

As I have since recognized, strong emotions such as those I felt for this woman cannot easily be dismissed. These "chance" meetings always seem to have a purpose. Many times I have left my house feeling as if I needed to call a certain friend. Over the course of the day, I will run into another person with the same name as the person I meant to call, or someone who is about to go visit that person. A scrap of paper with that person's phone number on it will pop out of my jacket pocket two or three times. If I continue to ignore the synchronicities trying to get me to call this friend of mine, and especially if the call is extremely important to one or both of us, the synchronicities will start to get even more obvious. Perhaps my friend will accidentally call a wrong number that happens to be an office where I am having a meeting.

Though I did not know it at the time, my meeting with this woman happened for an important purpose. It was the result of a deep connection between the two of us and would lead me to a path that I still follow today.

Confusing, contradictory feelings of guilt at deceiving my girlfriend and electrifying passion for this woman assaulted my senses. Perspiration beaded on my forehead and the rhythm of my breathing grew short and purposeful. Logic told me I was driving the car, yet I couldn't feel the steering wheel and had to force myself to concentrate on the flow of traffic. The sound of the young woman's voice echoed over and over in my mind, drowning out the sounds of car engines and horns. I drove around town until I was sure my girlfriend had left our apartment. The minutes seemed excruciatingly long.

About an hour later, I was at home and on the phone with the young, blonde woman. Her name was Françoise. I told her about my upcoming internship and about Isabella. She told me about her marital problems and that she had come to Santiago from Europe for a vacation. She had a young child who was staying with relatives while she was away. We talked of politics, philosophy and religion. We discussed our childhoods. We talked about our dreams.

While conversing with her, I was most certainly in an unordinary state of mind. I started having visions of another place and time. I saw myself in a Paris salon in the early nineteenth century. The salon was part of an eighteenth century chateau and had marble floors and red burgundy walls. I could see the patterns in the material of my garments and could feel the weight of the many layers of clothing I wore. A wig was on my head and I could actually smell the heavy makeup on my face. I could feel the coldness of the marble table top. There was tea that smelled of Ceylon and sweet bread that tasted like Christmas cake. I could hear the music of Mozart being played by an orchestra. And Françoise was there with me.

I had experienced feelings and visions of past lives before. As a young child, I often sat in my room dreaming my way through worlds I later identified as pieces of past lives. The first time my mother entered my room and saw me sitting in my chair in a very unusual posture with my extended fingers touching my knees, she went to a shelf of books in the next room and pulled a large volume off one of the top shelves. She came back in and told me she had a picture to show me. As she leafed through the book, I saw pictures of deserts and pyramids. Finally, she came upon a photograph of a temple entrance in Egypt, and she turned the book to show me. My posture was just like that of the giant statues at Abu Simbel in southwest Egypt. I sensed I had been a king in this land at the time the temple had been built, but somehow I had never seen the completion of the temple because I had fled into exile. I started to wonder what part of me could possibly remain the same from an Egyptian king to a French courtier to a child in Chile.

Talking to Françoise, I conveyed my impression that we had met in a past life. She said she was also sensing we had met before. We talked on and on, laughing, sighing in recognition. We started feeling so strongly that we belonged together that we questioned the plans we had made for our lives up to that point.

We arranged to meet the following day and over the next week we spent more and more time together. Our bond strengthened as we became lovers.

Feelings long since buried came rushing to the surface, including one of my earliest memories: my first birthday celebration. I was sitting on a yellow, wooden high chair at a table surrounded by my parents, aunts and uncles. "Doesn't he have his daddy's eyes?" and "His smile looks like yours" and other comments about my little body circulated the table. The table was set with Bavarian plates and teacups that had very colorful designs on them. Plates filled with a variety of colorful foods—cheeses, breads and a large variety of fruit—lay neatly on a white table-cloth embroidered with what I later learned was my father's coat of arms. To my right, near the end of the table, a pair of deep blue, pene-trating eyes looked at me. They were my grandfather's eyes. Something about Grandpa's gaze awakened me to the realization that "I am not this body." I was locked in that moment of time. Staring at my grandfather, I realized that the discomfort I felt at the comments about my body was caused by my knowledge that there was something more essential and unique beneath my physical appearance. At that point the birthday party took on a wholly different perspective. We were celebrating the anniver-sary of my transformation from pure spirit to matter. Looking back, I consider Grandpa the first of many teachers to come into my life.

Now Françoise reminded me of that early lesson. When she looked into my eyes, I sensed she saw beyond my body's physical features into my soul. Her penetrating gaze connected to my very essence causing my breath to catch in my throat. No one since Grandpa had touched me so deeply. My heart blossomed, nourished daily by my love for Françoise and the positive perspective she provided me on each waking moment. Parks and restaurants and other places I had been to hundreds of times suddenly seemed completely different; they became luminous and welcoming and safe.

I felt joy as I had never felt it before. Often while sitting in a cafe with Françoise, talking about something totally inconsequential—the weather, a threatened transportation strike, the arrival at the hospital of a long-awaited carton of cotton swabs—I would suddenly feel an unrelated, tremendous sense of joy. This joie de vivre was so power-ful I wanted to project it into eternity.

I couldn't specifically pinpoint anything causing my sudden joy. The sun was strong, the music flowed in a pleasing rhythm and my soul was happy. I was myself. Without any attention to my actions, thoughts or emotions, I experienced utter satisfaction. And best of all, the feeling was occurring with increased frequency.

At this point I started writing the journals that became my first book, *The Ebb and Flow of Living*. In it, I wrote to Françoise and described our meeting, the joy that made me feel like my soul was streaming light into the dark vastness of outer space and our journey together to Chile's Central Valley.

When Françoise first invited me to spend the summer with her in the Valley, I was sitting at home in the late afternoon. Not long after I hung up the phone, Isabella returned home from her job in one of the banks in downtown Santiago.

I could no longer deceive her, yet I didn't want to hurt her feelings or her sense of self-esteem. I wanted to break the news of my affair as gently as possible.

"Isabella, I don't think our relationship is working out," I said.

Without breaking her stride as she hung up her coat and dropped off some groceries on the kitchen counter, she replied, "We've been over this before. We just need to give it time. I am waiting for my promotion at the bank, and you've got to finish your internship. Then we can think about moving to a bigger apartment and buying a nicer car."

"No, I don't want to continue our relationship. Someone invited me to a hacienda in the Valley for the summer, and I have decided to go."

She stopped moving about the apartment but remained standing. "Is there another woman? Is that what you're telling me?"

"Yes, and you know I've wanted to end our relationship for a long time and haven't felt strong enough to do it until now. I'm sorry. I don't mean to hurt you."

She crossed to where I was sitting and sat on the edge of a nearby chair. "Well, I intend to keep the apartment."

"You may keep the apartment," I said.

"And you are not going to take all of our furniture. I will not live in a barren house."

"You may keep the furniture," I said.

"And I expect to keep the car. I need it when I go to visit my mother in Concepción."

"You may keep the car."

This meaningless exchange, a recitation of the laundry list of our collected material possessions, made me realize how dead I had become inside. I was so mired in my day-to-day existence that I actually became an observer rather than a participant in my own life. Looking at it from a new perspective was shocking indeed. This relationship had no real intimacy, no sense of openness or unity. It was much more than a lack of communication that ended it; it was a lack of communion with another human being. I had sacrificed my values for convenience. Unconsciously, perhaps, I had used Isabella's companionship to help me get through the rigors of medical school. We were never right for each other. Long after I realized our relationship was wrong, I had stayed in it. I didn't have the courage or the energy to risk finding real love. The "coincidental" meeting with Françoise shook me from my coma and made me realize that there could be a soulmate for each of us, a kindred spirit one is linked with throughout eternity. I was not sure if Françoise was mine, but she made me aware of that possibility.

Françoise and I left the city in her blue Fiat the morning after my breakup with Isabella. Françoise's friends lived in the Valley's farmlands. With the burden of laying to rest my relationship with Isabella lifted, I felt an even greater sense of freedom. As Françoise and I drove south from the capital city, the air cleared both physically and spiritually. We left the past behind. I saw every new stretch of road and every town we passed through as magical and exciting. We traveled the Pan-American Highway with the snow-clad Andes looming on the right and the lower coastal range on the left. We drove between the mountains into a valley of rich farmland with melons, wheat, corn and especially grape vines growing everywhere. The valley was cooled in the summers by Pacific breezes, so it practically gushed with flowers and fruit trees.

We sometimes felt as if we were traveling through a Van Gogh painting. Farmers wearing blue jackets and straw hats worked the soil, planting, hoeing and plowing behind teams of oxen. In the towns, fruit and vegetable stands vied for space with horses pulling carts and shoppers with their dogs, chickens and cows. A city boy my whole life, the scenery captivated me.

My mind and heart opened to each new feeling and experience. I stopped analyzing my feelings and thoughts, and instead allowed life to flow through me. I felt one with both heaven and earth. I stopped trying to solve the puzzle of the heart and instead worked to frame the exquisiteness of God's masterpiece through poetry and writing. I wrote *The Ebb and Flow of Living* in rich prose.

Deep in the Central Valley, we turned east onto an unpaved road. Only after we turned did I notice a small sign pointing the way. Dairy cows grazing in pastures looked up, startled at the sound of our car's motor. As we climbed a small grassy hill, the hacienda came into view.

The property, a thousand acres of farmland and another eight thousand acres of Andean foothills, had remained intact for hundreds of years. Colonial buildings made of white adobe—with wide verandas and ceramic-tile roofs—were settled between bright-colored gardens. This place was the setting for the awakening of a love that seemed to transcend time and place. As we pulled up to the main building, two peacocks strutted by screaming. We laughed at our unique welcoming committee.

Over the next two months, the two of us traveled from the farmland to the ocean and back. When we looked into the eyes of the peasants we met, we felt like we were glimpsing scenes of paradise. The spiritual wealth they held—uncomplicated lifestyles; their sense of connection with God, the land and each other—defied their lack of material possessions. It seemed the soul of the countryside evoked the soul in each of us. I was transformed and realized the love I felt was not just directed at Françoise. I was in a state of love with the universe.

This natural environment, and the simple lives of the people and animals there, conveyed a sense of timelessness. The cycles of nature—birth, aging, death and new birth—were more apparent in such a setting. Being in nature was yet another way to enter the timeless state in which I could connect with the soul and perceive the sacred. I realized the essential soul in each of us manifests itself in time through our interests, our qualities and our feelings. The lessons we learn at each step build upon what we already know as we grow and gain wisdom. The essential self that is one with every other living thing is unchanging; throughout our lives, however, our realization of it does changes. I was fortunate and determined enough to embark on a quest for the sacred in life and, consequently, my soul awareness grew stronger.

Many times Françoise described the joy she was feeling as a sense of freedom. She would often run ahead of me and then wait for me to catch up. One day—as we walked along the crest of a hill carrying our picnic lunch of champagne, fruit and chocolate rum balls—she suddenly took off down the hillside through the tall grass. When I finally caught up with her minutes later, she was sitting cross-legged beneath a small tree by a stream. We were both breathless. I finally caught my breath and asked her if this was where she wanted to eat our lunch, but she ignored my question.

"I don't care if I die homeless, poor and alone," she announced. "I would feel my life was wasted if I spent years in the same place. I could never buy land and feel tied to it. To me, freedom is much more important." She leaped up and started climbing the small tree.

"Everything relates to freedom," she called to me, "because it's a natural, central state. It has no form. It's the place where all things and events exist."

I set down our picnic lunch. "I think I wouldn't mind getting a home somewhere. I would like to be able to afford a place with a nice view and antique furniture and . . ."

"You need to reorient your mind," she interrupted. "You're too focused on things. Things tie you down, box you in. And you need to stop thinking. Try to just be. Just be here in the now."

The word "now" triggered a memory from my childhood. I had developed a sort of meditation one afternoon. I was on my bed, which was covered with a yellow blanket, doing my homework, when I looked up at the little baroque-style clock on my desk to see how long it would be before dinner. It was three o'clock. So I said to myself, "Now it is three o'clock." I kept repeating the word "now" over and over as I watched the hands of the clock slowly moving.

By focusing so intently on the movement of the clock's hands, the sense of time passing actually disappeared and it felt like I was experiencing one expanded, constant moment. My body seemed to grow and shrink with each breath, as if I was losing my "self" and then regaining it with each inhalation. More than an hour passed according to the clock, but I sensed it as one long moment, a single "now." Everything seemed clearer and less tense. When "now" is a mere

instant in the long march of history and the future, it is much more difficult to perceive our soul and its connection to other living things;
time goes by too fast. When "now" is long enough to shut out the distracting pull of flowing time, wisdom comes and the sacred is
revealed.

I once again entered that state. "Jetzt, aber jetzt, aber jetzt, aber jetzt
. . ."

Françoise climbed down out of the tree and came over, putting her
hand on my shoulder. I stopped my meditation and looked up at her.
"What were you doing?" she asked. "What is that word, 'yetst'?"

I pulled her down to sit beside me and put my arm around her waist.
"It's German for 'now.' I need to concentrate on this moment. I wan
to make it last forever." We kissed and then she asked how this meditation worked.

"As you concentrate on and relax into the present moment," I
explained, "you enter a state of timelessness. Repeating the word
'now' over and over helps keep your consciousness from sliding into
the problems of a past that's over or a future yet to be. When the inner
silence becomes complete, even for an instant, all your daily thoughts
and experiences become anecdotal. They seem like fairy tales you
heard as a young child, losing much of their power to evoke fear or
anger or frustration in you. They seem distant and insignificant compared to the essential essence you are connecting with."

I saw Françoise watching me as I spoke, listening intently. This
encouraged me to share more.

"I call this the 'I am' at our core that has no label. In this sacred
state of consciousness, thoughts and feelings are there, but they seem
to gently float past our awareness. We become a sort of unbiased
observer, a witness to what is going on. It's like bare attention."

"Bare attention?" she raised an eyebrow in curiosity.

"Bare attention is concerned only with the present. It teaches us
what so many have forgotten: To live with full awareness in the now.
To face the present without trying to escape into thoughts about the
past or the future. Past and future are not objects of observation but of
reflection. For some, the past and the future become ideas of religious
or wise reflection, but for most they become objects of daydreaming

and vain imaginings which are the main enemies of clear understanding or a clear mind."

"Bare attention," Françoise mused. "I think I've felt that way. Often when I first wake up in the morning, or sometimes just before I fall asleep at night, there's a sort of dreamy quality to my perception, though I'm conscious. I feel like everything that I've planned to do and everything that happened during the preceding day were far, far away, and when I get out of bed, I could find myself in an entirely different life."

There in the valley with my lover, I experienced the best of times. I sometimes thought about responsibilities and undone tasks awaiting me back at the hospital, but I believed I had to enjoy this opportunity while it was there. Too many times I postponed a chance for joy and happiness and found much of its richness and energy dissipated over the time I did something "more important."

Entering the hacienda felt like entering the gates of heaven. Françoise's friends furnished the building with brass beds, wood-burning cast-iron stoves, armoires, oriental carpets and hand-carved furniture. The beautiful surroundings added texture to our intense passion. Making love there opened me to an awareness of the soul that I never wanted to lose again. I didn't ever want to go back to the dependence on rationality and pragmatism that had characterized my life in Santiago. I tried to convince myself that what I was now feeling had as much or more potential for bringing me success in life.

I wrote in my journal:

This relationship has opened a perspective about a change I envision going on at this time for everybody on the planet. It is as if the feeling of being in love makes one believe that everyone is in love. But here is also a vision that a spiritual value change is happening in the world, or needs to happen at this time— recovery of soul and sacredness and spiritual values. The misery of the world is not being solved through society's old modes of change. There needs to be a new availability of solutions.

It is like a collective coming of a messiah or messianic-consciousness that is not singularized to any particular individual.

It is a new commitment, a new consciousness entering the world that will interconnect individuals through happenings like this encounter with Françoise. She is my wakeup call: awakening a deeper memory in myself, and awakening me to a positive psychology very distinct from what I have been living in current, everyday reality. I hope this chapter of my life never closes.

The manuscript describing my experiences with Françoise made its way to the Chilean presidential candidate, mystic and Nobel Prize-winning poet Pablo Neruda via a friend of mine. I didn't even realize Neruda had received the manuscript until I answered the phone one day. Neruda personally called to say he had read the manuscript and it deserved to be published. I almost fainted. When I composed myself enough to respond, he added that he would be happy to write a preface for it and find me a publisher.

I shared my surprise and joy with all my friends. The book was published only a few months later to widespread rave reviews. By this time, Françoise was gone. Her vacation had ended and she returned to Europe to resolve her problems there. I missed her terribly but I would always remember what this wild, free woman had taught me. It took me a long time to be able to love again as I had loved her, but she gave me a valuable gift: the ability to open up my heart to all circumstances. This showed me that I was capable of a deep capacity for loving.

The relationship returned me to my path by showing me how to incorporate the meaning of life's events into my essence instead of futilely trying to master the events technically. I opened myself to the urges of my spirit and surrendered the idea of manipulating the world to satisfy my perceived needs. Only after my return did I realize it was quite a challenge to keep this insight while working in the socialized model of medicine and dealing with forms, supplies and politics.

A year later, I was finishing up my internship at a hospital in Santiago. I lived in a high-rise apartment building near the hospital. This proximity to the hospital was a great benefit since I often returned from one of the 48-hour shifts that characterized most of my internship with barely enough energy to cook myself a meal and collapse. Being awake for these long periods was not the main factor in my fatigue, however. Chile was experiencing the chaos of political instability and 300 percent inflation. Consequently, doctors often worked without the most basic supplies like I.V. tubing, bandages and iodine.

These conditions also contributed to extreme overwork. Interns assigned to rural clinics were often given caseloads of 62 patients to see in a single morning. One of my first cases on such a day was a man who gestured wildly and spoke in broken sentences. When he told me there had been blood during coughing, I asked him to cough for me. He replied, "It's not me. It's my wife."

"Well, where is she?" I asked incredulously.

"She is waiting in the hall," he replied. "Do you want to see her?"

I took a deep breath, trying to remain calm as I calculated how much time I would have for 60 other patients. "Yes, bring her in," I said at last.

The woman was very large and literally bundled from head-to-toe in four layers of clothing. She looked like a stack of laundry with eyes and a nose peeking out. I got out my stethoscope and asked her to undress so I could listen to her lungs. We had been taught to examine patients with their clothes off, but the woman was taking so long to unbutton and untie all her garments that I just thrust the stethoscope down the neck of her sweaters and listened to her lungs in that awkward position in order to save time. I could tell she had a fever and her breathing was little more than a wheeze, so I immediately suspected pneumonia. I look back on that now and can't imagine practicing medicine with such time constraints.

One week before my internship ended, amidst the accompanying stress and insanity, I received a phone call at my apartment.

"I would like an appointment to speak with you," the woman said.

"I'm not taking private patients. You will have to contact the hospital where I work." I started giving her the hospital admissions department's phone number.

The woman's voice grew stern. "I am not calling for an examination."

"I really don't have time to see you," I said arrogantly. "I leave Chile in a week to start a residency in Boston."

"I must speak to you before you leave," the woman insisted.

Despite further tries to put her off or at least find out what she wanted, she told me she would call again and hung up. The following Monday morning before I even got out of bed, the same woman called to say she was "in the neighborhood" and would "drop by" in a half-hour. I had no idea how she got my address, and I considered not letting her in when she arrived. I decided to be cordial and got up to shower and dress.

Exactly 30 minutes later, I heard a knock at my door and a Middle-Eastern woman entered my apartment carrying a copy of my book, *The Ebb and Flow of Living*. She was a short woman but firmly built, and she exuded a tangible strength. Her long black hair was coiled on top of her head, and looking at her in profile she seemed to be of Greek descent. Middle-aged and elegantly dressed, she sat down and I noticed her dark, piercing eyes and thought she must be a very powerful person.

"I hope you don't mind me packing while we talk," I said as I put some books in one of the open packing crates on my table.

She pointed at the boxes. "That is not important. What are you planning to do with your life?"

When I started talking about my upcoming residency in pediatrics and my hopes of becoming a professor of medicine, she interrupted me. "No. What do *you* want to do with your life?"

I shrugged and shook my head. I am sure my disorientation was evident to her.

"Do you know who Gurdjieff is?" she asked very deliberately.

"No. I have no idea who you're talking about."

"And you don't know Ouspensky either?"

I was quickly becoming confused by this strange woman. "They both sound Russian," I ventured as my mind, grasping for straws, turned to the upcoming elections the Marxists were predicted to win. Was this woman looking for future candidates and if so, what did this have to do with my book?

"Do you comprehend the depth of what you have written?" she said as she gestured with the book.

"You have forgotten again," she went on. "Gurdjieff was a Russian mystic from Georgia, a man who left his homeland and founded the

Institute for Harmonious Living of Man. Ouspensky was a mathematician and something of a mystic himself. When Gurdjieff read Ouspensky's book, *In Search of the Miraculous*, he sought out the author and posed that question: Do you comprehend the depth of what you have written? When Ouspensky seemed confused by the question, Gurdjieff replied, 'If you would have known what you wrote about, I would have sat at your feet and followed you as my master, but you don't know what you have written.' At that, Gurdjieff left.

"I must say the same to you. I hope you wake up again." She stood up and left without saying farewell, slamming the door behind her. Astonished, I sat there staring at the door for several minutes. What did this mean? Gradually, I shook off my amazement and continued packing my things for my move to Boston.

My residency in pediatrics at the Children's Hospital of Harvard was characterized by constant work with very little free time. I worked part of the time in the city of Boston and part in a small hospital outside the city. Again I was back in the cycle of long shifts, but now even the time between was often filled with hours of library research. At least in Chile I had parties and dinners to go to when the shifts were over. Here I felt great loneliness. The people at the hospital seemed a bit cold, though there was little time to spend socializing with the few friends I had. When I did leave the hospital, the winter weather was cold and foggy. I felt like I was being tested. I was enduring this rat race in order to embark on an academic career that might eventually give me access to a full professorship at a top university, I told myself.

An important lesson I received at that time, one that which shaped my future destiny, ironically took place at the home of one of my professors. I was invited there one evening for dinner. My host was a renowned pediatrician whose publications were influential throughout the world. I had read his books while in Chile. His discoveries and papers seemed to be transforming the field.

I had expected to dine with the rest of his family, but when I arrived there were only two places set at the rather large dining room table. In South America, dinners are a nightly event for socializing, conducting business and meeting new people, so I felt this dinner for two would likely make for a lonely evening. My professor had prepared the meal himself, and it was simple and straightforward. We started with a salad and crabs, then had fish as the entree, and finished with coffee and dessert. After bringing our dinner out of the kitchen and serving the two of us, he opened a bottle of Scotch and sat down to share the miseries of his life.

As we drank together he told me his wife was dating another man. Being a Bostonian gentleman, the good doctor agreed to remain living with her, though they slept in separate bedrooms. His daughter was a drug addict living on the streets of San Francisco's Haight-Ashbury district. His son had fled to Canada to avoid the military draft during the Vietnam war. The family had no structure, no center.

I stayed overnight in his mansion. He accompanied me upstairs and told me, "You can stay in this room, if you want." The "room" was a beautiful suite with an enormous private bathroom and all kinds of luxurious details.

Even though I was very tired, I couldn't sleep. I gazed out the bedroom window of this beautiful mansion on a snowy beach, just an hour north of Boston. I stayed up for several hours and thought about the famous man living in the large, silent house. Was this the life I was preparing for myself? I reviewed my plans.

If I go on with this career, I told myself, I run the risk of high-tech medicine effecting my soul. I fantasized about how I would become less and less human each passing day. The pressure of competition would force me to specialize and devote myself to my career more and more deeply every day to survive in this environment. After finishing my residency, I would become an instructor. In three years, I might become an assistant professor. In three more years—if at all—I might become an associate professor. If everything turned out "right," I would have to sacrifice everything outside of my career specialization, but I would be deserving of full professorship and the same honors my host had achieved. But I would be deeply conditioned and foreign to everything except my technical specialty. I defined "foreign" as the state of consciousness in which one has completely forgotten oneself as a human being. It would not be a matter of lacking time for music, reading or sports, but something more like forgetting my breathing, or forgetting my essence. I felt I would not have a moment for the remembrance of the sacred self.

I wondered if I really wanted that for myself. I could see that this life could be empty, lacking spirituality, humanity and variety. It could also lack happiness, enthusiasm and thankfulness due to its pressures.

I thought about why I was in Boston. I came here to learn about human development through the study of pediatrics. I wanted to achieve greater insight into the transitional period of adolescence, and why so few Westerners complete that transition gracefully, if at all. I believed adolescence, which should be a fairly normal rite of passage, contained a great key to healing. From my studies of anthropology I knew that people who experienced adolescent initiations into adulthood led lives that were more balanced spiritually and materially. I also knew that these initiation rituals took place mainly in cultures defined as "primitive."

These cultures had rites and rituals that combined the hormonal and biological changes the adolescent was going through with the societal changes the child must endure in order to become an adult. These adolescents experienced the "death of the child" within themselves in order to precipitate the "birth of the adult." The West was definitely missing a key in the adolescent spiritual quest. The results could be seen in the high rates of teen delinquency that were already prevalent at this time.

I didn't find that key, but I did learn that an academic life too easily led to isolation and left little room for spirit. Perhaps psychiatry would be more open to the sacred, I thought as I finally turned off the ornate, brass bedside lamp. I had heard of an opening for a resident in psychiatry at a hospital in Chile during a recent vacation there. As I tried to fall asleep for the few hours remaining until morning, I resolved to apply for it.

I was accepted into the program in Chile a few months later and bid farewell to the cold intensity of my life as a pediatrician in Boston. I excitedly looked forward to the next step in my search for spirit and healing.

I had only been back in Chile a matter of days when I invited a beautiful young medical student named Jasmine out on a date. I felt a strange attraction to this rather tall, olive-skinned woman in her early twenties. She reminded me vaguely of someone, and I was drawn to her. Upon arriving at her house to pick her up for dinner, I was introduced to her mother. My jaw dropped. She was the mysterious woman who had stormed out of my apartment a year ago. Seeing mother and daughter together I definitely saw the resemblance.

A smile started to form on her face as she recognized me. "So, does our second meeting mean you have awakened again?"

I smiled back. "I have come to believe that anyone who defies all probabilities and comes into my life twice must have something to teach me."

I sat down and started talking with the woman, whose name was Layla and who turned out to be an esoteric teacher of Sufism, an Oriental mystical tradition that shares an inner core with many Western religious traditions, including Christianity and Islam. She told me that Sufi teachings were at the heart of the mystical tradition that flourished during medieval times, and many saints from this time, including St. Francis of Assisi, reflected Sufi ideals. As part of the purification process before battle, Christian knights of the chivalric order would repeat a prayer while laying prostrate before an altar. That prayer, "Forgive my errors O You the Most Powerful," is essentially a Sufi prayer. She shared various Sufi texts and teachings with me for hours that evening. These texts stressed the understanding of an evolutionary potential for soul development given as the "message of the mystics," and showed how an underlying design was operating in our lives.

One of the texts pointed to the balance of vocation and career; teaching, in ancient terms, that one should learn a livelihood to support oneself and spend the rest of the time cultivating awareness. It added that the Western world's preoccupation with material survival was harmful to awakening. It kept most of our attention stuck in the concept "all that matters is solid."

Once we began talking I knew my date with Jasmine would not take place.

"I read your book," Layla explained, "and I was struck by how perfectly you wrote about a state of being I have struggled my whole life to attain." She stood up. "Would you like something to drink?"

"Water, please," I replied. "What state of being were you referring to?"

She returned from the kitchen with a pitcher and a glass. "There is a technique known to the Sufi masters as the 'traspaso of baraka' or transfer of blessings. In your book you described looking into your lover's eyes. It was just like the masters staring into another human's eyes to see the divinity in that person and the portal to the universal consciousness that lies beyond them. It's a tool for enlightenment used to reach an ecstatic state of timelessness you described as soul awareness."

Layla placed the pitcher and glass on a nearby table, filled my glass and resumed her seat across from me. "Like the air that sustains us, we cannot see the soul. Like the air, we only become aware of our soul when it moves like the wind or when we feel we are suffering for lack of it.

"We're all born with a soul. It's the internal power that animates the body and brings consciousness to your worldly experiences. Every soul is perfect, and it contains the experience of many levels of life and of consciousness. But in order to experience that perfection we have to be awakened or activated so that we shift from a superficial identity to the essential one. Isn't that what you were trying to describe in *The Ebb and Flow of Living?*"

As I took a drink of water, she leaned forward and pointed her finger at me. "You are a doctor. What then is the difference between a living body and a corpse?"

I started to list the signs of life for her. A dead person's lungs and heart stop operating. The brain discontinues its electric nerve impulses. The body temperature drops to that of the room.

"No," she interrupted. "What causes all these bodily processes to shut down?"

"There are many causes for death," I said. "The lungs may become congested and stop supplying oxygen to the body. The heart may become injured or obstructed and the blood circulation may be cut off."

"Tell me," she interrupted again, "don't our bodies fight off congestion, injuries and obstructions for years and years? When people die, they have decided that earthly life is no longer where they want to be. Their souls leave their bodies, and then the body shuts down."

I thought back to when I was nine years old. My grandpa was getting older, and with age came the distress of disease and concern from his family and friends. Grandpa was a very pious and religious man, but the enjoyment I had seen on his face during prayer was rapidly declining. On a Sunday night when it seemed that all was coming to an end, Grandpa gathered the family together and blessed each of us. Later in the evening, around eight o'clock, he spoke to his wife of 60 years in a gentle, loving tone.

"Do not cry," he told my grandmother. "The Lord is calling, and I must go. I will not leave you here for long." He closed his eyes and left this world moments later.

I had already gone home by that time because my parents felt it would be too traumatic for a child to be around such a normal event as death. I sat in my bedroom and made a pledge with God to spare my beloved Grandpa. I felt I needed to sacrifice something for God to intervene and save him, but I had no idea what I could offer. I finally prayed, "Oh God, if I sacrifice and chew this piece of gum all night, please spare my grandpa's life."

But God did not enter my deal. I was deeply frustrated until two nights later. I dreamt I was in the presence of my grandfather. Smiling, he approached me and told me of eternity. "Don't worry about anything," he told me. "Life goes on, and I love you the same as before. All you must remember is the need for fundamental unity before what people call death."

Grandfather advised me to pray the Shema, which was his spiritual practice. The Shema is an anchor or pivot prayer on which an individual meditates. My grandfather prayed, "Hear O Israel, the eternal is the Lord, the eternal is one." He also reminded me to constantly do Teshuva, the prayer of repentance or return to the source. Real transformation, he said, means unity—the reconnection of the soul—and this shift can happen at any moment. He taught me a prayer of radical forgiveness. It went like this: "I hereby forgive all. May no one be punished on my account. I hereby forgive all. May no one be punished on my account."

I was thinking of this as Layla refilled my water glass from the pitcher while listing books I should read that would show me paths to awareness of my soul. I was intrigued with what she described as "reconnecting with the soul," since it promised to bring back the joy I had felt and described in my book. I asked her to teach me one of her techniques for reaching that connected state.

She told me to put down my glass, lean back in the chair, close my eyes and relax. "The Masters teach that there are two streams of energy that anchor soul awareness in the body. They are subtler than the physical, and even more subtle than the mental. One stream goes into the heart, and the other goes into the head. The stream going into the heart brings life force. The stream to the head enters near the pineal gland in the forehead and connects our consciousness with cosmic intelligence—the mind that connects all living things. Many cultures call this the 'third eye.' You will feel it as a subtle vibration. This is eternal force uniting you with all life.

"Move your consciousness away from this room and the sensations of your body," her voice soothed. "Orient your awareness toward subtler and more intimate phenomena. Raise your attention to the head. Go inward, into the area of the pineal gland in the center of your brain. This is still a physical focus but of a more inward nature. Concentrate and hold your attention at this spot in the center of the head.

"Next, go in even further. Don't make it difficult—just transcend the physical plane and imagine and visualize yourself moving to a subtler level of being. Move into the mental plane. Here you may experience a first indication that you are advancing toward the soul. As you move inward to each subtler, more abstract level you will sense a shift. The consciousness aspect of the soul is on the more abstract levels of the mental plane. Stay in here with your inward gaze focused at this point.

"Your attention is focused inward on the mental plane; now move to the abstract levels of the mental plane. In other words, keep moving to the subtler levels of being. The soul is a light body situated in the causal body. Try to consciously sense the soul's light, the higher vibration. This higher vibration flooding your body is like nothing you have ever experienced, and is the first clue you will have of the soul. You will remember this experience. Stay focused on this subtler level as long as you can.

"A sure way to know if you have contacted the soul, even if not visually, is the reciprocal energy or potency you receive from touching it. You will definitely be stimulated; your physical body will feel an increased potency.

"Imagine your center of being in your heart. Imagine the observer in you centered in your forehead. Now visualize a vortex of energy in your heart and your forehead. These energy vortexes feel like electric fire."

"I can see the vortexes," I told her, "but I do not feel any energy flowing."

"You must learn to surrender. You must give up your attachments to this world to perceive the world of the soul."

"What do you mean by 'attachments'?" I asked.

"Ah," Layla sighed. "You fear you must give up all the things you have known to reconnect with the soul." She paused. "No, you do not need to become a hermit. Once you reconnect with that higher part of yourself you will still have a body. You'll still exist in the world of emotions and sensations and physical manifestations. Your responsibilities to this world do not end when you enter the spirit realm. Perhaps you should think of attachments as expectations of how the world exists and functions. It may feel like a death, but you will discover that you never really died."

My mind turned to a class in medical school on embryology and obstetrics. The lecturer had pointed to a diagram of a fetus on the wall and said, "The child will not enter the birth canal until it has surrendered. It will struggle to stay in the aquatic world it has known, but eventually it will need to give up on that world before it can enter our world."

I inhaled deeply, returning to the present. A new sensation came over me, and I told Layla that I could now sense the burning energy in my heart and my forehead.

"Now imagine that these two vortexes are shaped like lotus flowers. Each has nine orange outer petals and three yellow inner petals folded around a center that emanates love. This is not sympathetic love, though. This is not an earthly love. When you feel a divine energy emanating from the centers of these two lotuses, you have entered a universe with very different laws from those of the physical world."

I thought back to the love I felt toward everything and everyone that summer with Françoise. This love was another way to recognize the state of soul awareness, I thought to myself. It feels timeless, and it feels like one is in love with the universe.

I sat and took in the feeling of lightness and serenity that washed over me. I felt calmer and more energized at the same time. I don't know how long I sat there in silence, but when I finally opened my eyes Layla was gone. I started to panic and feel suspicious. The feelings of lightness and serenity faded rapidly. I got up to find her. I called out, "hello," and she appeared from a doorway behind me.

"It is late," she said. "You must go."

"The sensation I felt was amazing," I told her, "but I have lost it."

Layla showed me to the door and said, "You'll be able to maintain that state of being only when you do the inner work necessary to stop seeing the personality that you identify as yourself as something separate and different from the soul you reconnected with a few minutes ago. This will give you a new view of life, one in which you will be in charge of the energy. This energy will respond to the way you think about yourself, life and the universe. In other words, through meditation you will see that the basic component of the universe is pure energy, and that this energy is changeable with your human intention. Your intention causes energy to flow and effect other systems. This is what the ancient mystics knew and the quantum physicists are discovering."

The Doorway to the Invisible School

2

I returned to my residency in the psychiatry department of the hospital the next morning. I had renewed hope that my chosen field would acknowledge the soul and the healing power that awareness of it can bring. I had heard that there was a change occurring at other hospitals and in psychiatry as a whole, that it was beginning to incorporate the human spirit into healing. Surely my experience and interests could be of service here.

I entered the psychiatry ward of the hospital that day, eager to see the signs of healing and soul awareness in my colleagues and patients. The scene was much the same as in my first few days there, however. Patients sat in their beds and on the hallway floors, some staring at their hands, some staring at the air in front of them, some talking or

29

whispering to unseen beings. Nurses stood at bedsides handing patients cups of water and dispensing pills one by one until they were all
swallowed. Other residents found empty examining rooms and stair-
wells to hide in so they wouldn't be disturbed by the patients and
nurses. Supervising physicians walked into a patient's room, checked
the medical records, left without speaking to the patient or the nurse
there, and tracked down a resident in the cafeteria to berate him or her
for not following the standard procedure for treating a particular disorder.

The only real difference in the psychiatric ward was that I was beginning to have a transformed understanding of the physical universe:
now I could see energies around the patients. This energy was like the
glow I had seen while meditating with Layla the night before. If I focused, everything glowed and radiated outward. The glow of the more
severe patients was opaque compared to the healthy nurses.

A couple of months after my evening with Layla, I received a phone
call at the hospital. I had arranged to have a local Santiago publisher
release a book of my poetry, and he was calling to tell me, "They're
here!" I immediately rushed downtown to pick up my first copies.

The publisher's office was in a fairly modern, two-story building.
In the center of a round, cobblestone plaza in front of the building
stood a statue of a military officer holding a bayonet rifle, which offered an unfriendly welcome.

I recalled my first meeting with the publisher months earlier while I
was visiting Chile on vacation from Boston. After passing the statue, I
found the rather cramped office on the second floor. In it, a balding
man with thick glasses was smoking cigarettes dangerously close to
several towering stacks of papers. After introductions, I had handed
him my manuscript. I sat in silence watching him turn the pages. A grin
crept across his face, and he nodded at certain points in his reading.

After reading almost half the manuscript, he finally set it down and
looked up at me. "I have to ask you something," he said.

"Please," I said anxiously.

"Were you high when you wrote this?"

"Excuse me?"

The publisher picked up my manuscript again and leaned back in his chair. "I was just curious. The insights and visions remind me of what one experiences on a mind-altering substance." He stubbed out his cigarette.

"I was probably in an altered state of consciousness when I wrote some of it," I said carefully, "but I got there through meditation, not through drugs."

"Have you ever tried hallucinogens?" he asked, letting his glasses slip down his nose a bit.

"No," I replied, a bit offended. "I never felt the need."

The publisher held up his hands in front of him. "That's fine with me. If you're really going through the sort of things you write about though, maybe you could use more help than your meditation."

He pulled several books off a filing cabinet in the corner behind his desk. He sat down again and looked at me very seriously. "You ought to try it sometime, but you should do it as I do, in a sacred manner. There are many substances that have been used in various cultures throughout history to effect a state of understanding that would otherwise take lifetimes to even glimpse. It is the substance itself that teaches; the shaman is simply the caretaker."

He pushed a copy of Aldous Huxley's *The Doors of Perception* toward me on the desk. "Huxley describes the psychedelic experience using a Catholic term, 'gratuitous grace,' and compares it to the apostle Paul's revelation on the road to Damascus.

"And here," the publisher said referring to a copy of Houston Smith's *The World's Religions*, "this professor calls it a 'religious experience.'"

At the time I told him his examples were not sufficient to change my attitude toward chemically-induced altered states. The subject hadn't come up during the book's production, though we had talked on the phone about a dozen times concerning corrections and cover designs and such. The publisher was standing with his back to me when I entered his office this time. In a canyon amid the paper towers on his desk sat two stacks of shiny, green paperback books with my name on them. Though this was my second book, I still beamed with pride.

"How do you like it?" the publisher asked as he turned around, adjusting his glasses and smoothing the hair over one ear.

I picked up a copy and sat down, trying to appear calm and mature when I was ecstatically happy. "It looks very nice," I said.

"As you can understand," he said as he sat down across the desk from me, "I've had the opportunity to read through the book several times in the past two months." He put a cigarette in his mouth and lit it. "I have the feeling from what you wrote here," he continued, pointing to the stacks of green books, "that you might benefit from meeting a friend of mine."

"Who is it?" I asked.

"Oh, the two of you have a lot in common," he replied. He took a small, yellow pad out of one of the desk drawers and wrote down a name and phone number. "Call this man," he said, "and tell him I thought you needed an initiation."

I took the slip of paper and about a dozen copies of my new book, thanked the publisher and left. I was suspicious but also intrigued by his suggestion that I needed an "initiation."

That night, I called the number on the yellow slip of paper below the name "Don Eduardo." An older woman with a refined accent answered the phone. I asked to speak with Don Eduardo. She paused for a moment and then told me she would go get him.

"Hello?" a man's voice said.

"Don Eduardo?" I ventured.

The man on the other end of the phone line laughed. "Please just call me Eduardo. And who are you?"

"My name is Carlos Warter," I said. "I am a doctor at the university hospital. I just published a book of poetry and my publisher advised me to call you. He said I needed an initiation."

"Why don't you join us for dinner tomorrow night instead?" Eduardo said. "I would like to meet you."

I agreed. He gave me his address and told me to arrive around eight o'clock. The man seemed friendly, and my social life was not yet busy enough, nor my finances substantial enough, to turn down a free dinner.

The foyer of Don Eduardo's house was a long, narrow corridor. An Oriental carpet ran its 15 feet in length. Lush green plants and purple and pink flowers hung in pots on the walls between the row of narrow windows on either side. At the end were two steps leading up to a perpendicular hallway. At the intersection of the two hallways a huge mask covered with bright paints and feathers hung on the wall, bathed in a stream of light originating from somewhere in the ceiling beams.

I was standing in front of the mask trying to decide which direction to go, when a man who appeared to be in his forties tapped me on the shoulder.

"Please come in," he said slowly and clearly, indicating the hallway to the right. Smiling, he introduced himself. "I am Eduardo."

Don Eduardo walked as if he knew there was no need to hurry. This was more slowly than I was accustomed to walking, so I had to pause one or twice so I wouldn't get ahead of him. As we walked down the hallway I could see that Don Eduardo was a distinguished looking mestizo; that is one of his parents must have been a native Indian. We passed a couple of darkened rooms on the left and eventually came to a brightly lit room at the end of the hallway. A huge fireplace decorated with statues and musical instruments dominated one wall of the room. In the center was a round, heavy wooden table set with three places and a candelabra. A woman dressed in a white blouse and mid-length dark skirt crossed to greet me.

"This is my partner, Teresa," Don Eduardo said as I shook hands with the woman. Teresa was tall and slim. The paleness of her skin was in stark contrast to that of Don Eduardo. Though I could tell she must have broken her nose at some point in time, this did not detract from her appearance but rather made her all the more interesting. I had the impression she was the type of woman whose beauty became all the more apparent as more was known about her.

"I told her you were a doctor of psychiatry," Don Eduardo told me in his patient, measured voice.

"I'm a psychiatrist, too," Teresa smiled, brightening her deep, dark eyes. "I'm working with a botanist on a research project. We're testing plant extracts for their psychoactive properties."

I smiled and said, "It's very nice to meet you." I had a feeling that the initiation my publisher and Don Eduardo had in mind involved taking some sort of drug.

We sat down at the table and were served by a surprisingly ener-
getic servant in her fifties. The conversation seemed to center
around my work with my patients and Teresa's work with experimental drugs. The meal was almost over an hour later when I realized that I had learned almost nothing about Don Eduardo except
that he liked to collect the art of indigenous peoples and that he had
a habit of pulling on the ends of his moustache.

"I feel like we haven't given you much of a chance to talk," I said
to Don Eduardo as the servant was clearing the plates for dessert.
"How do you spend your days when you aren't collecting art?"

Don Eduardo pushed his chair back and pulled on his moustache.
"I was trained," he said, "to pass along the traditions of the elders."

"I was one of his first initiates," interjected Teresa.

"What sort of initiation do you teach?" I asked Don Eduardo.

"There is a doorway to understanding the self," he replied, "a
threshold that can only be crossed through lifetimes of spiritual practice. There are plants that can teach what you need to know to cross
that threshold in a single lifetime. There are experiences that can open
the mind like no other."

We sat in silence as dessert was served. I waited for Don Eduardo
to say something more, but he simply ate the pudding placed in front
of him. When he finished, he stood up from his chair and began examining the various instruments and statues adorning the fireplace.
The servant came to clear the table and Teresa helped her carry the
dishes into the kitchen.

"I want to thank you for a wonderful evening," I called to Don
Eduardo. He turned his head slightly and nodded acknowledgment. "I
don't think I am ready for any initiations right now," I continued. He
nodded again.

"I will accompany you out," he said, leading the way back to the
front door with the same slow, deliberate gait.

As I drove home, I wondered whether I was being too closed-
minded about the initiation Don Eduardo seemed to be offering. I decided that I wasn't comfortable with the idea, and therefore shouldn't
pursue it further.

The next afternoon, however, I fell asleep while reading a research paper in the library. I dreamt I met a little man only half my height in a room with one door and no windows. He reassured me that no matter what I did, I would always be myself. He suggested my development was weighed down by the pain and confusion of my life's events. "You need to lose more of the you that you think you are, in order to discover the you that you really are," he told me, and then he exited through the door.

The dream startled me so much that I awakened. I started to consider that my spiritual development might need a jolt after all, and by that evening I was on the phone with Don Eduardo.

We arranged to meet on the following Saturday. I learned Don Eduardo had been initiated as a shaman by the Mapuche Indians. Using the knowledge he acquired from Mapuche, he led me on my first shamanistic journey. I focused on my intent to clear away the aspects of my "false self"—all those expectations, labels and judgments that obscure one's spiritual essence—and tried to relax my body and quiet my mind as Don Eduardo directed. Gradually, my body started feeling a bit numb and a detailed, expansive vision took form in my mind.

I was in a pasture with the sun gently shining down on me. A warm breeze caressed my skin. The breeze grew to a strong gust and then receded to near stillness. I felt a tremendous tranquility, a total detachment from my normal condition. I experienced all my feelings of fear and pain as if they were turned on to their maximum volume. But I was not in the midst of them; I was just observing them clearly. I once again felt as I had with Françoise, a joy and expansiveness I experienced as my soul was transmitted through the farthest reaches of time and space.

Then I felt myself descending. I realized I was inside myself, descending from my head into my heart. There I stood on an ocean beach. Two men that I identified as Jesus Christ and Che Guevara walked toward each other, embraced and melted into a beam of light shooting upward. I felt a sense of liberation that was both political and spiritual at the same time.

"And after that," as I was describing it to Don Eduardo later, "I saw angels who came to me and brought me aboard their golden light chariot. My spirit body rode with them up into the sky. I looked down and saw all the people on the ground far below looking up."

"What did you feel as you were in the chariot looking down at the world?" asked Don Eduardo.

"I was in tears because of the suffering of those below me." I paused. "I felt a deep desire to alleviate their pain."

"That last realization," Don Eduardo said as he got up from the grass where we were sitting outside his home, "is the golden key you have been seeking your whole life. It is very important that you remember this experience. With this key you will unlock your destiny. When you find the lock it fits in, you'll be ready for the next step in your spiritual development."

I felt energized. Everything I saw as I drove home had a numinous, sacred aura to it. I turned over the last part of my vision in my mind. Don Eduardo said that when I understood what it meant I would be ready to move on in my development.

It seemed service toward others had always been part of my life's purpose. I remembered a scene from when I was three years old. My mother was pushing me in a stroller through a park in Santiago. We passed a sandbox where several children were building sand castles under the protective gaze of their mothers or nannies. There was one little boy about my age and also in a stroller. While watching the other children, his head, arms and feet jerked in frequent spasms. I somehow realized that this other boy would never walk. I wanted to help him so that he could play with the other children in the sandbox.

The following day I sat in an afternoon clinical meeting while one of the psychiatrists, Dr. Max, described a patient of his as "an interesting case." A Jewish woman he was treating was in her late sixties and was a Holocaust survivor who suffered frequent bouts of severe, debilitating depression. Dr. Max had prescribed Elavil, an antidepressant, but his focus otherwise seemed to be entirely on diagnosing the exact point at which her "ego structure collapsed," not on alleviating the depression.

"Isn't it enough that she survived?" I asked Dr. Max. "Let's stop wasting our time trying to discover when she had her breakdown, and reinforce the spirit that helped her survive four years in a concentration camp."

One of the other residents—a very political socialist named Juan who later died on the same day that the military coup killed Allende—responded, "Worrying about spiritual well-being is a waste of time. We have thousands of patients. Just give her some medication and move on."

After the meeting, I accompanied Juan on his rounds. Although he and I often disagreed on methods and priorities in public meetings, in private we got along well because of our common focus on helping the poor: we both worked part-time in the same rural clinic.

In a room with four beds, Juan listened to his patient, a tired-looking Mapuche Indian woman in her fifties. She described the fear she felt at being discharged to her abusive husband and how the "little people" had told her last night they would not protect her anymore if she went back home. Juan asked her questions only when she stopped talking. He listened intently, making notes in her records every now and then. At one point, after some lengthy writing in her records, Juan stood up, announced that he had to go see other patients and left.

Even though much of psychiatry involves listening, the doctors didn't seem concerned with the deeper meaning of what their patients told them. Instead, they concentrated on whether what a patient said consistently fit an existing theoretical model, whether there was a drug they could prescribe to make the patient's problem less obvious or more manageable and whether there were sufficient personnel and available beds. Here, too, was a system that allowed for no creativity and no talk of intangibles like soul and meaning. A patient was assigned a diagnosis thousands of previous patients had received, given drugs and therapy almost identical to those prescribed in the rest of the hemisphere and discharged or transferred to make room for the thousands of new patients to come later. The context for healing one, individual patient was huge. Whether you were the patient or the physician, you felt small by comparison.

After observing my patient sleeping fitfully in the fourth bed, I looked at her chart to see if anything new had been added overnight. Evidently she was awakened at two in the morning and given pills to quiet her muscle spasms and help her sleep. Nothing else had oc-curred. I noted that the spasms were still continuing, but they seemed a bit less frequent.

Next, I went to a room with only two beds. The bed near the door was empty, so I sat down there to try to get some response out of the woman in the other bed. I had been assigned to her case after she was admitted and diagnosed as a catatonic schizophrenic. Her records stated her name was Carmen, that she lived with her mother in a small, rural town, and that she had not spoken at all since she was admitted two weeks before. Carmen sat upright in bed staring wide-eyed at the blank wall opposite her, with strands of her long black hair in her face. This was a position I often found her in when I came to visit. I took a look at her treatment records. One-on-one talking and group therapy had elicited no response from her whatsoever. Blood tests and exam-inations had revealed nothing wrong with her brain, thyroid or vocal cords. Carmen's mother was evidently at a loss to recall an event that might have triggered this catatonic state.

"How are you today, Carmen?" I ventured. No response. "Do you remember me? I'm Dr. Warter." The young woman's eyelids lowered slightly, but she neither spoke nor acknowledged my presence. If I could detect anything about her mental or emotional state, it was a sort of disillusionment that registered on her face occasionally. I noted that in her records. As I got up to go on with my rounds, I looked back at Carmen and decided to try something different with her that weekend.

Driving home from the hospital that night, I came upon a collision between two cars. Since the accident seemed recent, and there didn't appear to be a doctor on the scene or an ambulance on its way, I pulled over. One of the cars was on its side and looked like it had rolled over, so I checked that one first. The driver had been thrown to the passen-ger side of her vehicle and seemed unconscious. Blood ran across her face and down her neck. One of her legs was oddly twisted beneath her, suggesting a complete fracture.

The other car was upright, but it's front end was severely smashed from the collision. The passengers—a very young man and woman—were bruised but conscious, though their legs were pinned under the engine block.

When the ambulance arrived a few minutes later, I helped the paramedics extract and care for the three victims. The less experienced of the two paramedics seemed to appreciate my help greatly and asked if I would ride with her in the back of the ambulance. I agreed.

Within an hour of our arrival at the hospital emergency room, the woman in the car that had rolled died. Her mother, father and sister had seen me going into and out of the emergency room while the other doctors were operating on the woman. They stopped me to ask how she was doing. I felt obligated to tell them she had not survived the surgery. The mother and daughter started to sob, and a look in the father's eyes begged me to offer them the comfort he could not.

I searched my memory for the appropriate sentiments. I thought of my family's grief at my grandfather's death 15 years earlier. Two of my uncles seemed particularly devastated by Grandpa's passing. When I happened to mention the dream I'd had in which Grandpa came to me from the afterlife, these uncles wanted to know more.

In letters of consolation I typed on my father's old, black Underwood typewriter, I shared the communication from my dream, that Grandpa was on "the other side," happy and well. I wrote:

Grandpa told me that when he died he had been swept down a tunnel toward a bright light. Angels full of light pointed the way. His parents came to greet him and he felt peaceful because they seemed to radiate wisdom and contentment. He said dying is a part of living. We shouldn't be afraid of it. And he told me I would help others in grief now that I no longer feared death.

I tried to describe for the unfortunate woman's family how I believed the pain and sorrow of earthly life immediately left the body at the moment of death. I told them that even after a traumatic accident their loved one could find peace. One of the surgeons stood nearby listening. After the family left to sign some papers, he approached me.

"You can't worry about the emotional side of your patients," he advised. "Just fix them up, if you can, and send them on their way."

I thanked him for his attempt to be helpful and called a taxi to get back to my car.

Since I was scheduled to work the weekend shift, I came in two days later. After finishing the morning rounds, I went to the room of Carmen, the woman with catatonic schizophrenia. There was now a patient sharing Carmen's room. This other patient was in bed quietly working on some needlework. I found a chair in the hallway and brought it in next to Carmen's bed. Sitting down I noticed the bedclothes had shifted somewhat from the day before, but otherwise she was still sitting up in the same position, her gaze still fixed at the blank wall.

I had found that the simple act of paying attention to someone created a positive change in them, so I decided to try that with Carmen. There were three forms of attention I believed could help my patients in healing: the first was empathetic appreciation, feeling with compassion and heart-to-heart understanding what patients are going through; the second was respectful listening; and the third was emanating an effective healing presence through a vision of wholeness.

One of the books I received from Layla the Sufi woman suggested that the meditation she had taught me could also be extended to produce healing. It discussed four steps to facilitate healing work.

First, one must remember that one is really one's essence, higher self or soul. This centering work gives one the perspective needed to avoid reacting to the negativity and defenses the patient might direct toward the individual treating him. By remembering the soul, one is able to honor and grant validity to that part of oneself which shields the healer from the patient's layers of defenses and pain.

Second, one is aware of the patient as a whole human being, and envisions and discerns the essential self or soul within the patient. One must look beyond the labels—diagnosis, gender, situation—to accomplish this step.

Third, one examines the soul of the patient and acknowledges that the disease or discomfort can be an evolutionary step, that it can have purpose. The condition must be thought of as a transforming experience so that disempowering thoughts of victimization can be avoided.

And fourth, one suspends all judgments. One can not think about why the patient is not well, whether the healing techniques being used will work, why the patient is reacting a certain way or anything else that would get in the way of focusing on the person as a whole and sacred being. Sometimes it is difficult to silence that part of the mind that constantly judges things, people and events. It can be considered sufficient not to focus on those judgments, thereby decreasing their power to manifest.

This last step in preparation for healing seemed particularly important to me after seeing progress in another patient, Bernard, the past few days. Bernard was a working class man in his thirties who had been experiencing disturbing, vivid hallucinations. Though he was a strong man who had worked long hours at his job in the past, his current condition was completely debilitating. Although he was under the care of one of the other doctors, I usually said hello to him during my rounds. I had looked at his file the week before and found pages and pages of his doctor's notes describing in careful detail Bernard's various hallucinations.

Every time the doctor came he asked about Bernard's symptoms, that is, the hallucinations. I realized that this particular focus was keeping Bernard stuck in his hallucinations. I decided to shift Bernard's attention from his disease to his future, so that he would view his hallucinations as obstacles to his dreams instead of confirmation of his illness. When I asked him how he was doing, he responded with a list of his problems and fears. I told him those aspects of himself were only temporary. I was trying to get to know the real Bernard, I told him. I asked him about his plans for the future.

"I'm going to stay here," he told me, his large bulky body showing physical signs of fear.

"What are you going to do when you leave though?" I countered.

A look of pained confusion crossed the man's worn and acned face. "I can't leave here. I'm sick."

Although I couldn't get him beyond that judgmental labeling, I tried bypassing his defenses with a hypothetical situation. "Well, imagine that you are no longer sick. What would you want to do?" Over the following days, Bernard told me of his dreams of working in a motorcycle repair shop and earning enough money to buy his own motorcycle. Eventually, he saw himself on a long roadtrip with a friend to the Andes, eventually crossing the mountains toward Argentina. As Bernard's dreams of the future took more and more of his attention, his hallucinations decreased. His attending doctor seemed genuinely disappointed that Bernard rarely had any interesting hallucinations for him to write down.

With Bernard's progress in mind, I settled into the chair next to Carmen's bed and began the technique Layla taught me. I focused my mind in order to contact those energy flows in my heart and head. Carmen seemed to take no notice of me. I visualized the positive energy flowing from my heart to hers, sending the stream toward her with the suggestion that she communicate with me. I knew that I would probably receive her pain through my heart when she finally opened herself to me. Layla had explained to me the importance of sending the pain through the head out into the universe so that it did not remain trapped inside. Many psychiatrists I knew held the negative energy of pain inside and thus became sick themselves.

Hours went by before she even glanced in my direction. When she saw I was still focused on her, she looked away again. After another hour or more, she looked directly at me for a few seconds. After a few more minutes, a smile gradually formed on her lips. Then she went blank and looked away again, but now it felt more like a game of peekaboo than attempts to ignore me. She seemed incredulous that someone could pay her so much attention over so many hours.

I took a break and left Carmen to go down to the cafeteria to eat dinner. I watched two of my fellow residents trying to convince a table full of young nurses to accompany them to a party at the end of their shift. One of the other residents, Brigita Von Hoffenburg, a member of an old German family in Chile, came up and asked to join me. I was somewhat surprised by her request since for weeks she had gone out of her way to distance herself from me, often consciously avoiding my company while making nationalistic remarks. In listening to me speak about my approach to healing in clinical meetings, however, she developed so much enthusiasm for my methods she now treated me like her best friend. I told her about the experiment I was in the process of conducting with Carmen. She agreed to meet me at Carmen's room after I finished my meal and walked my evening rounds.

I met Brigita in the hall outside Carmen's room around ten o'clock, and the two of us went in together. The other patient in the room had finally put away her needlework and gone to sleep. I moved the lamp closer so that we could see Carmen's face better. She was still staring into space, but she seemed much more aware of my presence. I relaxed and reconnected with my inner energy flows and focused them on her once again. It almost seemed she kept her attention elsewhere as an act of will. After a few minutes, she again checked to see if I was still focused on her, and the smile reappeared. I couldn't keep from grinning broadly too. She wasn't talking, but at least she was starting to communicate. I renewed my commitment to getting her to speak. I almost completely forgot about Brigita's presence, the noises from the hall, the look of the room and the bed, the feel of the chair. My attention was more intense and more tightly focused on Carmen.

She looked away most of the time. She stopped smiling again. As it was getting very late at night, she seemed less able to maintain her upright posture any longer. She started to show signs of fatigue and sleepiness. She continued to check if I was still there and still focused on her. The progress she was making was more than enough to keep me—and Brigita, evidently—fascinated with this unorthodox type of therapy. I felt warmly empathetic as I paid more attention to Carmen.

I began to feel sleepy, too, but I felt I had to make a bit more progress before I gave up for the night. Around four o'clock that Sunday morning, Brigita was the first of us to speak. "We've been here for almost six hours. Aren't you going to say anything to her?"

I nodded. My impatience was getting the better of me, too. I spoke to the quiet, motionless Carmen. "Do you know who I am?"

She looked at me, but she did not speak. I thought I noticed one of her feet moving beneath the sheets. She seemed to be waiting for something more from me.

"I'm Dr. Warter. This woman is Dr. Von Hoffenburg. I'm willing to stay here with you all weekend if you want."

Carmen leaned toward me somewhat, her eyes scanned back and forth wildly, and she burst forth with a loud "No!" Brigita gasped, and the woman in the next bed stirred.

"You don't want me to stay with you all weekend?" I asked Carmen quietly.

"No!" she shouted back almost as loudly as before.

At this point, the older woman in the next bed sat up and peered across the room at the three of us. I tried to keep focused on Carmen. "Would you like us to let you sleep or would you like to talk some more?" I asked her softly.

Carmen closed her eyes and rattled off the word "no" over a dozen times much closer to my volume level.

"Can you tell me what you want?" I asked her, still focusing positive energy toward her.

"Go away!" she told me.

"Do you know where you are?"

Carmen made a sort of gurgling noise and then whispered something that sounded like, "Go away now."

"Do you know where you are?" I repeated.

"Bad place," she said much as you would expect a three-year-old to respond. Her breathing seemed faster.

"You're in Santiago in a hospital," I explained. "Your mother brought you here." I relaxed a bit but remained leaning forward in my chair.

"Mama, Mama," the young woman said. Her eyes scanned back and forth as if she were searching.

Brigita eventually had to leave and I took a much-needed nap before morning rounds. When I returned to Carmen later in the day, she continued talking with me in a sort of baby talk. By the end of the weekend, however, she had regained complete motor control of her body and was communicating virtually as a normal adult. She was out of the catatonic phase without medication. Love and presence seemed to work this miracle of healing.

By the time of our weekly clinical meeting on Wednesday, most of my resident friends had come to look in on the young woman who was suddenly telling stories about the abuse she had endured from her employer. It was remarkable how normal her speech and movement were after lying in bed like a mute mannequin for over two weeks. Some of my colleagues were curious, some chose to ignore what had happened, but some, thankfully, were very much with me and agreed that Carmen had been cured.

My happiness and pride accompanied me into the clinical meeting. When it was my turn to report, I shared what I had done to cure the catatonic schizophrenic woman, calling it "love therapy." I was reminded of the simple truth of the Beatles song popular at the time, "All You Need Is Love." I said that we needed to own the world of heart, that we needed a medicine based on relationships.

"Each person," I said, "is infinitely more vast in scope, more complex, than appears to the naked eye. A patient is not just his symptoms. We must begin, of course, with a good sense of who we are. In order to accomplish this and to get a sense of who our patient is, we have to employ a special sort of vision, a point of view that penetrates, like an x-ray, images that might otherwise pass unnoticed. We need to see the invisible world that effects the visible: the fantasies and values locked in the patient's past; the cultural viewpoint.

"The success of this particular patient's treatment pleased me because it wasn't cold and analytical," I continued. "Instead I read between the lines, so to speak, to develop an intimacy that allowed us to relate heart to heart." When I finished, the professor stood up to silence the whispering back and forth among my colleagues.

"I have, of course, looked in on the patient," the professor began. "I am quite pleased at how well she is now functioning, and I have signed off on your recommendation for discharge."

The professor took his seat again and adjusted his eye glasses on his nose. "However, there is no such thing as a cure for psychiatric illnesses. Since the patient seems well at this point, we must conclude, Doctor, that either the original diagnosis was in error or you are a genius.

"There is also no such thing as a genius," he continued. "Therefore this woman was never truly schizophrenic."

My smile quickly faded. My apparent victory suddenly became a reason for derision. Our professor showed me an even more disheartening fact of my chosen field. Not only is there no room for soul in psychiatry, there is no room for experimental techniques or for cures.

I later realized that a psychiatrist's identity is often so caught up in the doctor's omniscient, all-knowing role, that he or she loses the ability to come to a deeper understanding of the patient. Because of this unwillingness or inability to change perspective the psychiatrist often cannot empathize with the patient or admit there are answers to problems not found in textbooks, such as simply caring in the deepest sense for a person's spiritual needs. True spiritual healers, I knew, show profound empathy for the sorrowful conditions to which people are sometimes reduced by illness, wrong choices or unfortunate circumstances.

So, early in my residency, I was branded as a maverick in the field. I was often in deep trouble with academicians jealously guarding the diagnostic categories. For me, this closed-mindedness signaled the powerlessness of a system that knew how to define illness, but did not know how to bridge the hearts of the people involved. Medicine had become institutionalized by a language no one understood. People in pain and anguish were Borderline, Type 2. Patients were not sad or afraid; they were suffering from schizoaffective disorder or Huntington's Chorea. DSM labels and insurance categories had replaced empathetic understanding.

The institutional clothing—the patients' smocks and the doctors' coats—further emphasized the isolation and differentness of the patient and the healer. I was sometimes caught taking off the identification badge and the official-looking white labcoat when I talked with my patients.

Although I resisted it myself, it became clear to me that the medical system in which I worked was treating symptoms but not facilitating real healing. The system perpetuated and actually deepened the split between body, mind and soul. The list of chronic diseases lengthened as my fellow doctors, like the professor in the clinical meeting, lost hope in the concepts of cure and recovery.

From early on I realized we were in need of health-care reform; not just a reformation of specific functions, but a fundamental shift. We needed to go to the root of the matter: the recognition of the essential definition of a healer as one who alleviates the sorrow of others with compassion. To do this, we needed a transformation of our consciousness, a transcendence beyond education and cultural indoctrination.

I believed strongly that I could not be an effective healer if I were caught up in dramas and unhealthy behaviors of my own. I took to heart the old admonition, "Physician, heal thyself!" I began working on myself as Layla had suggested. Among the techniques and practices I started using at this time were lucid dreaming, yoga and zen meditation.

Whenever I found myself dreaming, I would take an active role in what was happening in the dream. I would ask questions of the other dream characters. I would go off and explore different rooms or buildings in the dream environment. A book Layla had recommended taught me yet another aspect of lucid dreaming. The book spoke of the sort of dream in which you are being chased by some person or monster. The Sufis try to stop running and face their pursuer in the dream. I found that the monster usually stopped too, and waited to see what I did next. The book then suggested asking the monster for a gift. When I did this in my dream, the monster would very politely hand me a box and disappear. In the box would be a key or a magnifying glass or a mirror or something else that represented the solution to the problem the monster represented.

When I awakened each morning, I did stretching exercises with controlled breathing from the tradition of Hatha Yoga. These included the well-known lotus seat in which the feet of the crossed legs rest on the opposite thigh. After practicing the lotus and a few other positions to prepare myself, I would bring out a small, round cushion and sit on it with my eyes closed and my legs crossed beneath me. This Zen Buddhist practice is called sitting in "zazen," and the objective is to empty the mind of thoughts and achieve "beginner's mind." I learned that this meditative state was analogous to soul awareness. In it, you observe every thought your mind generates without judging. You achieve the mindset of a young child, to whom everything is new and wonderful. Sometimes I would go to a community center nearby where they held Zen meditations on Wednesday nights. Eventually, I invited the group to meet at my apartment on additional nights.

I kept a journal at this time, too. In it I kept track of my daily practices. I checked off my early morning yoga and Zen exercises there. I checked off my Wednesday Zen meditations there. Although I found these Eastern techniques for self-exploration quite helpful, I saw a problem arising among my fellow Westerners.

The members of my Zen group saw in those Eastern traditions a hope for greater fulfillment than that offered by the traditions of the

West. They immersed themselves with great zeal in their newly chosen Eastern tradition: they busied their minds with learning new rituals and a new language. After years of study and practice, however, my fellow students became disillusioned with the Eastern tradition. The longing and emptiness that originally sent them searching returned.

Likewise, my spiritual teachers had become dissatisfied with the poverty and slow pace of the East and came West. They embraced the technology and materialism of this paradigm. Soon, they too were faced with the same lack of fulfillment, despite luxurious accommodations and adoring, devoted followers. They seemed to grow weary, losing the spark of joy and adventure they had felt at the start of their pilgrimage to the West.

In looking at this situation I came to the conclusion that the search for fulfillment was not about accepting teachings and winning salvation. Instead it was a process in which meditation or prayer was used to become more in charge of oneself. The process of spiritual connection or salvation was really the awakening of the spiritual consciousness. This connection was not an abstraction and could not be intellectualized. Rather it was the inspiration that comes when we truly love others and move forward on our true path. It became clear to me that in both Eastern and Western ideologies and religions, there was always a definitive moment which was the spiritual experience in and of itself. This was then followed by a methodology or a ritual that spawned an ideology or a belief system. I wasn't really interested in changing my belief systems, but in integrating the timelessness and the universal love that I had come to associate with spiritual consciousness and soul awareness.

While sitting on the little cushion I used during my Zen meditation one day, I started to feel the timelessness and universal love I had come to associate with soul awareness. I felt this was a beneficial way to prepare for my meditation because my mind realized the centered, quiet state the Zen Buddhists recommend; Zen masters often talked of the underlying energy which gave stability to the body and mind by just holding the meditation posture. My thoughts settled on the paradox of Westerners looking to the East and Easterners looking to the West in order to fill some void in their lives.

Zen masters teach the use of koans. These are opposing ideas—in my case East and West—are encouraged to argue with each other in one's mind. This produces a friction that, like two sticks being rubbed together, ignites a fire called satori. In the West, this concept is called the synthesis of opposites or the resolution of a paradox.

I found my meditations often gravitated toward this process of reconciling opposites. As I entered soul awareness, ideas that seemed at odds with each other—love and hate, change and satisfaction, giving and receiving—would blend into a feeling that these two were really expressions of the same principle. I came to realize that there were no polarities possible in the realm of spirit. When opposites became harmonious paradoxes, it was another sign that I had connected with my soul. In addition to a sense of timelessness and universal love, I knew I was in a state of soul awareness when I felt comfortable with paradoxes.

As I meditated on the differing paradigms of West (survival, change, parts) and East (transcendence, fulfillment, wholes), I was surprised to find no synthesis occurring. The more I tried to place the various aspects of the two paradigms in opposition, the more they seemed to fade and vanish from my thoughts. I was left with myself. I began to think I had failed in bringing East and West together in my mind, but a fleeting intuition caught my attention. Perhaps the fact that I was left with myself was what I was supposed to learn. Like the alcoholics with their wine or materialists with their jewels and fancy cars, searching for a new spiritual tradition was a form of external gratification. This "spiritual materialism" wasn't fulfilling because it temporarily relieved the pain and longing one feels, but it did not change the person whose life was fundamentally not working. I was left with myself in reconciling East and West because that is where the exploration and change needed to occur—within myself.

A few months later, I heard a friend of mine on the psychiatry staff explaining a new case to a colleague in one of the hallways. My friend had diagnosed a young woman with dementia praecox. She was studying physical therapy at our hospital and suffered an apparent breakdown under the strain of her demanding training. He felt her behavior had regressed to almost autistic characteristics in a desire "to receive affection for a weakened ego structure."

The organicist he spoke with uttered a long "hmmmm." He leaned against the wall and suggested the young woman undergo a series of electroshock treatments that would sufficiently confuse her to the point of being reeducated. The psychiatrist glanced in a folder he carried and responded that he favored giving her strong tranquilizers similar to Thorazine so she would become oblivious to her anxious feelings.

I thought back to an 18-year-old woman under another psychiatrist's care two weeks before. She was beautiful, blissful and the cause of great alarm in her family and in her doctor because she was in constant prayer and announced that she could talk to angels. To them, she was hallucinating; I wasn't as sure. The peace and calmness she exhibited extended to a depth I had seen in few people on our planet. Even her physical appearance took on aspects of the angelic: her limbs and fingers seemed inordinately long, and the trancelike state of bliss she lived in created an aura around her that was all but visible.

Between my rounds, I sometimes spent hours listening to her stories. She showed me her journals, and I often studied them in detail during my meal breaks. There seemed to be an uncommon wisdom in her writings, though the woman did not consider herself holy and wrote about her experiences with the greatest of humility.

She once told me, "Angels will again enter into the lives of human beings as a new era begins. Many of these angels will instruct humanity in etherial visions, in color healing, in realizing a super-conscious world, in developing superhuman physics, in celestial nourishment and in expanding consciousness."

I was deeply inspired by her message, but she was not my patient and I could not prescribe treatment. She was given electroshock treatments and, in her disorientation, forgot all about the angels. This wise, blissful young woman became tired, confused and, I thought, very unhappy. She was bloated, her face was swollen, and her limbs were now curled up and appeared to be palsied.

I went to see this woman after her treatment. The Carmelite nun who often made rounds at the hospital was in the room when I entered.

"Did you know this woman was subjected to electric shock because she was spending too much time praying and talking to angels?" I asked the nun.

"I am sorry if she had to suffer," the nun replied. "She must have been very ill."

"I'm not withholding anything from you, sister," I continued. "This young woman was diagnosed as sick because she believed she could communicate with angels. Perhaps we have silenced an undiscovered saint."

The nun glanced at the woman and then at me. "And perhaps not," she said as she turned and left.

With the memory fresh in my mind, I resolved at that moment not to let another misunderstood young woman's life be ruined.

I left the psychiatrist and the organicist at that point so that I wouldn't be caught eavesdropping. I found a nurse willing to tell me who the frightened physical therapy student was. The young woman's name was Katrina, and she was in a private room on the second floor. I had an evening shift that night so I decided to pay Katrina a visit.

I waited until after the orderlies had cleared the dinner trays to go up to the second floor. There I found the young, brown-haired, blue-eyed woman in bed with the covers pulled up tightly to her chin. She looked startled when I came in, so I immediately told her I was a doctor and that all I wanted to do was to talk with her.

I sat down in the chair next to her bed and introduced myself. She responded with a "hello." "Katrina, what are you afraid of?" I asked quite innocently.

For the next 25 minutes, Katrina told me the many reasons for her fear. The stories of difficult family members, threatening boyfriends, financial desperation and brutal teachers nearly overwhelmed me. No wonder she had been unable to handle the stress, I thought.

"Before you go on," I said interrupting her, "I was hoping you might help me out by writing out those things that make you so afraid." I handed her my pen and prescription pad. "On each piece of paper, write a few words to summarize the things that scare you."

At the end of an hour, she sat up in bed with a huge pile of papers in her lap. I reached into my pocket and produced some matches. Katrina smiled.

"If you had the power," I told her, "what is it you would do?"

She looked deeply into my eyes and shouted, "I would burn it all!"

I picked up a metal basin off the floor and scooped the pieces of paper into it. I put the basin full of papers back on her bed and extended the book of matches to her. "Go ahead," I said.

The slips of paper with her fears on them burned slowly. As I observed her facial expression in the flickering light of the flames, she seemed to acquire a look of serenity. She looked down and asked me in a soft voice, "Do you think I'm crazy?"

"No," I replied confidently. "You are a very strong, young woman who has a lot of hardships to deal with right now."

"I don't know if I belong here," she said as I took the basin of smoking ashes off the bed.

I wasn't sure what she meant. "You don't belong in the physical therapy school or you shouldn't be hospitalized?" She glanced away and didn't respond. "You can tell me. What do you want to know?"

Her deep blue eyes turned back toward me. "How long do I have to stay here?"

I looked at my wristwatch and she laughed. "No, I just realized that I have to finish my rounds soon. It's up to you and your therapist. I don't have any say in when you are discharged." She was gazing at the ashes of her fears and smiling when I left her.

Two days later, I was called into the office of the mental health department administrator. The administrator was an imposing woman in a gray suit jacket who sat behind a huge desk.

"I received a complaint about you yesterday," the administrator began. "One of the psychiatrists came to me and claimed that a young, inexperienced resident had changed the delusions of his patient. Evidently, the patient now believes she is well and wants to go home. From the patient's description, your supervising professor is convinced you are the resident in question."

The woman slid some papers on her desk to the side and leaned forward on her forearms. "Did you talk to this doctor's patient?"

"Yes, I spoke to her."

"I shouldn't need to remind you," she replied, "that you are not to interfere with patients under another physician's care. This incident will go in your academic file. You are not to make contact with this woman again."

I sighed heavily and asked if the woman was to be discharged. The administrator replied that, since she had admitted herself voluntarily, the hospital could not deny her request to be released.

Katrina's doctor refused to speak to me when we passed in the halls. At lunchtime I decided to take a walk to a nearby park. In front of the hospital I saw Katrina hugging an older woman. I went up to her as a man loaded her belongings into a waiting car.

"I heard you were being discharged," I told her. "Congratulations."

She introduced me to her mother, who said, "My daughter told me you came to her one night and helped her burn her fears away." She kissed me on the cheek. "You are a brilliant man. Thank you for helping my daughter." Katrina echoed her mother's gratitude and I waved goodbye as they got into the car and drove off.

By this time, I had been downgraded from maverick to troublemaker in the eyes of most of my professors. There was one professor who believed in my perspective, though, and I was fortunate to work with him for some time. We led groups of patients in healing circles. He had observed me working overtime one night, working with a single patient hours past the 50-minute time limit the psychiatric staff was asked to observe, and he decided that I would be perfect for this new outpatient program.

In the program all the participants sat in a circle, told their stories and prayed for each other. The professor and I led meditations to music. We brought in a dancer to lead the group in movement therapy. We brought in clay and the participants made bowls and vases as a sort of occupational therapy. We discovered a new school of thought called Gestalt therapy where the facilitators were asking patients to hold hands and hug each other, and we incorporated that into our group as well. We even rented a bus and took the participants to the ocean for one session. They seemed to relax and open up more there than when we met in the city.

Since the patients we saw did not have the severe problems of those in the psychiatric ward, they came voluntarily for our program and then went back to their lives between sessions. Word got out that we were not only allowing but encouraging our patients to touch each other. One of the nurses who had heard third-hand and therefore didn't realize I was responsible for the program was horrified to hear that "some doctor" had taken his psychiatric patients on a bus trip to the ocean where they were talking to trees! I joked with the nurse, "I heard many of them weren't talking at all before that, so I'd say talking to trees was an improvement." The nurse stared at me and walked away.

As my unusual methods slowly gained acceptance or at least familiarity, more of my colleagues came to observe my work. One of the older psychiatrists on staff, Dr. Perez, stopped me in the hallway near the end of the afternoon one day.

"I have been impressed with the results you've achieved here," the psychiatrist told me with arms folded.

"Thank you," I said. "They aren't all successes, I'm afraid."

"Don't be so modest," said Dr. Perez. "I think I know of a group that might be consistent with your philosophy. They meet here in Santiago. I think you might learn a lot from them."

"I'm always open to learning new things," I told him. "What does the group do?"

"It's a study group," Dr. Perez replied. "If you're interested, I can set up a meeting for you to talk to one of the people in the group."

"I'd like that," I said. "Thank you."

The next morning when I came on duty, there was a note taped to my desktop:

> *Be at the corner of Calle Iglesia and Avenida Libertad at 6 a.m. on Friday.—H. Perez*

Six in the morning? I groaned to myself. I considered tracking down Dr. Perez and asking for a later appointment and some description of the person I was supposed to meet. As he wasn't in that day, I eventually decided to go ahead with the meeting and see what happened.

My alarm clock went off at five o'clock that Friday morning, but I turned it off and went back to sleep for a half-hour. When I roused myself a bit and saw it was 5:30, I jumped out of bed and rushed through showering and dressing to make it out the door at ten minutes to six.

I drove down Avenida Libertad searching for Calle Iglesia, since I had never heard of the latter before. As Avenida Libertad approached the river the residential neighborhoods were replaced by warehouses. On the brick wall of one of the warehouses I spotted a sign that read "Calle Iglesia." I found a place to park at the nearest corner and sat in the car for a few minutes surveying the area.

The sun had rise, but it was still low in the sky, so the buildings, lamp posts and signs cast very long shadows. Through them passed the occasional laborer getting off the late shift or starting the morning shift. One very weary-looking man in a loosened tie and rumpled sports jacket staggered by my car as if he were still trying to find his way home from a party the night before. No one appeared to be waiting at any of the four corners of the intersection, however, so I decided to get out and make myself more visible. I checked my wristwatch. It was already several minutes after six.

When I got to the corner, I heard the calls of seagulls above my head and looked up. Two of the birds were making wide circles above the intersection. When they glided down Calle Iglesia toward the river, I followed. When I got a few steps down the alley, I noticed a one-story, adobe building with a bell and a cross above the door. I wondered if I'd found the church for which the alley had been named.

"Dr. Warter?" a husky male voice called from behind me. I jumped a bit in surprise. "I didn't mean to startle you. I understand you are interested in learning more about your true self, is that correct?"

I turned to face the man, who was about my height—well over six feet tall—and wore a black, wide-rimmed hat, wire-rim glasses and a gray tweed jacket. His features were germanic, he was well-muscled and I could see beneath his hat that his hair was cut short like an officer's. He had the air of an aristocrat and I was duly impressed. He carried a package in a Manilla envelope under one of his long, thin arms.

"Yes, that is correct," I replied.

The man handed me the package and explained, "In this package you will find two books and a card. You are to read the two books and write a report on each. Send the reports and a short autobiography to the address on the card. You will then be informed if you have been accepted into the group."

The man never introduced himself, nor did he stay around for questions. He handed over the package and started walking briskly away down the alley. He turned left onto Avenida Libertad and walked out of sight. By the time I followed him down the alley to the corner he was gone.

I returned to my car and opened the package. The card listed an address in England. The two books were by Idries Shah. I recognized one of the titles as a book Layla had recommended.

They were books of Sufi teaching stories. I took two weeks to finish reading them, then wrote down my reactions and sent the reports and a brief summary of my life to the address in England.

While I was waiting for a reply, I continued my initiation with Don Eduardo. The second session with him brought more visions, but I didn't feel any closer to the insight that would release me from the bonds of my past and of my fears.

On my third session with Don Eduardo weeks later, we met on a Saturday night at his home. He was actually waiting in front of the house when I drove up. When I got out of the car, he led me into the house in intense concentration, with one hand holding a small drum and drumstick and the other pulling on his moustache. We entered a room I had never been in. It was dark except for a single candle illuminating the center of a low table on which it rested.

We sat on the floor next to the table. Don Eduardo beat the drum as he led me through the breathing exercise and relaxation that preceded the shamanistic journeying sessions. I again felt the numbness in my body and the clearing of my mind.

Slowly a scene materialized. I felt a gentle breeze and the moist, misty air on my cheeks. I opened my eyes to see a woman in white robes standing on a flat, moss-covered rock next to a moonlit waterfall. She seemed to beckon me forward with her deep blue eyes. She invited me to let go of all my attachments, everything I thought I knew about myself and all my memories. Surprisingly, all the good things, the things I enjoyed, were easy to release. The painful memories and qualities about myself held on much more tenaciously. These painful memories, ideas and perceptions hung on like parasites, sucking on my vital identity, my soul.

Suddenly the woman disappeared. A flaming sword hung in midair where she had been standing. I stepped up and took the sword in my hand, using it to sever the parasites from my body one by one. I swung the sword with great fervor and could feel myself drenched in sweat. When there were only a few of the parasites left, I started to feel anxious, even scared.

What if I cut off the last of my perceptions and memories and found there was nothing left of me? I risked leading an isolated or indifferent life once the final remnants of my false self were removed. Casting these fears aside, I swung the sword again and the last of the parasites fell away.

I was alone. Even the waterfall, the rocks, and the sword had faded away. I was surprised to find myself calm. The solitude was actually peaceful and comforting.

At that realization, I envisioned myself in a sandy desert in the middle of the day. Sweat dripped from my body as the sun beat down upon me. There were no people, animals or even plants—just sand and sun. In the distance a door appeared. As I walked toward the door, it slowly opened to reveal an even brighter light than the sun above me. Then four guardian angels descended from above and gave me a box with a latched lid. They told me I needed the contents of the box to get through the doorway. When I asked what was in the box, one of the angels replied, "Faith."

When I stepped through the doorway with the box, the box disappeared and I felt myself floating in a void. With each exhalation of breath I was increasing my sense of surrender. Each exhalation brought more wholeness, more love, more ecstasy. I moved ever closer to oneness with the universal essence or soul.

But I could not completely dissociate from my body and join with that universal essence, tempting as that joyous feeling was. That complete dissociation comes only with death, I discovered, and that event was not up to me. That complete dissociation was up to a higher will than mine.

As I floated there on the edge of death, more overwhelmingly in touch with my soul identity than ever before in my life, an idea formed in my mind. I realized the most we can do while alive to connect to that universal soul is to perform service: we can act with kindness and compassion towards each individual on this planet. That, I decided, was the fourth sign of soul awareness. The universal love I felt in that timeless, paradoxical state of soul awareness manifested as an impulse to serve others. I was closer to my soul's path when I served others without the expectation of personal return.

I floated over pyramids and temples and churches and monuments. They were all built in a futile attempt to capture and house the inner peace I now felt, the builders jealously guarding their perceived storehouses of inner peace. The idea struck me as so funny that I laughed and laughed until my jaw started to hurt.

I landed at a crossroads that I perceived was inside myself. One avenue was painted with the word "Public," and the other with the word "Private." Beyond the crossroads was a temple. Again, the guardian angels appeared from above and urged me to approach the temple. When I opened the door of the temple, I experienced an intimacy and self-knowledge that was far deeper than either the public and private selves I had come to know.

I raised my hands to heaven and the clouds parted. Down came beams of colored light and a host of celestial beings. I had now experienced the initiation I was meant to have as a teenager.

When I came back from this shamanic state of consciousness and saw Don Eduardo sitting across from me in the dark room, I was surprised to look down at my body and find I was an adult, not a teenager.

"You are done here," Don Eduardo said. "Your path leads north now."

Interdimensional Awareness and the Ancient Wisdom of Plants

3

In one of the books the tall stranger gave me on that early Friday morning, Idries Shah spoke highly of Dr. Claudio Naranjo, M.D. When I was in medical school, Dr. Naranjo was the director of the Center of Studies of Medical Anthropology at the University of Chile where he researched non-ordinary states of consciousness in the arts and in spirituality. Dr. Naranjo's research in the United States for the National Institute of Mental Health (NIMH) focused on the therapeutic uses of psychoactive drugs. I mentioned this to Don Eduardo's partner Teresa, since her research seemed similar. She told me she knew Dr. Naranjo. The two of them had worked together in Chile years before, but he was now in California. Dr. Naranjo's name also came up in my studies of the enneagram, a Sufi system of nine personality types. When Don

Eduardo suggested I "go north," I decided a letter to Dr. Naranjo was in order.

He wrote back a few weeks later inviting me to come study with him, so I went to California during my three-month vacation that summer. Dr. Naranjo met me on the street in Berkeley. He was a skinny, shy man with hair that was quite long and an unkept beard. He had just returned from the Chilean desert where he studied with Oscar Ichazo. Ichazo was a Bolivian mystic who popularized the enneagram in Chile and founded the esoteric school Arica, named after the town where the school was located.

I saw in Dr. Naranjo demeanor a sadness coupled with mystery. It was as if he knew something he did not wish to share. While he was not overly friendly, we got along quite well considering our age difference.

It was evident from our conversation upon my arrival that the two of us shared not only a geographic past but also similar spiritual interests. He drove me to his house in Berkeley and told me it could be my base of operations for my entire sojourn in California, if I wished. He introduced me to the Esalen Institute in Big Sur, and during our week there convinced me to apply for a scholarship to their Gestalt therapy training program, a psychological system of dealing with both physiological and emotional traumas I had started to work with in the healing circles.

Dr. Naranjo told me that if I was awarded the scholarship, I would be immersed in a way of living quite in tune with the existentialists I had studied in school. This experiential lifestyle entailed certain characteristics: being centered in the present, in the here and now; focusing on what you have, not what you don't have; emphasizing the tangible, not the imagined; fully utilizing the senses and downplaying thought processes; expressing rather than manipulating, explaining, justifying or judging; surrendering to the full scope of feelings—pain as well as pleasure; rejecting others demands; rejecting the worship of idols; taking full responsibility for your actions, feelings and thoughts; and surrendering to your true identity.

The technique of choosing to live in the moment, sometimes called the present-centeredness technique, did not undermine the importance of consciousness and responsibility. Rather, it focused on wholeness,

awareness and actuality. When I employed Gestalt therapy in my healing circles I concentrated on an exercise called the continuum of awareness that is central to the therapy. Comparable to free association in psy-
choanalysis, the continuum of awareness involves looking at the past or
the future as though it were happening now. In this way an idea—a hope
or dream—could become a reality. If a patient came to me and said, "I
want to get well," I would have him rephrase and reframe his thinking
by saying instead, "I am well."

Claudio and I sat on his front porch one afternoon sipping herbal
tea and discussing the integration of various spiritual techniques and
philosophies. I explained that I had been looking for a good opportunity to balance my learning of Zen, of silent meditation, with expressive, communicative awareness.

"Your Gestalt training will definitely help you accomplish this. The
therapy allows the individual to more easily connect with others," said
Claudio.

"Could this connection be turned inward? I want to gain a greater
understanding of myself, similar to what I experienced in my love
affair with Françoise," I said.

Claudio thought for a moment and then replied, "There's a clear
connection between Gestalt awareness and the broad sense of zazen,
or Zen meditation, which embraces more that just correct posture.
Entering fully into every action with total attention and clear awareness is no less zazen. Basically, it develops and strengthens your
attention.

"I once read a parable that illustrates this point," Claudio continued.
"It went something like this. The master was asked by a disciple for
some maxims of the highest wisdom. The master took his brush and
wrote 'Attention.' The disciple asked, 'Is that all? Would you not add
something more?' The master wrote it again, twice 'Attention.
Attention.' Well, the disciple was irritated. 'I don't see much depth or
subtlety.' Then the master wrote it a third time, 'Attention. Attention.
Attention.' Half angry, the disciple said, 'What does that word
"Attention" mean anyway?'

"The master answered gently, 'Attention means attention.'"

I nodded in agreement, remembering my early Zen experiences.

My zazen practice began with counting the inhalations and exhalations of breath while sitting in a motionless zazen posture. This stilled the body's functions, stopped the mind from rambling and strengthened concentration.

Once I mastered this, I learned a more difficult zazen technique of following the inhalation and exhalation of the breath with the mind's eye only, in a natural rhythm. I was amazed at the state of equilibrium I achieved. I learned that zazen frees the mind from bondage to all thought forms, visions, objects and phenomena, bringing the mind to a state of absolute emptiness from which one can perceive the sacredness of one's own nature and the nature of the universe.

Dr. Naranjo also introduced me to a study group he attended, called "Seekers After Truth." The guest speakers I saw during my first few weeks of attending meetings represented a wide variety of traditions, including a Buddhist monk, a motivational consultant, an Indian meditation teacher and a fire-walker.

One speaker, who went by the nickname "Creature," seemed to embody in one person the variety of perspectives one would experience in several months of meetings. He had studied in India, Tibet, Japan, Indonesia, Mexico, Iceland, Scotland, France, Russia and Morocco. He had been a monk, an anthropologist, a fisherman, and now was a teacher of Sufism. Since I was also interested in Sufism and had been exposed to quite a few other traditions in my relatively short 25 years of life, I looked forward to chatting with this oddly named man after his talk.

With a name like Creature, one might expect a dark, hulking tangle of hair. In actuality, Creature was Anglo-Saxon in his features and almost a foot shorter than me in height. He was bald on top, but sported a large gray moustache. After his presentation he stood with his wife in the front of the hall. When I approached him, he locked me in a gaze so intense I became frightened and took a step back.

"You are too open," he told me as his blue eyes softened. "Do you let just anyone into your living room?"

I was at a loss for a response, but I didn't need to say anything because he went on after only a moment. "You need to be more closed. If you aren't a little more selective in what you let in, you may put yourself in danger. Pollution," he added, "is separation from radical unity. And this radical unity is the reconnection of the soul as a unit, as a oneness." His words reminded me of what my grandfather told me before he died.

I told him that all my experience and training thus far had encouraged me to be open. We talked for almost half an hour. When he heard I was looking into programs of consciousness study, he invited me to visit his training institute in the San Bernardino Mountains of southern California.

A week later I rode with one of Creature's students from the bus terminal to the institute in a dusty, red pickup truck. I was a bit nervous during the last part of the ride. The road was only one lane. It curved and twisted uncomfortably close to some rather steep, high cliffs.

The institute was a converted sheep ranch, I learned. Most of the conversion involved turning the ranch hands' quarters into guest lodging, but the beds were still bunks and the bathrooms were still communal, large and not especially clean. I slung the one bag I'd brought up onto the top bunk in my room and lay down on the lower bunk to rest until dinner time.

A light rain was falling when the dinner bell sounded, so I hurried with about two dozen other guests across the grounds to the main house where the meals were served. I scanned the sizable dining room for Creature, but didn't see him. One of the women at my table saw me looking around the room and anticipated my concern. "He doesn't usually eat dinner with us," she volunteered.

Evidently, he didn't eat breakfast with the guests either. Over our morning meal I asked one of the men when I might expect to see Creature. "He will be leading the morning meditation at ten," he told me as he took another helping of omelet.

I attended the meditation after breakfast. It was on attentiveness and I wasn't particularly impressed. The group was left sitting in silence for most of the session.

Creature approached me afterward. "Did you enjoy the morning session?"

I searched for something positive. "It was very straightforward," I said. He looked as if he wanted more feedback. "I found it very relaxing."

"Attentiveness is the main goal of my work here at the institute," he told me proudly. "I have to go take care of some paperwork right now, but perhaps we could talk further after dinner tonight."

I thanked him again for his invitation and told him I would look for him after dinner. He put on some sunglasses and headed for the main house.

The afternoon session was similarly uninspiring, so when I encountered Creature walking along the main road after dinner, I asked him if he could suggest any other teachers. He seemed unphased by the news of my impending departure, and told me of a great teacher and shaman he called Don Hector with whom he had studied recently in Mexico. He wrote out instructions on how I could get in touch with him.

In a phone call with Don Hector the next morning he told me to come visit anytime. I called Dr. Naranjo to let him know I was going to Mexico, then I asked one of the students to give me a ride back to the bus terminal.

Two days later, my Aeromexico flight landed in the Distrito Federal. I took a taxi to the address Creature had given me. I expected to find other students of Sufism there since I knew Shah had a study group in Mexico City. I was surprised to be very cordially greeted instead by a short middle-aged man with a receding hairline who introduced himself as Don Hector. He wore glasses, a button-down shirt and dark slacks. As he led me down the hall I noticed the firm way he walked. It reminded me of a puma or tiger because I could sense he was aware of everything around him and could spring into action with but a thought. When Don Hector showed me to my room in the back of the small house near the kitchen, I heard voices in a room next to mine. He explained that "others" lived there with him, though I never got to see their faces. On that first day he rarely spoke to me. He only looked at me and nodded when I encountered him.

On the second day, I got up and decided to go for a walk and wander around the city since Don Hector had not yet given me any instructions. As I left through the front door of the house and started down the street, Don Hector called out to me from one of the windows of his house, "Hey! Have you been to the museum of anthropology?" I shook my head no.

"That is where you will spend the day," he announced and pulled his head back in the window.

I asked directions on the street and made my way towards the museum. Mexico City was a dusty confusing place for a traveler. The streets were wide and full of heavy traffic. Many of the neighborhoods I passed were poor and in obvious decline. I ended up at the museum about an hour after leaving. I bought something to eat and then spent the next six hours going through the many rooms filled with anthropology exhibits. I practiced sensing the electromagnetic fields produced by the stones and artifacts as I passed from one room to the next. I mused that thousands of tourists had passed through these same rooms and had no inkling of the effects those electromagnetic fields would have on their systems. I began to believe that the ancient people who had produced the items on display here had been counting on their ability to influence people hundreds of years later. The ancients had "programmed" these relics with their teachings and with scenes from their lives. These programs could be "accessed" by a sensitive person who stood near the relics and "read" their electromagnetic fields.

That evening I had my first real conversation with my host and teacher. He talked of the mystical, lost continent of Atlantis and of the network of power points on the Earth. He said people always seemed to build churches and temples and shrines over these sources of terrestrial energy, usually unaware of why that spot demanded a sacred use.

I went to bed early on the narrow cot in my room, but I was restless. I tossed and turned half-awake or fully conscious for hours. In the middle of the night, I saw a face appear in my doorway. "There is never anything to fear," Don Hector said in the dim light from the hall and then disappeared.

I pondered that. There is never anything to fear. What did he mean by that? The house felt as if it were full of spirits or invisible guests. I did not see any of them, but I definitely heard conversations in dialects I couldn't understand. I thought about all the teachers I had met so far and wondered if it was my destiny to become a collector of teachings. Shortly after that, I finally fell asleep.

The next morning Don Hector stuck his head in my room and told me to get out of bed. "We're going shopping," he said.

He led me to the market of Sonora which I had heard about but never seen before. Thousands of vendors stood behind their stands which stretched for a half-mile along the roadside. Every kind of vegetable, fruit, herb, incense, powder, amulet and talisman you could imagine was being bartered, traded or sold there. "Hello, Don Hector!" was a familiar greeting from dozens of peasants we passed. I felt like I was being led through a movie set representing the sixteenth century; it seemed nothing had changed here in the last few hundred years.

The crowd was packed tightly in some areas, so it was sometimes difficult for us to see where we were going. At one point I stopped to buy some fruit at one of the stands. Don Hector turned to me and said with fierce conviction, "Plants were the first form of life on earth, millions of years before people. By the time humans showed up, plants already knew everything there was to know. My ancestors taught us that the green cover of the earth has a marvelous relationship with the sun—plants use their green chlorophyll to more directly synthesize solar rays into life."

We started walking again, and Don Hector continued, "This energy has information. The spirit of each plant knows how to become the source of all living processes. Through its vitamins and minerals, it produces a particular medicine.

"I will introduce you to a plant that has properties that can't be explained. It has a spirit that can carry human minds to destinies outside their understanding, back to their roots and beyond," he said mysteriously.

"We will meet a cactus," Don Hector explained, "that is the reason for your visit to this country. We have been watching you. We will continue to watch you as you go to a temple that borders the spiritual dimensions.

"Peyote is one of our sacred plants. These plants make bridges between man and the Great Spirit. Peyote is like a messenger because he can speak with the spirits. And more than that, this plant will leave an anchor in you so that the higher spirits can come find you later and whisper to you in your sleep what they want you to know . . . for the rest of your life," he added ominously.

He held out the palm of his hand and said abruptly, "Give me some pesos!"

I handed him the equivalent of five dollars, which he gave to a peasant in a poncho and sombrero. The older man gave Don Hector a brown paper sack. Don Hector gave the bag to me, then he laughed and called to the man, "Drink a beer on my health with the change!" I looked into the bag. It was filled with cactus.

Don Hector looked serious once more when he said, "I want to teach you something very important. It is a prayer of protection. If you say it when you are about to engage the spirit world, you will not have to fight the dark forces, nor will you risk absorbing their evil accidentally. Listen carefully because you will need to memorize it before tomorrow:

Spirits protect me! May the white light of knowledge surround me and protect me from ignorance! May the green light of healing surround me and give me strength! May the violet light of transmutation surround me and send, with neither love nor hate, whatever forces are not in resonance with these three lights back to its origin!

Now we must be on our way."

He gave me a quick glance and then darted through the crowds much faster than before. I actually had trouble keeping up with him on the way back to his house. When we got there, he dumped the contents of the bag out onto the kitchen table and gestured for me to take a seat.

"Do you trust me?" Don Hector asked with a smile as he sat down at the table. I told him I did.

"Even though you speak Spanish, you have la facha de gringo," he said accusingly in reference to my fair hair and complexion, "and do you know how little we think of them here?"

I felt that surrender was key at this point. "I do," I replied.

"You don't yet know what a plant is," he said as he picked through the pieces of cactus on the table.

"I understand how many plants are the source for the pharmacology of healing," I ventured.

"Plants cure because they are toxic," he explained. "The difference between a medicine, a narcotic and a poison is in the dose.

"The fruits of the gods are toxic to man, and you are about to eat one.

"Without losing consciousness, you'll enter into a dream state that will seem more vivid than everyday living. It is there that you will learn the purpose for your journey to Mexico.

"After you have this experience you must leave Mexico and travel to the old Inca fortress of Saqsaywaman near Cuzco, Peru. You will go all by yourself." He pulled an envelope from a nearby drawer and handed it to me. "There you will open this envelope and swallow its contents."

I looked down at the cactus on the table and said, "I am ready."

"You may be ready, but the plant is not," he said with a smile. "Today we prepare it, and tomorrow you can have your journey."

We cooked the peyote buttons for a long time and then mixed them with fruit and sugar to make a marmalade. He told me it would still taste very bitter, but the sugar would help. When the mixture had cooled, we spooned most of it into a yogurt container and put it in the refrigerator. By the time we finished making the peyote marmalade it was late at night and I was exhausted. I fell asleep quickly.

It was still dark out and I felt I'd just fallen asleep when Don Hector came and woke me early the next morning. He told me which buses to take to get to Teotihuacan, the site of some ruins about 60 miles outside of Mexico City.

"When you get there," Don Hector instructed, "you need to take your yogurt container to the top of the Pyramid of the Moon and eat the marmalade there."

"What?" I asked. "Alone in the middle of some old ruins?"

"Are you afraid?" He smiled.

"No, I'm fine," I lied, fearing he would tell me I was not ready.

"Mescal will guide you in your journey," Don Hector said in blessing. "May you speak with the gods and learn about us."

He thrust the yogurt container into my hands and commanded, "Now go!"

Three hours later I got off a bus and made my way through many bands of roving tourists. A multicultural melange, they seemed to come from every corner of the globe. I recognized Japanese, English, French and German phrases. Wiping the dust from my eyes, I headed toward the ruins with my marmalade, ready to climb one of the pyramids.

Don Hector had instructed me to go to the top of the Pyramid of the Moon, a ruin with 87 steps leading to its pinnacle, which was built at the opposite end of a long dirt road. Along this road stood the Pyramid of the Sun, a smaller monument flanked by other ruins. A sign in four languages proclaimed the road leading to the two pyramids to be the Avenue of the Dead.

It took me another hour and a half to get to the top of this exquisite monument and find a small "private" place for this sacred action. No wonder Don Hector had me start out so early, I thought to myself.

I repeated the prayer of protection Don Hector had taught me and ate the horribly bitter mixture we had made the day before. It was difficult to swallow, but I was determined to succeed, so I forced it down.

Despite the occasional tromping, huffing and puffing of tourists proud to have survived the climb to the top, I settled down on the smooth stones and started my journey.

Gradually the bottom part of the pyramid disappeared until all that was left was the top and the last few upper steps. I felt warmth and some sort of rounded enclosure forming around the top of the pyramid, as if I were in a huge womb. The pounding of some huge, celestial drum seemed to echo through the heavens. When I looked down and saw how far I was from the ground, I questioned if I would ever return to earth. There no longer seemed to be a way down from the pyramid.

Feeling very isolated from the rest of humanity, I floated there high above the ground. I thought back to all the times in school when I had felt this way. At parties, I would spend most of my time talking about philosophy to anyone who stayed long enough to listen before returning to the dance floor. I was given the nickname of "the Professor." In medical school and during my internship, I was shunned by many because my talk of the healing powers of love and of the soul made me seem strange. But this feeling of isolation that had brought me sadness and loneliness was now making me feel differently. The isolation I felt on the top of this pyramid stirred feelings of pride for some reason. I felt like I had won some honor, successfully completed an initiation.

As I began to feel closer to the rest of humanity, I gradually realized it was my "differentness" that was allowing me to connect with others more deeply. As I turned this paradox over in my mind, I also realized I now had a clearer understanding of the process of individuation. The concept had always seemed a simple case of breaking from the expectations of one's parents. I remembered that paradoxes were a mark of soul awareness, and perhaps this feeling of being unique and separate yet connected to others was another such marker.

I came to understand that as a person's true self is realized, the forces of heaven and earth rapidly come together to speed the individuation process. Life becomes rich and full as one naturally and spontaneously gravitates toward the activities and situations that are in harmony with one's own realization. Defensive, superficial and uninteresting activities and engagements drop away. It seemed to me that as more people connected with their essence, it would extend to the emergence of a new culture, a new way of relating, a new interpersonal ethic, that allowed for global realization. Life was a continuity of "being" instead of a string of events. When one was fully evolved the self naturally translated into the light of essence.

On top of this pyramid I was growing and understanding my true essence. I saw that there was a meaningful, synchronous order in the cosmos. I felt myself composed of light energy. It was a feeling that is difficult to describe, but I had an overall sense of "absolute knowledge." While in this state I knew that I would return to this same spot, the pyramids of Teotihuacan, twelve years later, a fact that was absolutely crucial in my future life.

Hours later when the bottom of the pyramid reappeared, the sky was dark. I climbed down to the ground quickly. It was late at night when I reached the Avenue of the Dead again. As I walked down the road, I felt like I was being followed by a beam of light. Slowly, I perceived crowds of tourists watching the nightly light and sound show and realized the lights following me were very much of this world.

When I got back to Don Hector's house it was after midnight. Hector was up waiting.

"How did it go?" he asked. His voice was cold and stern.

I told him I felt tired but okay. When I began to tell him what I had experienced on my journey he interrupted me. "Keep the gold for yourself so that it will strengthen your fiber."

"I'm surprised at the late hour," I told Don Hector. "I had no idea I was at the ruins for such a long time."

"You must understand," he said, "your attention was not earthbound. Galactic time and space is a completely different concept."

I enthusiastically talked of my insights on individuation and its role in the synchronous order of the cosmos.

Don Hector cut me off again, sighing. "There is still much that you must learn," he said. "You have already contacted the Tibetans and some of us, the Teotihuacanos. I advise you to learn from the collected wisdom of the indigenous peoples who have not become industrialized—the Mayans, the Hopis, the Kahunas, the Tibetans—and understand they have a notion of galactic time. The world is going to come to a point where the identity of the soul becomes a galactic identity. Later in history it will become apparent."

"I realize I still have a great deal to learn," I said. "But after today I feel I have a greater understanding of myself. I've always wanted to serve humanity, and now I know I'm on the right path."

We sat in silence for a few minutes, the sound of the ticking clock filled the void. Don Hector held his hands as if in prayer, bringing them up to meet his lips. Setting them down gently on the table, he leaned forward and looked directly into my eyes. "You are being trained now," he said. "Later you will form groups around the world to discuss these issues and to actively participate as a newly admitted member of a higher, galactic order. There will be a lot of light, photonic energy composed of electromagnetic radiation, coming into the planet. As it approaches our solar system, many people like yourself are being exposed and trained in order to ascend their perceptions from a third dimensional to a fifth dimensional reality. Photonic energy is what will matter."

"What is this fifth dimensional reality?" I asked.

"It is a new, integrated spirituality that is emerging. In your journey you are being trained in the substance of different spiritual traditions. This new spirituality is going to show that the disciplines of science, technology and spirituality can all merge. This unity is an aspect of fifth dimensional reality."

"I see," I said. "Am I in the right place to learn this knowledge? Is there one tradition I should be learning from?"

"No," Don Hector answered. "Don't be completely identified with any one tradition. Anyone who educates you to stick with one tradition is just brainwashing you. Toward the end of the century, which is the end of this karmic cycle, the traditions will merge into this new spirituality, a consciousness aimed toward the highest good of all: a mission of wholeness."

The next morning I packed my bags, including the envelope Don Hector had given me, and searched the house to say goodbye to my host. I found him sitting on the front step. He wished me well and reminded me to use the prayer of protection he had taught me. I set off for the airport.

My plane landed around noon in Lima, Peru. I had plenty of time to wander around the city before my connecting flight the next morning. I checked in at my hotel and then visited the Gold Museum, which housed relics of pre-Incan civilizations. At this museum I experienced a sense of cultural change, so to speak. Having been born and trained in the Western mode, Peru showed me that long before Western civilization invaded this country there were many sequences of civilizations that lived and loved and cared and worked and developed a life of their own, civilizations of which very little is known today. I was humbled, and realized there was a lot to learn. Western arrogance had made a false model of what it meant to be alive in the twentieth century.

I ate dinner at an outdoor cafe and stayed out late at a plaza where I watched and eventually participated in a ritual Incan folk dance. It was an almost ecstatically orgasmic dance, reminiscent of the original tribal rituals. The combination of music and dancing was so soothing I felt like I was in a non-ordinary state of consciousness. I didn't realize how tired and sore I had become until hours later when I stumbled back to my hotel.

The next morning, Saturday, I went back to the airport and boarded my flight to Cuzco. The view from the plane window as we ascended high over mountains was spectacular. Once we landed and I checked into my hotel room in Cuzco, an ancient Incan city 11,000 feet above sea level, one of the maids brought me a tea brewed from coca leaves. She said it would help me adapt to the higher altitude. "We give it to all our guests when they arrive," she said as she left. I drank the tea and immediately fell asleep for the next 24 hours.

I woke up late Sunday morning a bit light headed and very, very hungry. I checked at the hotel desk for suggestions about eating establishments, and the young man told me to try going to the nearby village of Pisac. "There's an open-air market with food and entertainment there every Sunday," he said.

As I walked through the city toward the bus bound for the Pisac market, I admired the three snow-capped peaks surrounding this valley. The city had been a center for healers since the days of the Incan empire, and I hoped that this market was the best place to meet them. Indians from various tribes came down from the mountain peaks and up from the valleys to sell their corn and potatoes and handcrafts, play the Andean flute, sing, dance and gossip. I had heard that the Quechua Indians often used the mind-altering ayahuasca vine in their rituals. Since I was interested in sacred initiatory substances, I tried to find one of these Indians.

"The soul is trying to contact you," called a strange voice.

I turned and saw an old Indian man sitting on the ground selling colorful ponchos. His wide cheeks and eyes were surrounded by deep lines etched into his face by Mexico's intense sun, and he wore one of his own ponchos over his dark, dusty clothes. He nodded when I looked at him, but his eyes quickly broke contact with mine as he scanned the area around him. I approached him and asked, "Do you know where I might find the ones who have ayahuasca?"

The old man looked away and didn't respond.

I retrieved the envelope Don Hector had given me from my jacket pocket. "Maybe I already have some ayahuasca," I suggested as I held out the envelope to the man selling ponchos.

He slowly leaned forward and took the envelope from me. His brow furrowed and he opened the envelope to sift through the brown powder in it. "Ayahuasca is called the Vine of the Dead. It helps those who eat it connect with the world of spirits," he said. He returned the envelope to me and continued, "You don't have a vine. You have a root."

I tried to ask the old man if he knew anything else about the brown powder or about ayahuasca, but he refused to talk further and waved me away. I stayed at the market for an hour longer and then boarded the bus back to Cuzco.

The next morning I ate a quick breakfast and set out with some water, some bread and my envelope containing the mysterious brown powder. The Incan fortress at Saqsaywaman, located on one of the nearby peaks, was visible from the street in front of my hotel. I headed in the general direction of the peak, and eventually I came across a dirt path leading up the hill toward the ruins.

It was almost noon when I finally reached the stone walls of Saqsaywaman. I had taken several rests on the way up, since the fortress was almost another thousand feet above Cuzco, but I was still breathless and sweating when I reached Saqsaywaman. I was completely alone at the fortress so I wandered about the site for a few minutes, around huge stone monoliths, through ornately carved trapezoidal archways. Then, I heard the sound of diesel engines approaching. Soon, two buses filled with tourists arrived. The visitors were quickly squealing at the majestic views and snapping photographs. I searched the ruins for about an hour before settling on a quiet location to perform the second part of Don Hector's initiation ritual.

I sat on a stone pedestal on the edge of the site on the far side of a seven-foot-high stone wall. I figured the location would give me a view of Cuzco and the rest of the valley below, give me shelter from the hot sun most of the afternoon and keep me secluded from most of the other visitors. I repeated the prayer of protection Don Hector had taught me and visualized the three colored lights descending over me.

Then I swallowed the brown powder and washed it down with water from my flask.

The first thing I noticed after several minutes was the brightening of the colors around me. The greens in the drying grass were more vivid. The sky seemed a brighter, deeper blue. The gray and red tones of the rocks looked as if they had been painted on with bright paints. I gazed down at the valley, and the city looked much bigger and regal, the river more forceful as it meandered along—almost electric.

The sounds of the tourists and the buses gradually faded away, and I felt very isolated and remote from humanity once again. I felt much more connected with the earth itself, a sort of consonance with the harmonies of life. As I stared at the landscape and the nearby rocks, the air seemed to shimmer as if it were very hot. There appeared an arching strand of energy just above the ground, stretching toward the horizon. Then more lines of energy began appearing. They started crossing. I saw some of the lines begin just above the ground in the ruins behind me. After a while, I found myself in the midst of a complex web of energy covering the ground as far as I could see. I felt that this web of energy was always present everywhere, that when we became centered and contacted our higher self, it was revealed to us.

Here was another mark of soul awareness, I thought. I remembered how connected I felt to the natural world when I had been in the Central Valley with Françoise, and I realized that it was the West's preoccupation with technology and human-built structures that actually made it more difficult to connect with the soul. As I studied the strands of earth-energy stretching to the horizons, I sensed that the earth itself was not only a key to our connection with our vital identity, but was also important in connecting with the souls of others. I felt this grid of energy was the foundation on which a new world with new values would be built. It was the structure that held everything in the third dimension together. Because all of humanity was held together in the third dimension this total sense of being, of "I am"-ness, was more dominant than the singular sense of personal identity. It was the essential identity of humanity which allowed for the understanding that we can be together as a human race.

I also perceived the presence of others. These beings were physical at other times, but here they existed as the custodians of the earth and lived in this other dimension. They were the keepers of knowledge—they understood these other dimensions that had subtly penetrated my own structures of awareness. An enrichment of my soul memory was surreptitiously taking place. Particles of information about this ancient wisdom were incorporated into my system, to be utilized at the appropriate times. These guardians were teachers working with me to unleash my heart's service.

Fourth-dimensional reality came from higher or more subtle ways of being that we, existing in the third dimension, could not grasp.

As the intersecting strings of energy started to fade, I noticed the sun was very low on the horizon. The buses and tourists had gone, and I was once more alone in the ancient fortress. I looked around the ruins one last time, took a deep breath, and headed back down the mountainside.

I later discovered the brown powder I swallowed that day up at Saqsaywaman was an African root called iboga, used by the Bwiti tribe of Gabon in a ritual to communicate with their ancestors and heal the soul of the community. It is now being studied by Western scientists for its ability to help addicts in recovery. It seems to gently show them the fears and childhood memories they are trying to repress with alcohol and drug abuse.

Because I still had more than a week before I had to return to my residency in Chile, I studied some maps back at my hotel in Cuzco. I realized I wasn't far from Machu Picchu, another famous Incan city. I inquired about transportation at the hotel front desk, and was told to be at the train station the next morning.

Late the next afternoon, I got off the train with my one suitcase in a small town named Aguas Calientes for the therapeutic hot springs there. The town was little more that a street lined with colonial houses, along which vendors sold jewelry, ponchos and the many other objects tourists are likely to buy. There was a small inn across from the train station, but the girl who greeted me at the inn's front porch told me there were no rooms available anywhere near the train station.

She suggested I try an inn on the edge of town, and she gave me directions to get there.

The directions weren't too hard to follow. There was only one street in Aguas Calientes, so I followed it to the edge of town in the direction the girl pointed. I easily found the two-story, yellow house the girl had described. When I entered the house, I walked into an old-fashioned parlor with Oriental rugs, tapestries on the walls, a ceiling fan, a love seat and chairs trimmed with tassels and fringe and a very large water pipe or hookah on a small, low table. A gentle breeze came through the two windows and made the wooden blinds tap in unison against their window frames. I noticed a poster proclaiming a Jefferson Airplane concert in San Francisco on one of the walls.

Eventually I was greeted by a short man with gray hair, a moustache and glasses. "Hello," he said. "Are you here for the hot springs or the ruins?"

"Both," I replied. "Is there a room I could have for the next few days?"

"Ordinarily not," the man said with a smile, "but one of our longtime residents, a younger mestizo guy, just left us to take a job in Lima, so the fourth room is open."

He explained there were two other Native Americans—he didn't know what tribe—that had been with him for several weeks. There was also an American couple who had arrived a few days earlier to study the ruins at Machu Picchu. He took money for the next two nights, asked me to sign a guest book and then showed me to my room. The room itself was so narrow I could touch opposite walls simultaneously, but there was a little cot, a shelf for my suitcase and a basin of water on a tall stand, so I decided it would suffice.

I met the inn's other four guests at the complimentary buffet in the parlor that evening. I got the impression the two Indian men didn't speak much Spanish, so I spent most of my time talking to the American couple in English. They were from California and were anthropologists who were making their way through Central and South America studying the lifestyles of the ancient Mayans and Incas from what was left of their cities, temples and writings. They were dressed in the hippy fashions of the times, and with their blond hair, blue eyes and pale skin seemed quite out of place in Mexico. The woman introduced herself as Lisa and her husband and colleague as Roger.

"What is your interest in the ruins?" Roger asked me.

I wasn't sure yet how open I could be about my interest in mysticism with these people so I claimed to be "just visiting."

"We've been spending the past few days up at Machu Picchu," Lisa said, "but tomorrow we are going up to Huaina Picchu. We have heard there are some carvings there that might add to our research."

"What have you found so far at Machu Picchu?" I asked.

"There seem to be a lot of references to two particular figures," Lisa explained. "We've seen them at other sites, but here you see pictures and references to Pachamamma, the cosmic mother, and to Wiracocha, the great spirit, everywhere. We see them as a sky god and the goddess of the Earth."

I finished my tea and set it on a nearby table. "So, what is there to do in Aguas Calientes on a Tuesday night?"

"After climbing up to and around in those ruins all day," Roger volunteered, "we always go to the hot springs to relax. We'll be going in a few minutes. Would you like to join us?"

I told them I would, and after getting some belongings from my room, I met them back in the parlor. The three of us followed a well-worn dirt path just off the main street to a series of pools along a stream running through a little valley. There were five others there at the springs, but the three of us found a nice, warm pool to ourselves and talked further about our travels and about the ruins I would visit that next morning.

The climb from my funky, little inn in Aguas Calientes up to the ruins at Machu Picchu the next morning looked a little too long to take by foot, so I boarded a small bus with a handful of other visitors at eight o'clock. I settled down in my seat and tried to relax as much as the bumpy, two-hour ride up the mountain would allow.

A couple of Quechua Indian guards greeted our bus when we reached the end of the road. They led our little group up a footpath from where the bus was parked. I noticed they were both armed with pistols.

We turned a bend, and from behind a cliff, the structures of Machu Picchu were revealed. It took us several more minutes to get to the sight itself. Some in our party felt fatigued, not yet adjusted to the high altitude.

The sight of Machu Picchu was truly awe-inspiring: it appeared to be a city grown right out of the mountain. The ruins were better preserved here than those at Saqsaywaman. Where before I had only seen a few walls and pedestals, here at Machu Picchu were complete buildings with roofs and windows and the suggestion of furnishings and decorations. The stone carvings were still broken and worn, but there were more of them to see and study. I tried to make out the figures of Pachamamma and Wiracocha that Lisa and Roger had told me about.

I found out from one of the guards that although the bus departed down the mountain for Aguas Calientes at two o'clock, I could stay another two hours if I wanted. "You will, of course, have to walk back," he said with a grin, "but you will have a better chance of finding what you are looking for when you are up here alone."

I smiled back and wondered if he really did know why I was there. There was a glint of recognition in his eyes that belied the macho ribbing and seemed to imply otherwise. I called out "Mucho gracias!" to him as he walked away to continue his patrolling. "I'll do that."

I followed a routine during my days at Machu Picchu: taking the bus to the site, walking back down in the late afternoon and taking a bath at the hot springs before bed. I started thinking I should try again to find an Indian to help me get some ayahuasca, but I couldn't communicate what I wanted to my fellow inn guests and the guards at the ruins seemed unapproachable. I wanted to get some further insight out of this trip, so I decided to stay up at the ruins overnight on the fourth day.

I took the bus up the mountain in the morning as usual. By the time the bus left with the other visitors that afternoon, the guards had become used to my staying behind and walking down later. When I started down the path toward Aguas Calientes around sunset that day, I could see the guards getting in their Jeep and heading down the road, too. I climbed back up to the site and found a building in which to pass the night. I put a blanket and some food I'd brought in the building, then wandered back out on the cliff to watch the setting sun and the rising of the nearly full moon.

As I sat there in the bright moonlight that evening, I scanned the shadowy ruins set into the cliff. Once or twice I imagined shadows in motion amid the stones, walls and buildings, but everything was so completely quiet otherwise I dismissed them. At first.

The moon was almost overhead by the time my eyelids started drooping and I trudged back to the building where I'd stowed my things. I laid down on the dirt floor and started imagining what the original occupants' lives might have been like here in this city on a high mountain cliff.

I was awakened almost an hour later by what sounded like footsteps! I held my breath and listened more closely. They seemed to stop. I carefully and quietly got up and moved to the doorway to see if there indeed were others out there. A couple of clouds rolled across the sky, but the moon still shone brightly on the ruins, which again seemed very still and abandoned.

I laid down again, but just as I was falling asleep I heard the footsteps. Instead of getting up, this time I remained lying down, listening. The steps were slow—walking, not running. There seemed to be groups of people going in different directions. The more I listened, the more footsteps I could make out. I started to worry that I was hallucinating. I lifted my head and sat up. The footsteps once again disappeared.

I got back to sleep and passed the rest of the night undisturbed. When the sunlight from the window reached my face the next morning, I woke up, gathered my things together, and ambled outside. The guards had already arrived in anticipation of the busload of tourists. One of the Quechua guards said something to the other and then started walking toward me. He didn't seem very threatening, so I was convinced that I wasn't in trouble.

"You decided to spend the night?" the guard asked when he was within a few feet of me. I nodded. "Did you hear the footsteps?"

My jaw dropped. "Yes, I did. What are they?"

"My people have a story," the Indian guard explained. "They say that one day, all the Incas disappeared. Maybe 20,000 of them disappeared.

Nobody knows where they went or what happened to them, but my people believe they never really left. They're still here. You just can't see them any more. There is an invisible holy sacred city where they live, in another dimension. They're waiting for the sign of a new world order. Evolution, from animals to humans, is based on the vibrations that will cause the re-emergence of the new civilization. Then the secret Incas will emerge and they will meet humankind: they will meet a new humanity."

The look of fascination on my face must have encouraged him because he continued, "They come up here from where they live down at Huaina Picchu, 'the new hill,' because this was an observatory for them. They come up here from their crystal city down in the valley to look out at the sky and the rest of the world for a sign. They're waiting down there in the Sacred Valley for the day when the ancient prophecy comes true. 'A new old world will come,' it says, and people will become disinterested in possessions. Matters of the spirit will become all-important. The need to control each other will disappear. All genuine seekers, from every land and religion, will gain the knowledge of the creator. That's when we'll be able to see them again."

The guard turned to go back to his post, then stopped and looked over his shoulder. "That's just a story, though," he called back to me.

The Seeker
After Truth

4

From Peru, I returned to Chile and continued working at the hospital. The successes my mentor and I experienced in the outpatient program—we called the program "healing circles"—must have improved my reputation among my colleagues somewhat. They started referring their more difficult cases to me. "Here," one of my fellow psychiatrists said handing a patient file to me, "since I'm not having any luck in helping this man, maybe you can do something with him." One day I found a patient file on my desk with a note stapled to it: "I don't think anyone can help this woman, but you're welcome to try."

The number of patients referred to me quickly grew to the point where I could no longer find spare time to see them individually. I

formed a private group that had many of the same features as the healing circles at the hospital. The successes continued there as well.

One woman in the group had incredibly low self-esteem. She was
intelligent, beautiful and married to a successful businessman. Yet she
often felt hopeless and even suicidal. During our work together, she discovered she was subconsciously comparing herself to and competing
with her husband. Within weeks she took on new responsibilities with a
non-profit organization and felt like she had taken control of her life
again. Her fears that having her own life would threaten her marriage
were unfounded; her husband was proud and pleased with her new
accomplishments and their relationship became a greater source of joy
than it had been in years.

One man in the group was plagued by shame and guilt. He never felt
happy or relaxed. During our sessions, we went over his past to find the
source of his shame. Other than some poverty he suffered about the time
he had met his devoted wife, there didn't seem to be any missed opportunity or cruel deed we could explore. In the middle of another participant's rather painful sharing, this man suddenly started crying. When
we asked what had evoked the tears, he said he hadn't wanted the group
to know his wife had been a prostitute. Although she was faithful to him
during their 25-year marriage, he believed deep down that every person
he met sensed his wife's past and judged him harshly for it. Through the
support of the group and some relaxation techniques I taught him, his
paranoid feelings and depressions started to disappear.

Another woman in the group felt resentment bordering on rage
toward her husband, who had no idea what he had done to upset her. In
tracing back to the start of her hostile feelings, they apparently started
about the time of her 28th birthday. Her husband had presented her with
a grand piano after discovering in one of the rare talks he'd had with her
estranged father that she had been an accomplished pianist as a child.
The rage the woman felt toward her father, who had forced her to play
the piano against her wishes, was evidently transferred to her husband
years ago. In exploring and releasing her fear and anger toward her
father, her marriage improved and she finally began playing the piano
that had been covered up for years in her parlor. In fact, I heard she later
gave concerts and recitals professionally.

In one session, we discovered that two men, a sociologist and an architect, had brought firearms to our group. The sociologist, we found out, was a radical leftist, and the architect was a member of the extreme right faction in the months before the coup against Allende. As the two men discussed their childhoods and their families, they discovered the humanity beneath the ideologies. In a later session both men broke down in tears, hugged each other and cried out, "I don't want to kill you."

During this time I recieved a reply from England in the form of a letter signed by Idries Shah, the author of the two books I had been given. He told me I was accepted into his study group and gave me instructions for my next task. The following Thursday evening, I entered the home of the tall aristocratic man who gave me the books and card in the warehouse district months before. His name was Horst Beckman. He turned out to be the leader of the study group which he called "the tariqa," Arabic for "the path." Horst showed me into his dining room. Five other members of the tariqa sat around a table—two women and three men, including my colleague Dr. Perez.

I attended meetings of the tariqa every Thursday evening. We met at Horst's home and read Sufi stories aloud to each other, mailing our reactions to those stories, and others we were asked to read individually, to England. Eventually, each of us was sent a new story to read and report on. This new story was different for each group member depending on how each of us responded to the first story.

After a few weeks of this, I grew a bit impatient with the teaching process. We were learning symbolic stories of three blind men and some grapes, for example, but I didn't see where it was leading. I voiced my frustrations to Horst after one of the Thursday meetings. "Is this all we do in this group?" I asked. "Read a story, report on it and read another story?"

"There are meditation techniques we teach as well," Horst said. "Perhaps if I teach you one of them now, it will help to address your intellectual frustrations. Because Sufism is based on a secret doctrine a real appreciation of its traditions must come with the help of a teacher. You must live Sufism to truly understand it."

"But I have been studying Sufi traditions for some time," I said.

Horst answered, "Sufism is not like a building: fixed and unchanging, left for future generations to learn from and study. It is more like a garden. It is active, changing and grows with the input of others. A Sufi school is born like any other living being. In order to flourish and not disappear—and to prevent itself from becoming mechanically ritualistic—Sufism is transmitted and activated by humans. So be patient, Carlos. Take the essence of this esoteric knowledge, and bring it, embody it, into your contemporary self."

He ushered me to a couch in his living room and led me through the meditation he called a self-realization technique. "The purpose," he continued, "is to learn more about your life's purpose. Remember, Sufism is not really Eastern or Western, it is the balance between the two. There are two ways to acquire knowledge: argument and experience. Argument brings conclusions but does not remove doubts. Sufism provides experience so that your inner life can be activated."

This sounded more like what I needed, so I settled back on the couch and asked, "What do I do first?"

"Whenever you have the opportunity to learn something," Horst said, "you must first repent."

"Repent what?" I asked.

"You said you are unsure of the value of our study meetings here, correct?" Horst said.

"Yes," I said tentatively.

"That is what you must repent," he said. "You must repent your objections to this group study."

"Okay," I said, "what if I agree to see this learning process through to the end, whatever that is?"

"You must still repent your objections. Even when you've agreed to learn something new, there remain in you objections to that learning. Make a habit of repenting your objections first whenever you are offered a teaching."

I nodded for him to continue and tried to relax and address my objections.

"Once you have repented," Horst went on, "you must return to rightness." He glanced at his watch and then at me saying, "Don't worry; we should have time to finish this." I sighed and tried to relax more.

"Returning to rightness," Horst explained, "means aligning your-self with your original intent, which was to learn. The next step is to renounce. You renounce all your little egos."

"Little egos?" I wasn't sure what he meant.

"I won't bother with the Arabic word and the whole explanation," he told me. "For now, think of them as all the little labels and ideas you have about who you are. Let's see. How would you describe your-self?"

"I am a Chilean. My parents were Austrian. I am a psychiatrist. I am tall. I have blue eyes. I enjoy going to parties. I do yoga and meditate every morning. . . ."

"All little egos," Horst interrupted. "You must renounce any labels used to describe you. They only get in the way of learning." He paused for a few moments. "So what do you sense is the end result of this meditation?"

I shifted in my seat and ventured, "I guess I need to submit to what-ever the teaching asks me to do."

Horst smiled. "Be sure you do not become a slave of the teaching. When the teaching becomes greater than you, it is of no use to you. The surrender you practice in this technique teaches you trust, not submis-sion. Fear and doubt take you away from your true self. Trust leads you to it and allows you to remain connected to your higher self and deep-en your understanding of that part of yourself. The content of the sto-ries you read is less important than your dedication to the process."

When the members of our group finished their initial training in Sufism, our Thursday routine changed from solely reading and dis-cussion to actual participation in Sufi ceremonies. Thursday night is sacred to the Sufi: it is when divinity and humanity come together. On these nights, members of our study group met at a Sufi shrine and entered a dimly lit room where a number of men gathered for the dervish ritual. As we did this, Horst, who embodied the leadership of the assembly, gave a signal to begin. Silently, 12 men formed two par-allel lines in the center of the room. The glimmer of the lamp in the darkness made their eyes come to life.

The spiritual exercise began with the zhikrs, the repetition of one of God's sacred names. These names are also attributes of God, so by repeating the name an individual brings the attribute alive in himself. Zhikrs are used to anchor a virtue—such as mindfulness, harmony, devotion, self-discipline—and to build character.

With a startling clap of the hands, Horst began swaying slowly from right to left. The men fell into the rhythm of his swaying. Every time they swayed to the left, they said, "Hu" in chorus. This dancing motion is very powerful, bringing closer communion with God.

Thursday nights were now in my consciousness added to the sacredness of Fridays, Saturdays and Sundays. At this point half the week was already a sacred time, as well as every morning and every evening. Life was recovering its sacredness.

A few months later, when I received the training scholarship in Gestalt therapy I'd applied for at Esalen Institute, I started making plans to complete my residency requirements there. I communicated my acceptance to Idries Shah and he wrote me a very brief, mysterious note that said, "Don't forget that not everything that shines is golden." It took some time for me to understand what this meant in practice.

A childhood friend of mine named Diego had also applied to Esalen and been accepted. Diego was three years older than me and had always been something of a hero to me growing up. I had modeled much of my early career after his success. I even dated his wife's sister for a time. He was now the chief resident in psychiatry at the hospital where he worked, and I looked forward to the opportunity to share this experience with him. A few months later I was on a 17-hour flight north to California.

After a couple of weeks in Berkeley I traveled down the coast to Big Sur, where the Esalen Institute was starting to develop an impressive reputation for consciousness studies—and for its hot tubs on the ocean cliffs. My friend Diego had already arrived by the time I got there. For the first time in my life I saw a side of Diego I had never witnessed before. He seemed somewhat nervous and was less sure of himself than I remembered.

While we were going through the intensive training program in Gestalt therapy, we had the opportunity to mingle with some of the most impressive minds in the field of consciousness research, including: Ram

Dass, who had just returned from India where he spent time with Nem Karoli Baba; John Lilly, the physician and scientist who had just returned from Chile where he had studied Arica training, the method of human awakening developed by Oscar Ichazo and based on the enneagram; and Gregory Bateson, author of *The Steps to an Ecology of the Mind*, former husband of world-renowned anthropologist Margaret Mead and pioneer in the field of family therapy, who was living in Esalen. Just being in their presence was an inspiration and an example of where human potential could reach.

For the Gestalt training, we met in small groups and used a variety of techniques with other students as our clients. If a student was having trouble expressing anger, she was directed to place a pillow or cushion on the floor and beat on it with her fists to the point of exhaustion, and eventually the buried anger surfaced. Another technique for getting past personal defenses and exposing repressed emotions was to have a student sit in the center of a circle composed of the other participants, who barraged him with questions and observations from all sides. A big part of the training also involved role-playing. One person played some part of another's personality so that she could have a dialogue with that part of herself. It was the early seventies, a time of great experimentation with various kinds of humanistic psychological techniques designed to free internal and external confusion.

At Esalen, I became familiar with a new context for the ecstatic moments I'd experienced in South America; Abraham Maslow called them "peak experiences," and the researchers at Esalen had begun cataloging dozens of triggers to these events beyond what I had experienced. The intense emotional, inner work of the Gestalt training brought up great sorrow as well, since I started realizing how I had a representation of my father, my mother and myself as a child within me that needed to be cared for and supported.

After completing the training, Diego and I decided to stay at Esalen a while longer to take in some of the other classes they offered. At an evening meal near the end of a conference being held there, Diego and I were approached by a German artist and therapist named Klaus Von Thuringen. Klaus reminded me of an ancient barbarian: he was hairy and heavily muscled, and spoke in a deep, resounding bass voice. He told us he wasn't planning to stay for the end of the conference and asked if we were interested in accompanying him back to his Sonoma County farm for what he billed as "the most complete lessons in surrender possible." Diego was a bit dubious, but we figured we had nothing to lose and agreed to give it a try.

Ego surrender is indeed too mild a term for what Mr. Von Thuringen had in mind for us. For three weeks, as we went to sleep nightly in his barn surrounded by cows and goats and only a thin layer of straw between our bodies and the cold ground, Diego and I referred to our daily "training" with our host as "ego annihilation."

For example, in the middle of one of our exercises, Klaus's young daughter came up to us and showed us what looked like a spider bite. The redness around the bite suggested the spider had been venomous. He asked us, as medical doctors, what we would do in this situation. I described how I would try to find the spider, rush her to a hospital and hope they had the proper antidote to the poison. Instead, Klaus viciously insulted us, put his mouth over the wound, sucked out some blood while his daughter stood there unflinching, took a leaf and crumpled it in his hand with some juice from the tobacco he had been chewing, applied the leaf mixture to the wound, and told us there would be no sign of the wound the next morning. And there wasn't.

The next day Klaus explained that he'd learned this technique from the Sioux Indians. White men had tried to study the chemical elements that composed the tobacco, the saliva and the juice, but had forgotten to add to their chemical and pharmaceutical products the human vibration, the essence that was really the healing element. "Until those in the West realize this," said Klaus, "bugs, viruses and bacteria will become resistant to technological stopgap measures by using their own life force to take in the chemical compounds and adapt them as nutrients. It's my vibration and the intention behind it that, when mixed with all the physical chemical elements, healed the wound. Intention and personal power are more potent than any manmade chemical."

It was the depth of Klaus' knowledge on subjects such as this that fascinated us and convinced us to follow him during these exercises. On one occasion, while we knelt on the ground with our shirts off,

Klaus threw guacamole dip in our faces and told us we were worthless. Anger and dismay mingled inside of me and internally I seriously questioned these surrender techniques.

On another occasion, Klaus handed me something to eat. I swallowed it and he told me to monitor my feelings. I felt fine for several minutes, but eventually I developed a severe stomachache. When I reported this to Klaus, he told me I had ingested strychnine, a poison I knew could kill me. I looked at him, ready to accuse him of being a madman, but in his eyes was a compassion and caring that helped me believe he wasn't really as sadistic as his teaching methods might make him seem. He taught me how to breathe and meditate to overcome the effects of the strychnine, and I had no more ill effects from it.

One night, Diego and I were sitting on the ground in a rigid lotus position when Klaus told us we could choose if we wanted to be ridiculed in front of his art students the next morning. I said I would try it. Diego was more hesitant. Klaus told us to close our eyes and maintain our sitting posture until he came for us early the next morning. At one point he came back and placed an antique Persian gold coin on my thigh and a large rock in Diego's lap. Klaus didn't come for us in the morning, though. We never saw him again.

Several hours later as the sun started rising in the sky, Diego removed the large rock from his lap and collapsed on his back. "Carlos," he moaned, "I would like to go home. This may be our only chance to escape." I started laughing and Diego joined me in this release of the previous days' tension.

So Diego left his boulder there, and I took my gold coin back to civilization. Diego got on a plane to Chile and I headed for a friend's house in Berkeley where I was to stay for my last several months in California. A week later, I was back on a farm, but this time I was with my friend Jeffrey and his friend Patty, and the farm was a very pleasant, comfortable, Buddhist retreat center.

Patty was a devout Baptist-turned-Buddhist, and she had convinced Jeffrey and me to go with her to see this "really cool lama" who was leading a weekend retreat on mental health. "With a subject like that and a recommendation like that," I joked with her, "how could I say no?"

The "really cool lama" turned out to be Lama Thartang Tulku Rimpoche. He was a roundish Tibetan monk with short hair, dressed in the traditional burgundy robes of his station. Everyone at the retreat could feel the energy he projected and we were all drawn to him. He shared with us several techniques and meditations from his Nyingma tradition of Buddhism. The first technique he taught us involved each of us approaching the front of the room one at a time. There he asked us individually, "What is your problem?"

When the student explained a personal challenge he or she was facing, Thartang Tulku usually broke out in a fit of giggles. He said he found Westerners' problems amusing in their insignificance. When he settled down enough to be serious again, he set a wooden box in front of the student and said, "I want you to imagine placing your problem in the box. Now, jump over the box. Where is your problem now?"

The student, of course, said the problem was now behind him. Thartang Tulku replied, "Good. Do you see it?"

When a student answered in the negative, the lama said, "Trust me. The problem is behind you. Leave it there."

Lama Thartang Tulku also taught us that meditation is self-healing. He said, "Many diseases are the result of blockages in our physical bodies caused by our emotions. In Tibet there are very few cases of cancer because the environment is tranquil and life is less stressful."

"How can meditation cure these diseases?" asked one student.

He said, "Meditation is a process of deep understanding of our mind and our nature. A calm mind is like a still pond; we can see our problems like waves and our self-image like a reflection. A beginning meditator needs to still the mind and retrain it to be the observer. A more advanced meditator can learn to relax, let go and just be, without effort and without attachment. It is then that we discover the mind itself does not exist. This natural state is the state of self-healing. Visualization, the natural attention of seeing, produces light and a flow of positive energy to those areas which are harmed or diseased."

"I understand that stress can cause blockages and thus disease, but all organisms must die," said another student.

"Yes, this is true." said Thartang Tulku, "But we must therefore learn about transcendence so that we can find our inner peace. Modern technology has given us a lot of comfort, but our needs and habits trap us. Therefore, it is very important that we go beyond it."

In a meditation on impermanence, the lama told us, "Visualize a yellow light entering your circulatory system. Now focus your attention on the individual red blood cells, white blood cells and platelets." After a couple of minutes, he continued, "Because the blood is fluid and constantly in motion, it is difficult to focus on a single element of it. In the same way, you should concentrate on the whole of life, not on the circumstances of individual beings—yourself and those around you."

My favorite meditation, however, was the one he called "inner massage." The object of the exercise was to make sure the flow of life force was not becoming blocked anywhere within ourselves. In it, he asked us to relax our bodies and minds so the edges would be softer. Then we were to imagine fingers massaging our bodies and minds from both the inside and the outside.

The lama Thartang Tulku was able to express some of the teachings of the ancient Tibetan traditions in terms compatible with my Western understanding. The teaching of re-identification or detachment was one of the most important things that I learned from him.

I asked him once, "How does one know the job one needs to do?"

He replied, "It doesn't matter what job you do. The important thing is the attention you give it. It's like the sun, which always gives light and never gives darkness. Always be aware, alert and attentive. These actions are of the utmost importance because they do not accumulate darkness or emotion, habits or suffering. Alertness is like the lotus. It has its roots in the mud, but its flower is always pure. To develop you need to know how to meditate, and then you need to transcend your meditation. And then, you need to know how to renounce meditation."

"I should stop doing my spiritual exercises?" I asked, puzzled.

"No," he answered. "I mean renounce all conceptual ideas of meditation and be alert and attentive."

I began to see a connection between all the spiritual teachers I had learned from thus far. Attention was the great metaphysical tool used to keep oneself in balance.

A few weeks later, I was walking up one of the rather steep streets of San Francisco when I saw an older man with bright, blue eyes leaning against a car. As I was looking at him, the man asked me, "Can I give you a ride somewhere?" in a slight French accent. When I nodded, he unlocked the car doors and I got in.

"Where are you going?" my driver asked.

"I have a meeting up the street, near Van Ness Avenue," I replied.

"I meant, where are you going in life?"

"I'm studying the soul's power to heal. I'm a psychiatrist."

"Who is your teacher?" the man asked, sounding more interested.

"I am studying Sufism with Idries Shah," I replied.

"And what path do you follow?"

"Is there more than one path?" I said, waxing philosophical.

"There are many paths up the mountain," he said, "but they all con-verge at the summit. There lies the key to the Golden Path." I thought back to what Don Eduardo told me. The man parked the car. "This is where I have my appointment." He scribbled an address on a piece of paper and handed it to me. "I am giving a talk this weekend. If you are interested, be at this address at one o'clock Sunday afternoon."

I thanked the man for the ride and he shuffled into a nearby hotel.

That Sunday afternoon I showed up at the address he had given me, a house in Oakland not far from the apartment where I was staying. The house was filled primarily with women in their forties and fifties. One of the women asked me who had invited me. I spotted the old man who had given me the three-block ride sitting in the next room and pointed to him. The woman seemed very impressed that I had such an influential friend.

Someone told me his name was Alain Naude, but that meant noth-ing to me at the time. As he talked about "beingness," I envisioned a golden globe hanging in the air before me. In it was a large golden key, the same key I had seen during my initiation with Don Eduardo. The key entered my sternum, turned and opened my chest as if it were the gates to a beautiful palace. The feelings of inner awareness, love and satisfaction that washed over me were remarkable. In the midst of the deep emotions and gratitude I felt, I approached this man after his talk and asked him if I would see him again.

"It probably isn't necessary," he replied. "You have already received the essence of the teachings."

When I returned to Jeffrey's apartment, Patty was there visiting. They asked me where I had been all day, because they had been waiting to take me to a movie in Berkeley. When I said I had gone to hear some man named Alain Naude speak, Patty felt slighted. "You had a meeting with Krishnamurti's closest disciple, and you didn't tell me?" she complained. "Where do you get all these invitations?"

"I'm not exactly sure," I answered. "I really don't go searching for these invitations or meetings. They just seem to happen to me ever since I surrendered to the flow of life and to my own essence. Each encounter I have leads me to the next step, as long as I don't try to direct or control the situation. I have come to believe there's a message that the ancient mystics knew, and I feel I'm completely guided to find this mystery. As long as I listen to this guidance, I'll continue on this path."

"If that is true, I guess I need to start listening more attentively," Patty said with a smile.

Forgiveness and the Maturation of the Heart

My most confronting, nontraditional and challenging teacher during my year in California, however, was a man I met in a fruit bar in Berkeley. I was happily eating the cup of fruit I'd ordered and reading a flyer someone on the street had handed me when a large, gray-haired black man at a nearby table called over to me, "You're not going to get enlightened by eating that."

I looked over at the man and noticed he was eating the same thing I was, so I laughed and tried to ignore him. He continued to talk to me saying I needed to love more, learn more, become more humble. I didn't respond.

Finally, I finished eating and got up to leave. "I'll see you again soon," he called to me.

"Maybe," I acknowledged as I left to go home.

The next day I went shopping. When I returned home late in the afternoon, I found a note from Jeffrey asking me to call an Otis Lee Jefferson back. I had no idea who this Mr. Jefferson was, but called the number and asked to speak to him.

"You must be surprised about my calling you there," a vaguely familiar voice said with a chuckle.

"Do I know you?"

"We talked at the fruit bar on Telegraph Avenue yesterday, Doctor."

"How did you get this number? And how did you find out I was a doctor?"

The man on the other end of the line chuckled again. "You may place limits on your perceptions of who you are, but I know everything about you: your inner conflict, the way your energy flows. Our meeting isn't just a coincidence. Remember, there's something operating under everything you see."

"So what is it I need to learn from you, Mr. Jefferson?" I asked, intrigued.

"In order to be a good doctor you must focus on more than the survival of yourself and your patients. First you need to learn how to clear the past so there's no part of yourself trying to control or dominate another part. Your emotional, physical, intellectual and spiritual sides must all operate together, you know, as one unit. If you don't do that you'll feel disconnected, out-of-touch with the source of all life."

"But how do you know so much about me?" I asked again.

"I can't answer that right now," he said. "You think about what I said Doc," and he hung up.

I put the phone down, turned to Jeffrey and asked him if he knew this Otis Lee Jefferson. He said he didn't, and he had no idea how the man could know I was staying at his apartment.

Two days later, a package arrived at Jeffrey's, addressed to me. In it was a book by a psychiatrist titled *Love or Perish* stapled to a long letter from the mysterious Mr. Jefferson. The letter began:

I can help you. I worked for 30 years as an orderly in a psychiatric ward. Every doctor I saw there was missing his heart.

You need to get cured of the pain inside you. I see in your eyes, your face, that your inner child, as well as that of your mom and dad, never grew up. Neither have you. You've got to grow up, or you will do more harm than good. How can you fix somebody else's brain if yours is all screwed up?

The next day, I went to the post office to buy airmail stamps. When I came out, the seemingly ubiquitous Mr. Jefferson was standing on the sidewalk with a colorful, knit beret on his gray-frosted hair.

"Carl," he called to me. "I'd like to talk to you."

I heaved a heavy sigh and approached him. "What can I do for you, Mr. Jefferson?"

"Other than call me Otis," he replied, "I don't think there's a damn thing you can do for me. Well maybe there is just one. I would like you to come with me to my home over in Oakland, I'll make you lunch, maybe even give you a little concert. I think you might learn a thing or two. Besides, you don't have anything better to do with your time, now do you."

I looked at this man who was insinuating himself into my life. I didn't know a thing about him, I didn't know where he lived or what kind of man he was. All I knew for sure was that he had some knowledge he felt he needed to share with me. And in truth, I didn't have anything better to do.

"All right Otis, if it is that important to you, I'll come with you."

"Well Carl, it's not as important to me as it is to you. But follow along now, and try to keep up."

He led me to a bus stop and we caught a bus to Oakland. Otis pointed out all the sights to me as we passed by the Oakland Bay bridge. We transferred buses, and continued on into his neighborhood. As we moved closer to his apartment, I couldn't help noticing that the area was getting worse.

"This is our stop," Otis said to me as he pulled the bell cord. We were in the middle of the worst neighborhood I had seen in my entire stay in California. I could see prostitutes on street corners with their pimps, drug dealers pushing their wares, children that from the look and sound surely were suffering from tuberculosis.

"Don't let that little boy inside you get too scared Carl," Otis qui-etly said to me, seeing that I was somewhat disturbed by my surroundings. "Ain't nothing going to happen to you in my neighbor-hood. I'll make sure of that. My place is in this building over here."

We walked down the street to a brick building. Entering the build-ing we ran right into a Pakistani man yelling at the top of his lungs as he evicted tenants from a ground floor apartment.

"My landlord," Otis said to me. "Hello Mr. Gupta. How are you today?"

The man stopped yelling at the cowering couple who were moving their possessions onto the curb. He turned to the two of us, smiled and said, "I am very fine today, Otis. How are you?"

"I'm always doing well Mr. Gupta, you should know that. I want you to meet a friend of mine. This here's Carl. You'll probably see him around a bit in the near future."

I shook Mr. Gupta's hand and said hello. As Otis and I made our way up the stairs I could hear Mr. Gupta begin berating his ex-tenants once again.

Otis unlocked the door to apartment 7G and we walked in. His apartment was in complete contrast to the neighborhood and the building it was a part of. It was clean and elegantly decorated. There were beautiful rugs on the hardwood floors and quality furniture placed with care about the place.

"Most of this furniture came from my parents or their parents or their parents' parents. It's one thing they passed on. This is another," he said as he walked me over near a window. In the corner of his living room stood a piano. Otis sat down and started playing, and I could not believe my ears. He was playing and singing a folk song I had heard my grandfather sing when I was a small child. When he was done with that he sang *Eli Eli L'ama Sabachtani* (Father, Father Why Have You Forsaken Me), and followed that with a negro spiritual.

When he finished he closed the piano keyboard, spun around on the bench and said, "I want to talk to you about these people you've got inside you. You know about them?"

I thought back to the dialoguing work I had been doing at Esalen with my Inner Mother, my Inner Father and my Inner Child. "I think so," I replied.

"Seeing yourself just as a doctor and forgetting your humanness can be a disease," he postulated as he stood up and started walking around the room. "If you became a doctor because you wanted to help yourself, that motivation comes from a place that we will call negative love. It's like a child who acts up just to get attention, even if it's negative. You get this desire from your parents and it makes it very difficult to be a healer. If you became a doctor to be famous, to 'publish or perish,' then you're emotionally immature and that stops you from being a true healer. You need to heal yourself before you can really help others."

"I became a doctor because I truly wanted to help others," I said. "I was, and am, very sincere in my efforts. And my parents never . . ."

Otis interrupted, "Like I said, you get this need for negative emotion from your parents and, like them, you pass it down to your kids. But when you become a doctor, you don't just give it to your kids, you give it to all your patients too.

"Humans compete for energy. In the name of helping other people, it is possible to harm them instead by unintentionally stealing their energy. We learn to do this in childhood by mimicking the first competitors for energy we know in life—our parents. I know you have seen these energy fields at work in your medical practice, even if you didn't realize what you were truly seeing. You need to understand these energy fields in which you function and become conscious of them. To accomplish this, I can guide you through a process of cleaning the attachments to your biographical past.

"This leads me to something else I noticed in you," he continued. "You don't have no compassion. I kept hearing all these doctors saying it was 'publish or perish' in their business. It's like that book I sent you, though—'love or perish.' You've got to start feeling the love or you're emotionally dead."

"You don't think I'm compassionate?" I said trying to humor him.

"Have you ever refused to see someone who was sick?" Otis asked.

I felt a twinge of guilt as I remembered times when I was tired or I wanted to go home to bed, and there were other doctors available to see the patients. "In some cases," I admitted.

"Have you ever given up on one of your patients?" Otis asked.

"Only when I knew there was nothing more I could do," I countered.

"How do you know when that is?" Otis said as he stopped walking and faced me. "How do you know the next thing you tried wouldn't cure that guy, if you'd been creative and not a quitter? I always say, `If you can't, you must, and if you must, you will.'"

"What do you mean by that?" I turned to face this stranger who kept on attacking me.

Otis sat back down on the piano bench and struck a pose looking down and slouching with drooping shoulders. "This is 'I can't,'" he announced. "You ever notice that's what kids say all the time when you ask them to do something for themselves? Since parents figure they're there to teach and care for their kids, they trudge on over and do it for the kid. In their minds, they taught their kid how to do something for himself. But that's not what the kid learned. He learned that if you cry and whine enough, eventually someone else will do it for you."

Otis sat up, looked up and threw his shoulders back. "This is 'I must.' When you say 'I can't,' you're giving up your will. When you say 'I must,' you're just making a choice to take control of your life again. When you're in that space, you keep trying to succeed until you reach your goal, or you realize that you were doing the right thing but you were working on the wrong problem."

Otis stood up, looked up to the ceiling, and raised his arms above his head. "And this," he concluded, "is 'I will.' You have to get beyond the idea of trying. You need to get in a space where you're so damn sure you're going to succeed, there isn't any doubt left. Trying gets you started in the right direction, but knowing you will succeed is what gets you there."

Otis sat back down on the bench in his 'I must' posture and asked me, "How many times have you prescribed a drug because it was the easiest thing to do?"

"I have no idea," I said with an exasperated sigh.

"Well, I have an idea," Otis said tapping his temple with his index finger. Otis continued to talk to me about my medical experiences. After an hour or so he served me a lunch of avocado and artichoke salad, bean soup and collard greens with oranges and bananas for dessert. I was convinced that he could teach me something useful, though I wasn't sure exactly what that might be. I agreed to meet with him once a week so he could share with me the technique he had learned.

On a visit soon after my initial meeting with Otis, he finished up another impromptu concert, this time playing classical pieces by Bach and Chopin, and turned to me. "Get yourself over here. I'm gonna teach you how to survive and be productive in this world." Reluctantly, I joined him on the bench.

"Many doctors I've watched," Otis explained, "were like little children playing doctor. They never really grew up. They never learned how 'cause their parents never grew up. Look at all the negative habits your mother and father had. You are angry because out of negative love you adopted the same habits yourself. Now my parents were dead for 20 years when I figured that out, so I had to find some way to go back in time and fix my relationship with them so I could grow up right, even though I'm . . . How old you think I am?"

"You look like you're in your mid-forties," I said truthfully, "but you would have to be older than that to have worked at the hospital as long as you said you did."

"Sixty-eight," he announced proudly. "I retired three years ago, and that's when I met this Indian guy who taught me how to break the curse."

I waited for him to finish, but when he didn't, I asked, "What curse?"

He grinned as if he had been waiting for me to ask that. Otis started laughing. "Not bad, Carl. You sometimes slip back into being like a little kid, see? The kid growing up has no idea of what's right or wrong, so he looks to his parents to check how he's doing. If they get mad and spank him, he figures he did something wrong. If they smile and give him a hug or a treat, he figures he did something right.

"Now, as the kid gets older, he sees other people doing something. He doesn't see any harm in doing it too, so he copies what he sees. It's like my little grandson. He has this problem with swearing now. His mother is hitting the roof because he breaks out in his cuss words when there's company over, and she gets all embarrassed, like it's her fault he's using those words. To him, though, he heard somebody using those words and nothing bad happened, so he thought he'd give it a try too. After all, he's never seen anybody cry out in pain or start bleeding over a word.

"This starts a tension going on in the kid," Otis continued. "Mom says what he's doing is bad, but it doesn't seem bad to him. Eventually, everybody rebels against their parents' wishes to some extent, but somewhere in the back of their adult minds, they can see Mom watching and judging their every word and movement.

"We have to move beyond this if we ever hope to become a true adult. The Indian guy told me to imagine my mom standing inside my heart. She probably looks a little sad and scared. Do this with me! Close your eyes!"

I closed my eyes and tried to imagine my mother inside my heart.

"Then," Otis continued, "you imagine yourself comforting her, making her feel better. Tell her everything's going to turn out just dandy. Then you have to imagine her parents standing behind her, and their parents behind them and on back through your whole family tree. Every generation not growing up and passing the curse on to the next generation."

I visualized myself comforting my mother, but I started feeling anger rising in me. Why was I wasting my time listening to this guy? I have other things I need to be doing, I thought to myself.

"Then you do the same with your father. Try to make him feel better and imagine all his ancestors standing behind him."

As I visualized my father and attempted to show him support, I had trouble concentrating. I felt this was a futile exercise. Why should I be showing him all this love and support when he always seemed okay? I was the one with the problems!

"How are you feeling, Carl?"

"Very angry," I admitted.

"Good," he responded with a chuckle. "Now you've got to get over it."

I opened my eyes and looked at him. "How?"

"You're going to have to think about that until we meet again next week." At this Otis got up and showed me the door.

The next week I returned to Oakland. I had spent the week thinking about the anger I felt, trying to determine where it came from and how I could get over it. After another enjoyable concert, this time Tchaikovsky, Otis once again sat me down.

"Close your eyes. I want you to relax and go back to the place you were last week. Now do you remember the anger you were feeling the last time you were here?"

"Of course I remember," I said with a hint of sarcasm. "I've been thinking about it all week. I can't figure out a way to get over it now that you've brought it up." I opened my eyes and look straight at Otis. "I hope you know how to get rid of it."

"Close your eyes! I said I was going to help you with this."

I closed my eyes and tried to relax and center myself again.

"Next," Otis continued, "you look inside your heart for this little kid—whatever age you were when you first expected your parents to be there for you and they weren't. That little boy is probably crying and scared. And he's probably pissed that his parents left him all alone and didn't love him like they were supposed to."

I thought for a moment and then remembered a painful experience from my childhood. I visualized a time when I was seven years old and had decided to find out what was on the top of the bookshelf in our living room. Wanting to show everyone I was a big boy and could get to the top by myself, I began to climb up the bookshelf. There were a few obstacles in my way, various knickknacks and porcelain vases. Still, I was undeterred in my efforts. I reached the top, pulled out an interesting book and began my descent, awkwardly trying to hold on to the book. I could hear my mother in the kitchen and wanted to hurry down and show her what I had done all by myself. In my haste, my right foot slipped, hitting a beautiful antique porcelain vase that was one of my mother's prized possessions. It fell to the hardwood floor below and shattered into shards. I lost my grip and tumbled along with it, hitting the floor with a thud. I immediately burst into tears.

My mother came running from the kitchen and found me sitting in the pile of broken glass, the book at my side. My little legs were bleeding where the shards of the vase had poked my skin. Certainly Mama would fix me up and make me feel better. After all, I had climbed to the top of the bookshelf all by myself. She would be proud that I was becoming a grown-up.

But Mama didn't quite view my exploration as the big right-of-passage experience I had. "Carlos!" she screamed, "What were you trying to do? Don't you know how dangerous it is for little boys to climb so high on something so unsteady? And look, you broke my favorite vase."

I looked desperately at her through tear-filled eyes. "But Mama," I wailed, "I'm a big boy!"

"No. You're still a little boy, Carlos. You must ask me if you need something," she said as she led me to the bathroom to pull out the pieces of glass that were stinging me like little needles. The calmness I was trying to maintain once again turned to anger. Because I was an only child and spent so much time with adults I had always thought I was an adult, just like my mother, father, aunts and uncles. But my parents often reminded me that I was a child, and didn't let this small adult come through.

"Let out all that anger that you're feeling," said Otis. I could feel my face grow warm and my jaw clench.

"Come on, Carl. Make some noise, man! Don't hold it in. You're gonna kill yourself if you do that. Let's see that Latin fire!" he barked like a drill sergeant.

"I'm a big boy. Treat me like an adult," I yelled, slapping the bench with my palms. I could feel the veins in my neck popping to the surface. Anyone in a nearby apartment must have thought something truly strange was going on in Otis' place.

"I think we're starting to make some progress here, Carl. You're really showing some improvement. I want you to try something this week. Put yourself in your parents place. See if you can figure out what they were thinking during this time, what they were feeling."

Once again I left Otis' apartment with a homework assignment for the week. I looked forward to our weekly time together, and I could feel something inside me opening up. Though I couldn't put my finger on exactly what it was, I knew that it was a part of me that I had somehow lost along the way.

I returned in a week, and we started where we left off the week before. Otis said in a tone that suggested tenderness, "You're back to Carlos the seven-year-old boy. Now you've got to see that little boy going up to the mom and dad inside you. He's asking why they didn't treat him like a big boy. What do they say back to him?"

I visualized the seven-year-old Carlos approaching his mother and father and asking why they didn't love him for who he was. "They're telling me they never learned how to love that way," I reported.

"You see all their parents and grandparents behind them?" I nodded. "If that little boy asks them the same question, they'll say the same thing. From one generation to the next, none of them figured out how to love their kids, and the curse of emotional deadness keeps going until you figure out how to be your own parent."

"How do I do that?" I asked. My interest in the process he was teaching was growing.

The old man got up from the bench and said, "You mean you haven't read that book I sent you yet? Read it! And then meet me at the post office tomorrow. I only gave you the first three steps—awareness, anger, and understanding. You've got four more to go."

When I got home, I finished some letters I had been writing and dug the book Otis had sent me out of my suitcase. "Love or Perish," I read aloud to myself as I looked at the front cover. I meditated on the significance of the title for a while and then began reading it.

Later in the afternoon, Jeffrey came home. I looked up from reading and said hello to him.

"You decided to read that book?" Jeffrey asked as he peered at the cover.

"I was ordered to read it," I chuckled. "I went to the post office this afternoon, and Mr. Jefferson was lying in wait for me."

Jeffrey took the book from my hand. "So is it any good?"

"I've been studying directly with teachers and masters for so long, I'd forgotten that books were capable of transmitting wisdom as well. Yes, it's pretty good."

Jeffrey started paging through the little paperback. "What's it about?"

"It talks about the importance of love," I explained, "and how to get past obstacles to it. Some fear or hurt from our past usually blocks our experience of love and connection. The first step is awareness. What was the event that started the fear or sadness?"

"Uh-huh," Jeffrey grunted as he continued to scan through the book.

"Second," I continued, "we have to let the anger out. It may be anger toward someone who hurt or neglected us. It may be anger about all the time and happiness we lost by not facing the issue sooner.

"Third, we have to come to an intellectual understanding of why the event occurred. For example, we have to understand our parents didn't mean to hurt or neglect us. They were doing the best they could, even if that wasn't enough. We have to see what happened to us as a logical result of all the events that happened before."

I watched Jeffrey read through more of the book for a few seconds. "Oh," he said suddenly, "what is the next step?"

"I was hoping to find that out too," I said. I held out my hand, and Jeffrey gave the book back with a sheepish grin.

I managed to read all but the last chapter by the time of our next session. When I arrived at Otis's place he sat on the piano bench. Without looking up, he called to me as I approached, "Don't dawdle, Carl. Get over here."

I walked over and sat down.

"You ready for your next lesson?" Otis said.

"Yes," I replied. "The next step has to do with empathy?"

"I remember where we left off," he snapped. "Lean back and close your eyes. I'm going to lead you through this.

"I want you to go back inside yourself. Look in your heart. Your mama and papa are standing there in front of your seven-year-old self.

Behind them are their parents and grandparents and all your ancestors before them. They're telling the little boy that they never learned how to love unconditionally. Now you may understand that and still feel angry, right?"

"Yes."

"Now you've got to stop identifying with that little boy and try to see things from that woman's perspective. She had a hard childhood, too. Nobody seemed to love her like she wanted. Nobody really understood her. She was left alone a lot. Your mother grew up and met your dad, and she felt the same kind of love her parents had for each other, so she married him. And they had lots of problems getting to know each other. And they had a little boy who they didn't seem to understand. He would spend hours alone by himself, and he seemed to enjoy it."

I thought back to the times I had gotten in trouble on purpose so I would be sent to my room. I would sit on my bed or in my chair and dream of angels and people from other planets. A couple of times, my mother or my aunts were disturbed to find I had locked myself in my room.

"And look at your father in there," Otis continued. "Look at things from his perspective. He had to deal with crazy, demanding parents who didn't seem to understand or love him like he needed to be loved either. They wouldn't let him play. His parents made him study, and when he wasn't studying, they made him work hard. He also never grew up. When your dad became a man, he tried to do things to make his parents proud of him. He met your mom, and though his parents were nice to her, they didn't really approve of him marrying her. And he and your mother had disagreements. And he had a little boy. He tried to show that boy he cared, but his son just went off in his own world. He couldn't understand him."

As I tried looking out through my mother's and father's eyes, thinking back on what their lives might have been like as children, my anger faded. Tears welled up in my eyes.

"Now you can't blame yourself here," Otis went on. "You were just a little boy. You couldn't know what they expected you to be. You had to just be what you were. You have to forgive yourself for not being a better son. You were doing the best you knew how."

I opened my eyes and looked at Otis. "I can't blame my parents for not understanding me either."

"Close your eyes!" Otis said. "That's right. You can't blame your parents either. You've got to forgive them too. They never were parents before. This was all new to them. They were doing the best they could."

A feeling of compassion emerged. I saw the presence of my spiritual inner guide, the angel who had been in the corner of my room, showering me with the ability to understand my parents and myself. At the same time that I felt compassion for their predicament, I also felt deep compassion for my inner child and for all inner children in humanity.

Then I felt this compassion being transformed into strength. A determination to voice the inner dialogue between my inner child and my understanding aspect and bring it to fruition grew within me. I resolved not to blame parents or others, not even myself, for my destiny, but to develop instead a firm resolve to change—to leave infantile modes and shift to the maturation of the heart.

"This is as far as I got in the book," I admitted, making sure I kept my eyes closed. "The author was talking about forgiveness and compassion toward yourself and others. I feel that now, but I don't know what comes next."

"Well, then, you're going to be kept in suspense until you finish that book. When I give you an assignment it's something you need to learn, and I expect you'll do what I tell you. Now go home and read the rest of that book."

I left Otis' and went home and finished *Love or Perish*. When I returned the next week Otis sat me down and said, "I'm not going to keep you in suspense any longer, Carl. The last thing to do is go back as an adult and be the kind of parent the child in you needed all those years. You've got to help that child grow up. We don't want any children running around inside the hearts of adults. That's what's made us so screwed up in the first place. We must stop blaming the inner child for the integrated spiritual responsibility that is missing from our adult lives."

Otis began drumming a steady beat with his hands on the bench. The vibrations traveled up my spine. "How old are you now?"

"I'm 26," I replied.

"Imagine yourself at 26 coming up to that seven-year-old you. You give the boy a hug and tell him it's time for him to grow up. He starts getting older and bigger. He's eight now. And you're there to help him with all the challenges of being eight. And when he becomes nine, you watch him live his life as a nine-year-old, and you're there to comfort him and teach him when he needs it. And as he turns ten, eleven, and twelve, the twenty-six-year-old is there to show him how much you care and how fully you accept him for what he is. And you give him a big hug and tell him you love him as he's growing through his teenage years. And eventually, the boy is gone. He has grown up and become you. And now you can look back at your childhood and remember that the adult you went back in time to help you through."

The tapping stopped. I sat in silence, taking in the feeling of wholeness Otis's meditation had brought to me. Slowly, I opened my eyes and looked around. The room, the street outside the window, the people on the sidewalks below, the buildings, the trees, everything I saw seemed brighter. I looked over at Otis and asked, "Did the sun come out in the last few minutes?"

"No," Otis said with a grin. "It's still pretty cloudy out." He got up from his piano bench. "Today's lesson is over. Here are some books I want you to read. I'll see you around Carl." He walked me to the door, and quietly closed it after me.

I thought about my childhood on my way back to Berkeley. I had always believed it was a fairly normal one. I knew my parents cared about me. I was punished when I broke the rules, but I was never beaten. I always thought I had a close relationship with my mother and father. I tried to account for the anger my child-self had felt, but I finally gave up. The meditation had taught me at the very least that every child is the complex integration of two complex parents, and it was wasted effort trying to distill all the child's fears and motivations into one idea. The relationship between myself and my parents didn't need improvement. I just needed to recognize and accept it for what it was, in all its complexity.

The thoughts of forgiveness made me remember the prayer my grandfather taught me, the prayer of radical forgiveness. "I hereby forgive all. May no one be punished on my account," I recited. The link between two seemingly disparate people—Otis, a straight-talking stranger I had just met in California, and my grandfather—reminded me of the interconnectedness of all things.

A few weeks later, I was walking down Telegraph Avenue after another session with Otis. I passed by the Shambhala bookstore Jeffrey had guided me to when I first arrived. Looking through the window and seeing the bookshelves overflowing with wonderful works, I decided to go in and browse. The store had a large selection of books on the world's religions, so I often looked through the books on yoga and Sufism to see if there were any new ones to add to my collection. I was paging through a book in the section on Sufism, a collection of meditations, when I heard a loud thud on the floor behind me. A copy of the Koran, the holy book of Islam, was lying on the floor a foot away. Just beyond it down the aisle was an older man in blue jeans with reddish-brown hair and a mustache. He was holding a book in one hand and looking down at the Koran on the floor. He looked up at me as we both reached for the book.

"The remembrance of God, blessed be He," the man said with a smile, "is not limited to a moment, a period of time or a definite place. We must learn to remember Him in all places, in all times, in all moments, without any restrictions."

The man had a Scottish accent and spoke slowly, in a deep bass voice. He picked up the copy of the Koran and put it back on the shelf. "Of course," he continued, "there are some places that are much better than others for practicing that remembrance."

I wondered if he thought the book's fall was such a reminder of God's presence. "Are you also interested in Sufism?" I asked.

"You could say that," the man said. "Have you ever come across this book?" He pulled a volume off the shelf with the title *The Book of Strangers*.

I took the book from him and shook my head. "I think you might find it interesting," he told me as he turned and headed down the next aisle. I glanced at the book, noticed that it was yet more Sufi teaching stories and put it back on the shelf. I had many such books from the

Sufi master Idries Shah, I thought, what do I need with another by some unknown writer named Ian Dallas?

When I got home from the bookstore, I brought the mail in. As usual, most of the mail was for Jeffrey, but there was a postcard addressed to me in very elegant handwriting. I had written to a group in London, England, about a teaching program specializing in Sufism, and this postcard invited me to tea at the Sufi center in Berkeley.

The next day, I took a bus to College Avenue and then walked down to the address on the postcard. There was a house at the address but no sign identifying it in any way. It looked very much like the other residences on the block. I checked the address again. Yes, this was the right place, I realized. I rang the doorbell, and the door opened to reveal a young Arab man in white turban and brown cotton robes. He stepped aside and motioned for me to enter.

The young man led me through a living room carpeted in Oriental rugs, with flags and banners adorned with Arabic writing hanging from the walls. Other men in turbans and the same kind of long cotton robes, which I later learned were called jalabas, were sitting down reading or engaging each other in animated discussions in a language I didn't recognize.

When we entered the dining room, the young man pulled out a chair from the dining room table and indicated that I should sit there. I eased into the chair, feeling somewhat out of place in my Western attire, and looked at the other faces around the table. They were all men in their twenties, thirties and forties. They sat drinking tea, seemingly waiting for the man at the head of the table to say something.

"You have made your way to a better place in which to remember God," the man at the head of the table said as he picked up his teacup. The reddish mustache and the Scottish accent made me look twice at this older man in the turban and black jalaba. I hadn't recognized him as the man from the bookstore until he spoke. I introduced myself and told him about the program I had applied to.

"You know that you must give up your worldly possessions and move to Morocco?" the Scottish man asked.

I was familiar with this stage in learning Sufism—giving up one's possessions—and the brochure I'd responded to mentioned the Sufi community itself was in Morocco. "Yes, I know. I've been studying Sufism under Idries Shah while in Chile."

"The community in Morocco is one of the best places in the world to practice the remembrance of God," the man who appeared to be the leader of this group said. "And Sufism is one of the best scientific traditions for that awareness of God to take place. Most of the enduring religions of the world teach that there is one true God. Certain traditions, though, like those of the Hindus and the Greek philosophers, began to place God at so high, lofty and powerful a setting, they felt He was too great and overwhelming for the average worshiper to comprehend. Sufism believes each person should have direct access to God, unmediated by priests. It's an especially useful tradition at this period in the history of the world, one in which we are all called upon to become what your teacher Mr. Shah refers to as 'practical mystics.' Everyone must have their own relationship to the divine now. We need to develop our ability to function practically in the world, while experiencing the sacred in our own lives, not taking all our commitment to God from faith based on parables and stories."

He waved at one of the young men to go bring in some more tea. "Do you know what the zhikrs are?" he asked me.

"I learned a couple of them," I said. "They are the 99 attributes of God."

"And they are, therefore, the 99 attributes of humanity as well," the Scottish man continued. "The zhikrs, when you repeat them, help you to connect with that higher part of yourself we sometimes call the soul. They remind you of that consciousness all things spring from."

"Ian," one of the other men at the table said to the Scottish man, "we've been told that all creatures must unite with God. How then do the dog and the bird and the snake find this union if they cannot recite the zhikrs?"

"God is manifest," the leader answered. "He shows his presence and his attributes in nature constantly, in the process of creating new life, in the changing of the seasons. Even the insects can appreciate these things."

Over the course of the afternoon, I learned that Ian was Ian Dallas, the author of the book he had pointed to in the bookstore and that he, too, had studied with Idries Shah for a time. He had been to the Sufi community his group ran in Meknes, Morocco, many times over the years, so he was able to answer all my questions about the lifestyle and teachings there. I became more and more enthusiastic about going, for it promised to provide still more experience in connecting with the vital identity and using it in healing work.

"Now, you must go clean up your things in South America," Ian said to me as I prepared to leave, "and then we'll meet you in Morocco. You are young and have left many loose ends. Your past ties you to the image that you have of yourself. You will introduce yourself to an ancient fire that will consume your past, but will not burn you. You will erase your personal history like a serpent lets go of its skin. This is what has happened to you over the past few years, you're letting go of your old skin to emerge in that which you will become."

When I returned to Jeffrey's apartment that night, I announced to my roommate that I was moving to Morocco.

"That's great," Jeffrey told me as he patted me on the shoulder. "When do you go?"

"I have to go back to Chile first and liquidate my assets."

"Liquidate your assets?"

"Give away everything I own."

"Are you becoming a monk," Jeffrey asked. "With the vow of poverty and chastity and all that?"

"Actually," I said with a smile, "I think I'm going to be a fakir. The poverty and chastity will be circumstantial, from what I've heard."

"What do you mean?"

Just then, the phone rang. I was close to it, so I answered it. "Hello?"

"Carl!" It was the unmistakable drawl of Otis Lee Jefferson. "Get over here. We've got to meet one more time before you take off."

I rolled my eyes at Jeffrey. "How do you know I'm leaving California, Otis?"

"I saw you walking down College Avenue tonight," Otis said. "Your mind and your body were thousands of miles apart, I could tell. Where are you moving?"

"Morocco."

"Meet me at the fruit bar tomorrow at noon. I've got one more thing I've got to teach you." At that, he hung up.

When I walked into the fruit bar where we had met, I saw Otis wearing one of his colorful berets and eating his fruit salad. "You're never going to get enlightened by eating that crap," I called to him.

He turned and smiled at me, and I sat down at his table. "I read to get enlightened. I eat so I don't keel over," Otis explained.

"You said you had something you wanted to tell me?"

"What are you going to do once you leave Berkeley?" Otis asked.

"I'm going to Morocco," I replied. "I already told you that."

"No, I mean after that. What are you going to do with your life? Do you have any clear goals for yourself, things you want in life?"

"I'm a good psychiatrist and I do have clear goals in life. I'm just being moved by a force that is more powerful than my ability to reason. This force is moving me along according to my plan. I feel like I'm being trained by different traditions so that I can put together the pieces of this puzzle that is my life. Then I can truly be of service to others."

"There's a maturity of the heart I'm trying to teach you, Carl. It's difficult to pay attention to what your higher self wants you to do if you got all this interference from these voices of your mom and dad, or anybody else you consider an authority figure. The child inside you has to grow up and be a separate person.

"I just want to make sure you understand the process completely and how important it is. Only then can you help others with it. The first thing you have to do is recognize the negative habits of your parents, and recognize your anger because you have developed these same habits. Then you must express your anger. Only after you have given expression to your anger can you recognize that, though your parents are guilty of passing down these habits to you, they are not to blame because their own parents passed the habits down to them. This pattern of passing down negative habits can be traced back generations.

"Once you recognize this you can feel compassion for your ancestors—from your parents backwards—and begin to heal. This also allows you to feel compassion for yourself. With this self-compassion comes taking responsibility for yourself and your own behavior, which in turn allows you to forgive that inner child that lies deep inside you. Then you can help your inner child heal and grow up. With this inner child grown, you can then forgive your parents, seeing them simply as the human beings they are. This allows you to integrate the aspects of your self, and then establish self and spiritual awareness. This is the path to maturation of the heart.

"There's another thing you should do. Now that you've forgiven and expressed your love to your parents in your heart, you need to do it in person. This is the only way you can complete your journey. Do you think you can do that, Carl?"

"I do have some time before I go to Morocco," I answered. "I must give away all my possessions before I go, and most of my possessions are in Chile with my parents. Yes, I can do this for them, and for me."

"Good. That's real good. Now then, you say you want to serve the world, right?"

"Yes, I do."

"In order to serve others, you have to relate to them in meaningful ways, but without getting all tied up in their problems or their lives. You have to be able to connect when you're interacting, and then you got to disconnect. There are too many people—and many of them are doctors—running around this world carrying a half-dozen or more folks on their backs. There's a story that my Indian friend told me that will explain what I'm talking about.

"There were these two monks traveling across Asia. They had both taken vows of chastity, so they weren't supposed to talk to women, much less touch them. Well, when they got to a fairly deep mountain stream they noticed a beautiful woman looking out at the river and crying. She needed to cross the river, but she feared the current was too fast and she might drown. The older of the two monks told the woman to climb on his back, and he carried her across the stream. On the other side, she thanked the monk and went on her way. After the two monks had continued their journey another hour, the younger monk said, 'You have taken vows of chastity. How come you carried that woman across the river?' The older monk replied, 'I set her down once we had crossed the river. Why are you still carrying her in your mind?'"

I laughed. "I see your point. I need to serve the world without feeling joined or fused to it."

"That is emotional freedom," Otis said. "When you achieve it, you're not angry, you're not feeling guilty and you're not all caught up in yourself. When you're really in touch with your deeper self, you know who you are. You don't need to define yourself by what other people say about you, or how they react to you. And you know what the big payoff is, Carl?"

"What?"

"Strange as it may seem, once you disassociate yourself from the rest of the world, when you don't need anybody else to tell you what is right or wrong and just being yourself makes you feel good and whole, that's when somebody special will appear who knocks your socks off! See, it's this sort of paradox, Carl. When you no longer need someone else, that's when you're finally ready for intimate relationships. Then you can respect yourself and that other person as two whole and perfect beings who come together to learn more about themselves."

Retreat to the Self

6

I had several weeks before I was expected in Morocco to continue my study of Sufism, so I flew back to Chile to visit my friends and family and to give away my possessions. My parents picked me up at the airport, and I told them of the inner process I had experienced with Otis. I also gave them my forgiveness and my love. I spent my first night at their home talking with them about my personal journey.

The next morning, I drove their car to the high-rise building in Santiago where I had kept an apartment for the past three years. I got into the elevator in the building and started hunting for my keys in my suitcase. I arrived at my floor before I found the keys, so I got off the elevator and walked down the hall to my apartment door. I tried the door handle, and it wasn't locked. I opened it and carried my bags inside.

Cushions, pillows, books, papers and cassette tapes lay in heaps all over the floor. It appeared the friend to whom I'd lent the apartment during my year in California, a friend I had met during my years in college when I was active in the student movement, was no longer living there. It also appeared that someone had broken in. The chairs, sofa and table had all been turned over or were on their sides. As I surveyed the scene with my mouth open in shock, a woman who lived down the hall entered and said, "The junta has taken them away."

I was shocked by her words. I knew the junta's coup against the Allende government occurred while I was in the United States. I heard the junta had burned all literature related to socialism. Since my book *The Ebb and Flow of Living* contained a prologue by Pablo Neruda, and since Neruda, even though he was a mystical poet, had been a communist presidential candidate, it was not a complete surprise that my apartment was turned upside down by the junta. But I wasn't sure who the woman from down the hall meant by "them." She explained that my friend, who was also a psychiatrist, had invited one of Allende's relatives to stay with him while I was in California. When the coup occurred, she said, the two of them were "disappeared" by the police.

"Do you know what happened to them?" I asked with obvious desperation. I knew that if no one had heard from them they were probably dead.

She shook her head. "Many who were taken in the past few months are never seen again alive. May God have mercy on their souls." She backed out of the apartment and left.

I looked around my apartment and began to cry. I did not care about the broken furniture, I was going to give it all away. But I knew I had lost another friend to fear and the inability of men in power to see that we are all connected with each other. My countrymen were killing each other and I was powerless to stop it.

I thought back to a dinner in Berkeley months before. I was out with Jeffrey, his friend Patty and an Armenian friend named Anton. Anton was a writer, and Patty said he was feeling very depressed, so the three of us had met with Anton, talking with him for hours about his problems and fears. I confided in Patty at one point when Anton had left the table that the young man seemed like he might commit suicide, so she might want to check on him regularly over the next few days. Eventually, the discussion shifted to politics, and from the political instability of Anton's homeland to the instability in mine. Patty had read that President Allende's rule was being challenged by the military generals, and speculation was running toward a coup in the making.

"The CIA has a grudge against Allende," I said, "so if there is a coup, he is sure to be killed. When I was serving as a medical officer in the Chilean air force, I was stationed in Panama. One night at a bar, I heard some CIA agents talking. I was with a group of Chilean soldiers and the men from the CIA—who were very drunk, I might add—told us that if we would kill Allende ourselves we would save them a lot of time and effort."

The day following our meeting with Anton, I returned home from a meditation group meeting to find a note from Jeffrey next to the telephone. He wrote that Patty had called to tell me I was right, that "he" was dead. I tried calling Patty back, but there was no answer. I phoned Anton, who answered the phone still a bit depressed, but nonetheless alive, so I realized Patty had meant President Allende's death.

I wondered how many other friends had been "disappeared" for their political affiliations.

I walked into the bedroom of my ransacked apartment. Here, too, were clothes and papers strewn about the floor. I noticed a corner of my mattress on the floor underneath everything, so I cleared off the mattress, found a sheet and threw it on top, and lay down to rest and meditate after the long journey from the United States and the sudden emotional turbulence of coming face to face with repressive life under the junta's rule.

The next day, I had my telephone reconnected. I started calling all my friends to find out if they were all right. Over the course of the week, many of them came by to see me. I managed to leave the apartment pretty empty when I set out for Morocco. Whenever friends came by, I asked them if they wanted any of my things.

I also visited my parents that week. I brought my diplomas, licenses and other important documents for them to hold for me. And I had them store a Persian rug that had been my grandfather's and that I felt a deep connection to. My parents were still in good health and doing as well as could be expected in the midst of the political and economic upheavals. I had dinner at their house on several occasions, and I sensed some change in our relationship. We did not talk about it, but we seemed to treat each other differently. There seemed to be more friendliness and respect in our interactions than I had ever noticed before. And I saw wisdom and strength in their faces when I looked at them now.

Driving home to my bare apartment on my last night in Chile, I recalled how much more open and expressive my mother and father seemed at dinner. My father told me some stories of his youth I had heard many times before, but this time I listened with a different heart. For the first time, my mother told me with openness about her relationship with my father before I was born. At one point, my mother told me she was glad I was exploring all these different religious traditions.

"I thought you disapproved," I told her.

"Oh no," my mother replied. "Since I was a little girl, I always wanted to taste some of the other traditions. Buddhism, Sufism, Hinduism—all of those fascinated me when I read about them in school, but I never felt like I had a chance to try them out like you're doing. I have something from your childhood I would like to show you."

My mother left the room and returned with a pillow. My mother had embroidered a design on the top of the pillow when I was a baby, a design that I later found was based on an oriental design which came from Qalandar. She told me that when I cried as a baby one of the only things that calmed me down was looking at this design. The pattern on the pillowed seemed to calm my brain and cause me to relax. It was a positive surprise for me to see that my mother was interested in and had read about many of the traditions I was experiencing firsthand: my life had become a living expression of her own visions.

I kept asking them questions about what they had experienced in the year I was in California, trying to figure out what had caused them to become more open and centered. Their answers were somewhat brief, and I could tell they were using discretion in order to save me from experiencing their hardships. They said it was similar to what they experienced during WW II, that they felt the same type of fear. They had continued to work, visit relatives, and maintain their house and garden. Certainly the takeover of the government by the military had been frightening, but it hadn't substantially changed their particular lives.

"Nothing has changed for you in all this?" I asked in frustration and amazement.

"There are no more lines for bread and milk," my mother replied.

"There is a curfew," my father volunteered, "but we haven't been out that late in quite some time."

It was not until that night, lying on my mattress, that I realized what had happened. The inner healing work I had done with Otis had transformed my relationship with my parents. This realization enabled me to clearly see the changes that had been wrought in our relationship. Although a large number of people have worked with their inner child, most of them have become attached to justifying negative experiences of pain in their lives with their inner child, thus perpetuating their addiction and their need. Otis showed me how to mature my inner child, how to maintain my qualities of a child-like nature but remove my childishness. I decided to incorporate this process into my own therapeutic bag.

My relationship with my parents became a means of uniting with them. It transcended the family and cultural programming, as I later discovered, and opened me to true soul identity. I understood the respect and the honor I gave my mother and father—their honest, loving presence in my life—unlocked a door inside me. This door took me from a world shaped by my parents' influence—their DNA, their life experiences, their humanness—to a world shaped by cosmic DNA, that which is life itself and has been passed down from the first life on this planet to all living beings. I was no longer just the son of my mother and father; I was a child of the universe, of the life force.

I thought about the Fourth Commandment God gave to Moses: "Honor thy father and thy mother." I had always suspected that particular commandment had more to do with maintaining the social order than maintaining a connection to spirit. But I started to realize that when you honor your parents, you are indirectly honoring your-self. I used to joke that I was "the product of an egg and a successful sperm," but we are all more than that. Through our genes and our childhood experiences, we are very much a blend of the good and bad qualities of our parents. When I respect and honor the good qualities my parents passed on to me, I honor that part of myself too.

This made me think of the wonderful characteristics that my par-ents passed down to me in my early childhood education. They taught me the importance of speaking my thoughts freely and honestly, with-out fear, and of honoring freedom of expression in all people. They taught me tolerance: standing firm enough in one's own beliefs to be comfortable with, and not threatened by, the different beliefs of oth-ers. Through their bond of unconditional love they showed me how to be committed and engaged in pursuit of my goals through self-disci-pline. My father was a man who always kept his word and always car-ried through on his commitments because he was self-disciplined and had a sense of responsibility.

They also taught me about courage; courage to be oneself and to persevere. They were engaged to be married during World War II in an area called Bucovina, now in the Ukraine and Romania. They had to survive not just the physical adversity of the war but also the strain on their relationship. My father was captured by the Nazis and deport-ed. This separated my parents for seven years, but they honored their commitment to each other. They also taught me about faith: faith in a higher power, in our personal path or destiny, in God.

After my work with Otis the values that I received from my parents were purified or cleansed of misunderstandings, and I could now appreciate them. I also realized that the process I had been through was needed in the world at large; the same values and characteristics passed down to me needed to be cleared of misunderstandings associated with them so they could benefit all of humanity.

During the time I spent with my mother and father I wrote entries in my journal detailing the changes that had transformed my life and my relationship with my parents. I collected these writings sometime later and they became a book of poetry titled *Child of the Universe*. This time with my parents was a crucial follow-up to the inner child work I did with Otis and completed the healing process. My stay in Chile brought me much closer to them, which they also sensed and responded to with even more openness.

The next day, I was on a plane crossing the Atlantic Ocean. Because there were no direct flights to Morocco I chose to change flights in the Canary Islands. Alfredo, one of the friends I had made while studying at Esalen, was a native of the Canary Islands and had invited me to visit him. I planned to stay with him for three weeks, relaxing and learning more about the self-development center he was starting.

My flight landed in Las Palmas on Gran Canaria Island, but since Alfredo lived on Tenerife Island, I had to transfer to a small nine-seat, twin-propeller plane to Santa Cruz on Tenerife. When I got out of the little plane on the airport's single runway, Alfredo was there to greet me. He was a man in his fifties with thinning, gray-and-black hair. He wore a short-sleeve, white, button-down shirt, shorts and sandals.

"Carlos!" he said as he gave me a hug. "It is so good to see you again."

"It's only been a few months, my friend," I told him. I picked my single suitcase off the luggage cart and we walked toward the terminal building. I passed quickly through customs and put my suitcase in the backseat of Alfredo's dusty, white jeep. We set off down the coast from Santa Cruz to his ranch just outside San Miguel on the southern tip of the island.

We caught up on what we had been doing over the several months since we met at Esalen, but eventually he told me to enjoy the scenery and he drove in silence. I was pleased to follow his directive for the scenery was spectacular. He told me that the Canary Islands include seven different climates, and I had already seen two. The drier foothills of Santa Cruz were changing into a virtual rainforest as we headed south. The trees and other vegetation on our right, and eventually on both sides of the road, were thick and filled with the calls of monkeys and exotic birds.

I thought back to my days at Esalen several months before. I had met Alfredo during the second week of my training. At that time he had been in Northern California for several months, and was seeking

out individuals who might be interested in recreating the atmosphere
of Esalen at his ranch in the Canary Islands. He had actually lived in
Pondicherry, India for several years, during which time he had
become a disciple of the Hindu guru Sri Aurobindo. Over the following weeks, he told me more and more about Sri Aurobindo and gave
me his guru's book, *The Adventure of Consciousness*. Before meeting
Alfredo, I had always seen the practice of yoga as a physical and emotional practice. Through some yoga meditations Alfredo had taught
me, however, I was starting to realize that yoga also offered a path to
self-attainment, or soul awareness. I was particularly intrigued by a
meditation technique he called "The Eyes of God."

In it, you imagine looking at the inside of yourself from imaginary
eyes near the back of your head. You watch your real eyes as they look
out and observe the world around you. This reminded me of a Sufi
meditation Horst taught me at one of the meetings of the tariqa in
Santiago. The Sufis believe there is a concealed head behind and above
your real head. It is through the eyes of this concealed head that you
can look down on yourself from above and observe what are you are
doing, as if you were observing someone else. You see others and yourself from a higher perspective, less caught up in obscuring emotions.

The ranch covered several hundred acres at the foot of a steep cliff.
The road to the main house was rather bumpy, but thankfully, it wasn't
too long. The main house had a lovely garden in front and overlooked
the ocean from the top of a big hill. Alfredo parked the Jeep and
directed a servant to take my suitcase toward one of the many cottages
nestled further back against the foot of the cliff. The two of us proceeded into the house for late afternoon drinks.

Over the course of the next couple of weeks, Alfredo introduced me
to others he had gathered there to start his personal growth center.
There were therapists, bodyworkers, healers and meditation teachers.
The setting was as idyllic as Esalen's. "We even have hot water to
soak in with a view of the ocean!" Alfredo crowed when I pointed out
the similarity.

Alfredo told me I would be welcomed if I decided to stay. On several occasions my enthusiasm about staying would build, then something would happen to urge me on to Morocco. One day, Alfredo and

I rode camels down to a cabin on some property he held on the other side of the road down on the ocean shore. I was feeling quite engaged by this majestic environment when I happened to notice one of the camels snorting and pushing something that looked like a book around with its nose. I went over and picked up the book. Many of the pages were wet and torn, and the cover and first dozen or so pages were missing. I turned to the first dry page, somewhere in the middle of the book, and started reading the Spanish there:

You need to find yourself. This should never be a hobby. You should not rest from the search. The search is the most important thing.

The words seemed prophetic, and at the same time, familiar. This is what I needed to hear. I couldn't give up the quest for knowledge so early in life, I thought. I needed to go on to the Sufi community in Morocco, I decided once more. As I paged through the rest of the book, a female character the author loved intensely reminded me so much of Francoise that I finally realized I had happened on a copy of my own book, *The Ebb and Flow of Living*. Fate had once again reminded me of my original intention. I set a date to leave.

On the eve of my planned departure I finally got to see the hot springs Alfredo had been telling me about. Despite my earlier decision, once again I had been wavering back and forth on whether or not to proceed with my plans to go to Morocco. Here, I rationalized, with much urging from Alfredo, was a perfect environment for me to work and teach what I had learned in healing and soul awareness. But there was an unsettled feeling in the pit of my stomach. My mind was drawn to stay, but my soul kept urging me to move on.

As Alfredo and I rode in the jeep up the road to Pico de Teide, the huge, steep mountain in the center of the island, Alfredo was once again pressuring me not to leave in the morning for Morocco. "You could set up your own clinic," he said. "People would come to see you from all over the world."

"If these hot springs are as wonderful as you've said," I joked with him, "perhaps I'll change my mind and stay after all."

As we climbed to the higher altitude on the mountain, the palm trees gave way to shorter trees and shrubs, and the air grew colder. Looking up, I could see a glacier making its way down a crevice between two peaks. All of a sudden, the jeep's engine died. Alfredo immediately set the emergency brake and tried to restart the engine, but it would not kick in again. We both got out and lifted the hood, trying to find out what was wrong with the vehicle.

Alfredo propped the hood open, and as we stood there scanning the engine, I heard a voice call out, "I have released you from bondage! Do not place yourself in bondage again!" I looked at Alfredo. He looked at me warily.

"Did you hear that?" Alfredo whispered, his brow wrinkled inquiringly.

"I heard . . . something. What did you hear?" I said.

"I heard a voice say something about keeping out of bondage."

"That's what I heard," I exclaimed. "What do you think it means?"

Wondering if our senses betrayed us, we started looking around to find the source of the mysterious voice. We looked in the scrub and bushes but we did not see anyone or anything around us. We seemed to be alone on the road. "I think it means you should stop chasing around all over the world at the beckoning of your ego," Alfredo said. "You should settle down and work in a free environment . . . like my center."

"I'm not sure what it means," I replied, shaking my head incredulously. "All I know for sure is I did hear it. It's a sign of some sort."

We stood in silence pondering the mystery.

Eventually, our attention turned towards the car again, "I smell gasoline fumes," I said, "I think the engine is flooded. We should just let it sit awhile before restarting it."

"That sounds like as good a plan as any," Alfredo replied with a smile.

I was grateful for the chance to think more about the voice and what it had said. About ten minutes later we were on the road again. We soon arrived at the hot springs. On a plateau just below the tree line a stream flowed, steam rising from its surface. The spring was very hot, so it took some time to build dams to regulate a more tolerable water temperature. We took off our clothes and sat in the steaming water for a couple of hours, rarely talking. I looked out at the clouds, the ocean and the other islands in the distance and found myself once again in confusion. Was running away to yet another new place a form of "bondage" as Alfredo had suggested?

After my prayers and zhikrs, or repetitions, the next morning, I made my decision in earnest. The voice had been reminding me of my earlier intention just as the copy of my book had days before. It was not yet time for me to give what I had learned to others. The quest for greater and more consistent soul awareness had to continue. The "bondage" the mysterious voice spoke of concerned my being too settled in the past. I was in danger of going back to a routine that obscured my essential identity.

I informed Alfredo that I would indeed be leaving. I left with him some journals I had written and tapes I had recorded while working with the Israeli physicist Moshe Feldenkrais in Northern California. Feldenkrais had guided me through a month-long personal training program on body awareness and mature behavior. The written and taped record of this work was my contribution to Alfredo's center, and left open the door for me if I wanted to return sometime. He drove me back to the airport in Santa Cruz. He wished me well and invited me to come back whenever I wanted, but I never stepped on this farm again. Within two hours, I was on a plane bound for Casablanca, Morocco.

Customs inspections in Casablanca, luckily, were also relatively brief, since I had only minutes to catch a connecting flight to Tangiers. There, representatives of the Sufi community would take me to Meknes. As I was in line to get on the airplane to Tangiers, however, an older man just ahead of me in line collapsed. As a doctor, I had taken an oath to render aid wherever and whenever it was needed, so I went to the man and checked his pulse and breathing. His heartbeat was irregular and his breathing was fast and shallow, so I assumed he had suffered a heart attack. A crowd started to form around the fallen man and me, so I urged the onlookers back, asking one of them to help me move the man out of the way. I glanced up several times while waiting for paramedics to arrive, but the airline refused to hold the flight and it took off without me.

When the man was conscious and safely in an ambulance, I looked into another Royal Air Moroc flight to Tangiers and found that there wasn't one for several hours. There was no way to contact the representatives scheduled to meet me in Tangiers. I left my name with the airline after I reserved a seat on the later flight, in case the members of the Sufi community called the airport looking for me.

When I arrived in Tangiers late that night, I hurried to the place where I was supposed to meet the representatives from Meknes, but they were not there. I was, after all, several hours late. I found a room for the night and tried, as I have learned to do, to find the lesson in this particular bit of adversity. I fell asleep thinking I probably wouldn't figure it out until later.

The next morning, I headed toward the train station to see if I could get to Meknes on my own. I entered the crowded and chaotic terminal building. I couldn't read the signs. No one seemed to speak Spanish or English, and so I couldn't get directions from anyone. Eventually, I found myself on one of the train platforms, still being pushed and bumped by the crowd. A young man suddenly burst through the crowd, put his hands on my shoulders, and steered me toward one of the trains saying in Spanish, "The train to Meknes is leaving! You have to hurry!" By the time I got on the train, the young man had disappeared, but upon checking with the conductor who sold me my ticket, I was indeed bound for Meknes.

The train ride took nine hours. The distance to Meknes was rather short, but at every stop passengers pushed through the crowded platforms with their sheep, goats and dogs to get onto or off the train. And vendors walked up and down the length of the train selling their wares to passengers leaning out of the train's windows. We also stopped four times in the middle of the desert, and I and all the Moslem passengers —that is, almost everyone on the train—disembarked to face east and say prayers. I had learned the prayers and the excerpts from the Koran in Arabic from Ian before leaving Berkeley.

When the train got into Meknes that evening around sunset, I took my suitcase and my sleeping bag into the terminal and tried to gather some information on the location of the Sufi community. The map was, thankfully, in Arabic and Spanish, so I determined I needed to go to the old city, the Medina. I left the terminal and looked for a bus stop or taxi stand, but there was none. I saw a young man waiting along the road. A car stopped a few feet beyond him, and he went to the car and got in. I figured I would probably have to hitchhike into the Medina as well. I planted myself where the young man had been and stuck out my thumb to the passing automobiles.

After a few minutes, a Moroccan man driving a red Fiat pulled up beside me. "Hop in!" he called out in English.

"Thank you," I said as I put my suitcase and sleeping bag in the back seat and sat down beside him on the front seat. "Can you take me to the Medina?"

"Ah," he said with a broad smile, "Do you speak Spanish?"

"Yes. Why?"

"I thought so from your accent," the man replied. "That is much better. I need more practice with my Spanish. Close the door. I can take you to the Medina."

He was a student and seemed overjoyed to have someone with whom to practice one of the many languages he spoke. He occasionally substituted a Portuguese word—another of his languages—but for the most part, his Spanish was as clear and idiomatic as his English. He gave me a brief history of the area and told me about the local architect. The homes in Morocco all look the same from the outside: they are square buildings with no windows. It is very difficult to distinguish the home of a pauper from that of a prince. It is only when you go inside, when you see what lies within the walls, that you can tell how your host lives. Each home has an open courtyard in the middle, usually with a lime tree and garden growing there, and it is the beauty that exists here that a Moroccan homeowner is most proud of. He dropped me off at the gates to the old city, and sped off with a wave and a smile.

I wandered through the stone gates, scanning the narrow streets for the few pedestrians visible in the twilight. I spied one man wearing a Western-style suit amid the many men in turbans and jalabas, so I approached him saying the name of the community I was seeking. "Habibya Zawya?"

The man's face became a mask of disdain. He spit at me and cursed me. It was not until several weeks later that I learned the motivation behind his hatred. He had been happy to help me, a Westerner, which he aspired to be himself. When he heard me say I was looking for the Sufi community, however, his admiration disappeared. Here I was, a Westerner with all the advantages, throwing away my life and material goods to join what he viewed as an antiquated, primitive cult.

I wandered deeper into the Medina where the streets became more narrow and the street lights further and further apart. At one dimly lit intersection, a crowd watched four men playing some game of chance on the cobblestones. I stood and watched for a few minutes. Then I noticed the crowd was being drawn from some sort of plaza not far down one of the streets, so I proceeded in that direction.

When I reached the plaza, dozens of people were milling about, walking from one eating establishment to the next. I tried saying the name of the Sufi community to those I encountered, but none of them seemed to pay attention or understand me.

Suddenly an old, bearded man in a black jalaba grabbed me and started dragging me down an alley from the plaza. "Are you taking me to Sufi community?" I asked. He didn't answer, but kept leading me. Since I hadn't received any kind of response from the people in the plaza, I figured I couldn't lose anything by seeing where this stranger was taking me.

Soon, however, I became anxious. There was a light at the entrance to the alley, but as the man led me further and further down the alley, I could barely make out the doorways we passed because of the lack of light. I heard the snarling of dogs and the groans and snores of unseen men. Although I knew I could easily break the grasp of the old man, I started worrying that I was being led toward an ambush in which I would surely lose my meager possessions if not my life. I started repeating the zhikr meant to instill me with courage. The old man continued pulling me down the dark alley.

Finally, we turned a corner and stopped. I heard him knock on something, and then a huge, wood-and-brass door opened. The light from behind it illuminated a fairly young boy, who said to me in Spanish, "So there you are at last."

Someone called to the boy from inside, and he called back, "The blind man brought him!"

I turned and looked at the old man beside me in the light from the doorway. For the first time, I noticed he had no eyeballs. I was shocked. My breath caught in my throat, and I couldn't move. As I stared at his disfigured face, a smile formed on the blind man's lips.

The boy beckoned the two of us inside, where he exchanged words with a man in a brown jalaba and white turban. The man introduced himself in English as Abdul Rahman. The boy and the blind man left down a hall to the right as Abdul Rahman explained that the mukadem had been very concerned when I hadn't arrived at the appointed place in Tangiers. He gave me a jalaba and turban to wear and asked me to give him my suitcase for storage. The wall behind him was an intricate, repeating pattern of diamond shapes, and he removed the front from one of the dozens of diamond-shaped compartments in the wall, put my bag in the opening, and replaced the front. Seconds later, as he stepped away from the wall, I had trouble remembering where Abdul Rahman had placed my belongings. I gathered that I would have no need of them in this place.

I picked up my sleeping bag again. Abdul Rahman showed me to a huge, dark room. A half-dozen candles glowed at various points on the floor illuminating dozens of men sleeping, praying, or reading on reed mats or sleeping bags. As he stepped back and went back into the hallway, Abdul Rahman advised me to get some sleep because I would start the daily routine in the morning before sunrise.

When he left, I stepped back into the hallway and took off my shirt and blue jeans and tried on the turban and jalaba. The jalaba was made of light-weight cotton and was cool and allowed me free movement. I was amazed how comfortable I was after throwing off the constraints of my Western clothing. It took me a couple of tries to tie the turban so that it wouldn't slide down.

Eventually, I entered the sleeping chamber again and laid my sleeping bag out on some empty floor space near the far wall. A narrow slit of a window projected moonlight from the courtyard into the room. I heaved a big sigh. I felt like I had finally arrived at the end of a very long journey. I was in a place where there was no Westernization or Easternization of teaching. Here was a place where people simply lived lives of spiritual awareness and dedicated themselves to the science of self-discovery and the science of service. I thought about all the teachers I had encountered that seemed to be preparing me for my life here in the zawya. I recalled the mysterious Layla I'd encountered in Santiago. Then there was Horst and the tariqa, and the Sufi author, Ian, I'd met in Berkeley. All of them were people with big hearts.

The transformational process that was guiding me was a path of the heart. I had studied other techniques and traditions along the way, but it seemed the path of the heart had been the most obvious one I was following, and it didn't matter in what frame of reference or community or belief system or ideology it was immersed, there was always a quality of heart that was central to the experience. My thoughts turned to my parents, and I prayed they were happy and well.

This reflection came to me: All around planet Earth, people were yearning for change. This, I knew, was the outward sign of the coming spiritual grace. I felt exhilarated knowing I could travel anywhere on the globe and the spiritual energy would find me.

The wonder of this realization was similar to when, in my early adolescence, I discovered the meditation, "Now is the time." As long as I was focused on this "nowness," I could see that the interface between the earthly and heavenly worlds was developing. I prayed to be filled with those things the soul longed for: love, compassion, peace and joy. I put my awareness in my heart's center and felt these qualities.

When I did this, I felt a shift in the energy inside my physical body. I acknowledged this and my being, my essence, became solidified and empowered with the knowledge of the true being. I knew it did not matter where I was. I could be in the mountains of Peru, Morocco, North America or Europe. The essence was getting stronger as I continued my journey. As I moved on I was further awakened to my responsibility for the depth of my own heart.

But my prayer was not just for me. I prayed to expand, and I experienced a different energy vortex outside my physical body. On one level it was a cellular physical energy change. I felt lightness and was filled with joy in a holy community that extended to the whole planet. I could see and feel the light of the planet, could sense the planet alive in myself.

I heard an inner voice say, "You are not alone. The power, awareness and passion of everyone who has ever walked this blessed planet are all available to you if you can transcend the body and the mind.
Of the millions who have been released from the limited state of
awareness the body and mind allow, many have chosen to assist those
who seek the soul. When you call the masters of the past, the present
and the future, you will be answered. When you ask to be filled with
a consciousness that allows you to love everything you see and every
thought you think, it will happen. You have never been alone. But the
present wonder is that you are now closer to us than you have ever
been, and this makes us grateful."

I slept soundly that night after the many hours of travel without rest.
Much too soon for me, though, I awakened in the darkness of the huge
room. Someone in the courtyard outside my room was chanting loudly over and over, "There is no God but Reality. There is no Reality but
God." I opened my eyes wider and propped myself on my elbows. In
the moonlight that still shone through the narrow window, I could see
the other men in the room getting up, rewrapping themselves in turbans and jalabas and heading out the door. I got up to look out the narrow window. A man circling the fountain in the center of the courtyard
called out to the other narrow windows on the courtyard walls. I retied
my turban and went out into the hall to see if I could find out what was
going on. For all I knew, there was a fire, and we were being evacu-
ated from the building.
    When I got to the hall, the other men were calmly making their way
toward the prayer room, so I followed. In the prayer room, the rest of
the community had already arrived, and, as was the case in everything
I was to do in this zawya, the women were on one side of the room
and men on the other. I took my place on an empty rug in the front of
the room with the other men and faced East, where a piece of parch-
ment with the word Allah, or God, written on it in Arabic calligraphy
hung.
    After a couple of minutes, a very tall, young man in a black jalaba
and turban entered and stood on a more ornate rug in front of the altar.
Everyone else in the room rose, and I recognized the prayer ritual I

had seen several times in Berkeley and in the desert during the train ride the day before. I followed the prayers, chanted in Arabic, and performed the usual rituals of prostrating myself, touching my head to the floor, sitting and standing.

A long silence followed the prayers, and I noticed everyone sitting with their eyes closed. This was a time for meditation, and I tried to relax and calm my thoughts. I again prayed for the health and happiness of my parents and friends and also for the betterment of all humanity.

Then, hearing another prayer beginning, I opened my eyes. In a minute it was over, and everyone started leaving the room. As I stood alone, the tall, young man who had led the prayer approached and introduced me to an older man with eyeglasses, a beard and thick, dark eyebrows. "This is Hassan," the younger man explained, "and he will be your teacher for the time being."

As I shook hands with Hassan, the tall, young man left. "Have you already met the mukadem?" he asked.

"No. Which one is he?"

"That was him," Hassan said with a smile. "You must understand that he is very busy in running the zawya, and does not always take time to properly introduce himself to the new arrivals. Are you hungry?"

In fact, I had not eaten in over 15 hours and I was starving, but I simply said, "Yes."

"You are in luck then," my bearded teacher replied. "Now we go to breakfast."

Hassan led me out of the now empty prayer room across the courtyard to the dining room. There, again, the separation of men and women continued. We sat at the men's table, and were immediately served a small bowl of some hot cereal, a grain called couscous. The man to my right asked me to pass him the pitcher of water. I reached forward and grabbed the handle with my left hand, and Hassan yelled at me, "No! Put it down!" I put the pitcher down and looked over at the man at my right who looked somewhat aghast. Quickly, one of the servers took away the pitcher and gave the man a new one. Later, in private, Hassan explained that one never offers one's left hand to someone or passes food with the left hand in Arab countries, no matter how clean it is.

The routine of that first day was the same on every day at the zawya from then on. We awakened before sunrise for the morning prayer and meditation. Before every prayer, five times a day, everyone trooped into the courtyard to wash their hands, feet and face in the fountain. Some scrubbed as if they were really trying to clean up, and others barely dipped their hands and feet in the water before moving on. Hassan explained to me that this was called the wuzu, and it is meant to be a ritual cleansing. Most of the members of the community bathed in private.

The next part of the mornings we broke into small groups to study and recite the zhikrs. I had learned a couple of the prayers with Horst back in Chile, but there were 99 of them, so there was much to learn. Each prayer represented a name of God which corresponded to an attribute of God. Though there is only one God he has many names, just as a man can be called husband, father, son, brother or friend. Hassan taught the Arabic prayer, what it meant in English, and the conditions under which it should be invoked.

"Every quality of essence, every quality of God," Hassan taught, "has an effect like a medicine when it's repeated. For instance, when you say 'al-Afuw,' it means 'the Pardoner.' The Arabic I will teach you means, 'He who pardons all who repent sincerely as if they had no previous sin.' This is one of the qualities of God, and you can invoke the quality in yourself by repeating the zhikr of the Pardoner. When you repeat 'Ya Afuw,' all your sins become pardoned.

"Let me give you another example. Let us say a couple is having a relationship problem. If one of them says the zhikr of the Lover, al-Wadud, which means 'He who loves those who do good and bestows on them His compassion,' a hundred times over some food that is then served to the other spouse, the quarrel disappears. You say 'Ya Wadud' over and over, and that quality in you will come forth."

I came to learn that Hassan was also a healer, and that was why the mukadem had assigned me to his study group. Hassan saw a great many of the world's troubles caused by a lack of self-esteem, and so he often instructed those in his care to repeat "Ya Kabir" or "I am great" 100 times each morning. Ya Kabir is the zhikr of the Great One, al-Kabir, Hassan explained.

"You must understand," Hassan said, "that Kabir means the greatness of the soul. It is not meant to make one vain or boost one's ego."

When someone's troubles are physically manifested, whether it is fever or coughing or more serious symptoms, the healer often uses the zhikr of the Peaceful One, or zhikr al-Salam. The healer repeats "Ya Salam," meaning "I am at peace," 100 times over the ill person to invoke the quality in him or her. With a peaceful state of mind comes health, Hassan taught.

In the late mornings, we were called to exercise, which everyone did in their own way. I did some yogic stretching and took walks around the grounds of the zawya. After that, we were divided into new groups to prepare lunch. Lunch was a much larger meal than breakfast, and often involved four or more courses. But the noon prayer came before we could eat lunch, much like the morning prayer but without the silent meditation.

After lunch, we were assigned chores just for the afternoon or chores that remained the same for weeks at a time. I was most often called upon to fix furniture and, because of my height and long arms, to pick lemons and oranges from the fruit trees in the courtyard. I was grateful that the chores seemed to be a part of the devotional life there, and not an interruption. "Manual labor is an extension of God's work in this world," Hassan taught.

Invariably, I would have my arms full of fruit or be in the middle of recaning the seat of a chair when the call to learn was sounded. At that point, I had to drop whatever I was doing and go to a group meeting. There one of the teachers from the zawya or a visiting teacher told stories and talked about various principles of spirituality. When the speaker was Arabic, visitors from Great Britain often translated into English. For several weeks, Ian, the red-haired man Scot, served as translator or teacher at these sessions.

When the group study session ended, everyone went back to their chores until they were interrupted again by the mid-afternoon prayer. Dinner was served just before sundown. The menu often included grains and fruit. On Thursday nights, the Night of the Poor, we had a special dish similar to honeyed lamb. Dinner was a leisurely meal.

Before each bite of food, everyone whispered "Bismillah"—"in the name of Allah"—under their breath. When everyone finished eating, we remained at the tables for more stories and teachings. Here, however, there was more opportunity to ask questions than during the more formal afternoon study sessions.

One recurring theme in many of the teachings and stories involved the use of techniques to achieve greater soul awareness. I was taught a metaphor: When you drink something, you pay attention to the drink, not to the bottle from which it came. Over and over, the stories told of followers who became so focused on the techniques they were learning they performed them like automatons. They were doing the motions and saying the words, but the goal of the technique or prayer had become lost to them. It gave me a new orientation to the various practices I had learned and was learning. Whenever I felt myself performing a meditation, technique, prayer, or ritual automatically, I dropped it until I could do it with the goal clearly in mind. Hassan often said, "The magic key of one is the millstone of another."

One of the first prayers I learned at the zawya dealt with the subject of soul awareness quite well, I thought:

He who knows and does not know that he knows he is asleep, let him become one, whole. Let him be awake.

He who has known but does not know, let him see once more the beginning of all.

He who does not wish to know, and yet says that he needs to know, let him be guided to safety and to light.

He who does not know and knows that he does not know, let him through this knowledge know.

He who does not know but thinks that he knows, set him free from the confusion of that ignorance.

He who knows and knows that HE IS, he is wise. Let him be followed. By his presence alone, man may be transformed.

After dinner, we would gather for the evening prayer. After the usual prostrations, bowing and standing, however, we formed a circle called the hadzrat. First we would sit facing each other repeating the zhikrs, trying to reach a level of ecstatic surrender so profound it would cause the body to shake and move. Then we would all stand up, join hands and continue the shaking.

I used the breathing and chanting I learned with Ian in Berkeley to achieve a stae of mind and body where I could see the others in the group as bodies of light and could spontaneously shake with the rush of energy being evoked. I clearly experienced everyone as part of a connected energy field; we were all beings of light. I overheard Ian, during one of his visits, explaining the process to an older man who was another newcomer.

"I feel a little self-conscious during the hadzrat," the older man told Ian during dinner one night. "What should I be doing differently?"

"You should not be consciously making your body shake," Ian explained in his low voice and heavy, Scottish accent. "It is an ecstatogenic technique. An inner force, an inner energy wakes you up. Through the repetition of the zhikrs, you short-circuit the connection between the left and right halves of your brain. And as the left and right brains become a more unified field, the unified field allows for perceptions not available in ordinary states of consciousness."

After the hadzrat, we retired to our rooms. From there we heard the call from the courtyard after sunset for the night prayer, which we did in private. During my time at the zawya, I rarely left the estate, and the routine stayed much the same. It was the routine that seemed to confound all the "nafs," the little egos Horst had started to explain to me at the tariqa meetings in Santiago. Arrogance, hostility and pride gradually faded from my experience as I began to lose myself in a more essential, communal identity.

One of the only exceptions to this routine were the rare visits with the sheik whose wealth supported the zawya. He was a man in his seventies with four wives, six children and about a dozen grandchildren. But even when the rest of his family was not around, the presence of the sheik could be felt. Even though he was deeply wrinkled and walked with a cane, he exuded a feeling of wisdom and peacefulness. The first time I met him in person, I introduced myself. He immediately said, "Intention is the true elixir!" I turned and watched as one of his servants closed the doors behind me and left us alone together.

"Intention gives you strength," the sheik continued. "When you are searching for God, when you are studying the holy teachings, it is being in the presence of one who has dedicated his whole life to a specific intention that strengthens your own intention.

"Our cosmology of the self and higher consciousness is not well understood in the West because it is multidimensional in nature. When your heart is open, you will embody the teachings. You will be like a bee that carries pollen from one plant to another and leaves honey wherever it goes. The heart is meant to revolve. It should always be in motion. If it turns and revolves, and does not fixate specifically on any one thing, it will not be pulled or attached to any one situation."

I listened attentively as he went on, "You can become a free being who is capable of love and is not attached to any particular setting, not even this one. If you can accomplish this, it will be of use to you when you have to make your decision. Your task is to keep your heart turning. When something changes, your heart must turn so that nothing can adhere to it. You can use it like radar or an antenna that receives and transmits signals and always stays connected to the source of love. If your heart is stuck, your ability to help and serve will diminish. This subtlety of the heart is where the truth lies—the truth about your existence and your ability to be a useful member of your community.

"On the other side, the highest reason will perceive reality and its connection to the divine cause. The highest reason for being is stabilization of consciousness. It never turns. It is always fixated in the Creator."

As the sheik continued his teaching about intention, I marveled at the opposites his presence embraced. Outwardly, he was not very beautiful, but inwardly, his peacefulness, wisdom and compassion were astounding. Outwardly, everything about his manner, his clothing and his surroundings indicated a strict adherence to discipline, but inwardly, his mind ranged from one idea to another, never settling on one perspective as being the right one.

I felt so at peace and was learning so much in this place that I couldn't conceive of leaving. I was quite happy and content. But on the morning of my 200th day at the zawya, Abdul Rahman retrieved me from my study group. He took me to the courtyard and explained that I needed to make a choice at that moment. Then he led me to the prayer room where all the other members of the community were facing the altar and chanting "La ilaha il Allah," which means "There is no God but Supreme Reality."

"What am I supposed to decide about?" I asked Abdul Rahman as he had me stand next to the prostrate mukadem before the altar.

"You must leave Habibya Zawya today," Abdul Rahman whispered. "You must choose whether you will commit to your life as a fakir in another community in Egypt, or if you will take what you have learned here back to the West."

I stood there while the rest of the community chanted for nearly an hour. I had no preparation for this sudden change of plans. I had never heard of anyone being faced with a decision like this before. I felt very comfortable at Habibya Zawya. When I tried to picture myself living the rest of my life as a Sufi fakir in Egypt, I realized I had forgotten my intention once more. It was not yet my time to settle down and give back what I had learned. I felt in my heart I had much more to learn, so despite how much I intellectually wanted to continue this particular path, I finally turned to the mukadem and announced, "I will return to the West."

Immediately, the chanting stopped. The mukadem stood up and gestured to two of the others there who took me to the sheik's apartment.

As I stood before the sheik one last time, he asked me, "What have you decided?"

"I will not go to Egypt," I replied. "I will return to the West."

The sheik rose knowing exactly that I had made the right decision and crossed to me. He put his hands on top of my head and said, "Mash Allah. Be the will of God done." At that moment, visions of my path up to that point rushed into my head. I again saw "the bigger story," and I knew I was doing the right thing.

Minutes later, I was in the foyer of the zawya with Abdul Rahman. He reached into the wall compartment in which he had stored my small suitcase and took back my turban and jalaba. I changed back into the shirt and jeans I had been wearing when I arrived over six months ago, and he opened the door to the street and repeated the sheik's blessing, "Be the will of God!"

Sacred Love
in Daily
Life

That afternoon, I boarded the train back to Tangiers and stayed overnight there. The following morning, I telephoned the only phone number I had with me at the time, a friend I'd met at Esalen who lived in Paris. Laurent was very glad to hear from me, and said I could stay with him as long as I needed to reorient myself to life in the West.

I booked a flight from Tangiers to Paris with the credit card I had not used in almost a year. The plane left that afternoon for Madrid, where I would have a four-hour layover before changing planes for the flight to Paris. I felt a vague anxiety by the time the plane landed in Madrid. With so much time before the next plane departed, I decided to take a walk to get some exercise and find a place to relax.

The sound of people shouting, the bright, flashing lights, the roaring of engines, the blare of car horns and all the motion of people running to catch flights, truckers delivering crates, conveyor belts and escalators moving every which way assaulted my senses after the quiet, slow routine of my previous months at the zawya in Meknes. My head ached and waves of nausea washed over me, so I ducked into a public rest room. I found an empty stall and stayed there for a couple of hours, so sick and disoriented I was certain I would die there. I then started to cry thinking how sad and embarrassed my parents would be to hear of my death in a public restroom in Madrid.

I glanced at my watch to see I had only an hour before my flight for Paris left, and I started to panic because my stomach was still in knots, my head throbbed and my muscles were as exhausted as if I had been clinging to a rope over a cliff for hours. I slowed my breathing and tried to calm myself. The panic subsided to nervousness, so I stumbled squinting out of the restroom and into the hot, bright afternoon sun toward the airport.

Once I'd boarded the plane the cooler air in the jet relaxed me further, and I felt like melting into my seat. I actually slept most of the short flight to Paris, and my dreams placed me once again in the courtyard of the zawya smelling the flowering orange blossoms and bathing my feet in the cool water of the fountain.

But it was the same shock all over again when I awoke and found the plane had landed in Paris and the passengers were crowding down the aisle to disembark. I entered the flow reluctantly, and quickly found myself standing in the Paris airport. I stood there for several minutes just taking in an environment that hadn't seemed nearly so alien a mere half-year before. There were huge billboards and neon lights everywhere, and I hadn't seen either for months. And there was a sort of sexual, sensual smell in the air. The scent of women's perfume made me notice how men and women were flirting with each other and kissing and hugging. It was if I was rediscovering one of my senses, and I realized I had just gone through the longest period of sexual celibacy in my adult life.

After passing through customs and exchanging some money, I called Laurent from one of the pay phones in the airport. When he answered the phone, he seemed very glad I had arrived and asked me how much luggage I had.

"A small suitcase and a sleeping bag," I answered.

"Oh, good," he said. "I hope you don't mind riding on the back of my scooter. The traffic this time of day is horrible. We'll cut an hour off the trip this way. Meet me at the entrance to the parking garage. I should be there in 30 minutes."

I asked directions to the parking garage and, after picking up my belongings, I only had to wait ten minutes before Laurent arrived. I recognized his long, gray beard and paunch at a distance, so I called hello to him as he drove his white Vespa up to the curb where I had been waiting. He wore jeans, a black leather jacket and mirrored sunglasses. He strapped the sleeping bag to the back of the scooter and asked me to hold the suitcase on my lap as we rode.

When we got to Laurent's spacious Left Bank apartment a few minutes later, he showed me to my room. I immediately lay down on the bed and jokingly asked him not to wake me until lunch the next day. I was so relieved to be in a quiet place and to be horizontal, I fell into a deep sleep that lasted 14 hours.

I awoke quite refreshed late the next morning. When Laurent saw me stir to find the bathroom, he called to me, "Lunch won't be for a couple of hours yet, I'm afraid." I remembered my request from the night before and chuckled along with him.

After a very light lunch, Laurent packed a small backpack he asked me to wear and we were on the road again on his little white scooter. We took small, country roads in the direction of Reims and within an hour or so, we turned onto a private road. Cows grazed in the field on one side, glancing up for only a moment when the high buzz of the scooter's engine whipped past.

Laurent was a filmmaker, with quite a bit of money and free time. He had rented a chateau, and when we drove up to the building, I spotted small groups of Asian-looking men in orange robes wandering around the grounds. "Who are they?" I asked pointing toward the brightly robed men.

"They are Buddhist monks," Laurent explained as we got off the bike. "They're refugees from Tibet. The Chinese have stepped up their torture and murder of the Tibetans in Lhasa, so many of them come here first until we can find new homes for them here in France or in Germany or Belgium. Come inside, and I'll introduce you to the others."

Among the others there was a young French woman named Clarisse, an anthropology student at the Sorbonne in Paris. She was a woman of medium height with freckles, green eyes and reddish-brown hair cut in the pageboy style that is so popular in Paris. She was by no means a frail French woman of fashion, but wore a loose fitting dress and appeared to have adopted not only the heavy, grounded way of walking that Tibetan monks use, but also their bodybuild. She was a collection of full, round surfaces and had attained that bouyant, blissful demeanor of the Buddhist monk. I got settled in my room for the weekend and went back downstairs to talk to this attractive woman. She was talking to two of the monks in the kitchen when I came back down. I waited in the doorway until she was finished, and she approached me with a smile.

"Are you looking for me, or have you been overcome with ravenous hunger?" she asked.

Before I could answer, she had shuttled me into the hallway. "Never mind that," she said with a grin. "Answer this for me: How long will you be staying here at the chateau?" She traced a line with her finger down my arm.

"I'm here with Laurent," I replied. "He has to be back in Paris on Monday." I was somewhat surprised at her forthrightness after my encounters with the more demure women in Morocco.

"If you'd like to stay longer, I could take you back on Tuesday. I don't have any classes until that afternoon." Clarisse leaned back against the opposite wall, still smiling.

"Are you here to study with the Tibetans?"

"Yes. Buddhism has interested me for some time."

"If you want, maybe I could share some of what I know about Buddhism with you later this afternoon."

Just then, Laurent joined us in the hallway. Clarisse nodded at him and then answered me, "I think I would enjoy that." She shook my hand, holding on for just a bit longer than the standard handshake, and went off outside taking my attention with her. Her scent lingered in the air where she stood only moments before.

Sensing the sparks between us, Laurent turned to me and said, "Be gentle with her, my friend. She has been celibate for a very long time."

"So have I," I countered with a chuckle.

"I will tell her to be gentle with you too, then. I overheard you say you would be teaching her something about Buddhism later today. That would be interesting to witness, my friend."

I folded my arms and gave him a quizzical look. "Why is that?"

"Well, let me see," Laurent began. "I believe you will find that Clarisse left home at the age of 13 and hitchhiked through Turkey and Persia to India where she met the Burmese Theravada Buddhist master Goenka and studied about three schools of Buddhism and the relativity of time and space for eight years. She returned to France last year to enter the Sorbonne on a scholarship and publish a book on the confluence of the teachings of Rumi and the Buddha. She is here to teach the monks metta-meditation, or heart-meditation, so it will be interesting to see what you can add to her knowledge of Buddhism."

Laurent left chuckling. I felt sure this woman was attracted to me, but I obviously had to find some other way to gain her respect. There was a reception for some new Tibetan immigrants that evening, so after dinner I was only able to speak with Clarisse for a minute or two at a time before she was whisked off to be introduced to someone or another. She seemed very poised and serene for someone only 23 years old. I talked to Laurent for a while, and he suggested I sit in on her meditation class in the morning. As I climbed the stairs to go to bed that night, I noticed Clarisse bowing to yet another orange-robed monk in the hall.

Laurent knocked on my door early the next morning. "It is sunrise, my friend. You said you wanted me to wake you for Clarisse's meditation class. Do you want to change your mind?"

"No," I replied, as I struggled up to a sitting position, "I'll be there."

"We meet in the garden. Go out the front door and follow the path to the right."

Within 15 minutes, I was dressed and heading down toward the garden. Behind a hedge, I suddenly came upon a sea of orange robes. Approximately 30 monks were already gathered on the lawn along with a few Westerners like Laurent, all in silent meditation. I picked up a mat from a stack near the hedge and joined them as unobtrusive-ly as possible. I spotted Clarisse's pulled-back, brown hair in front. After a minute or so, Clarisse, seated facing the rest of us, opened her eyes and gave the invocation, which was a bit more inclusive than the one I had used with my healing circles back in Chile:

> *May all sentient beings have happiness and its causes.*
> *May all sentient beings be free of suffering and its causes.*
> *May all sentient beings not be separated from sorrowless bliss.*
> *May all sentient beings abide in equanimity, free of bias, attachment and anger.*

After this, there was another period of silence, and then she began the meditation.

"Our task today is not to pray or meditate," Clarisse began again. "I am not here to teach you to meditate."

She fell silent again. Heads started to turn, gauging the reactions of others to this statement. Did she really mean that she was calling off the meditation?

"I am here to make your life a meditation," she resumed. "You must focus your attention on your heart, not on your mind. The mind will keep you from burning your hand on a flame or walking off a cliff, but it is the heart's intelligence that will keep you healthy and fulfilled. Many of you find that place of wisdom when you sit like this to medi-tate. I tell you, you must try to maintain that focus at all times. When you eat, you focus on your heart. When you bathe, you focus on your heart. When you talk with someone else, you focus on your heart. There can be no split between your 'ordinary' life and your spiritual life.

"Many things can take us away from a focus on the heart, that essential part of ourselves that does not change over time. The most common distraction is action. When you see the wind blowing through an open window and causing your papers to flutter off your desk, you might immediately go to the window and close it. I believe contemplation should precede all action. When I come upon such a scene, I watch the graceful twisting and floating of the pieces of paper as they fall to the floor. I feel the currents of air spreading throughout the room. I might go first to the desk to see what pages remain there, and then to the floor to see what the wind has put there. Perhaps the wind has decided to sweep aside the letters and plans that have been distracting me from my life's true purpose. Perhaps the wind has uncovered the letter I most need to return or the book I have put down and stopped reading for too long. What a great teaching I might have missed if I had simply acted to close the window and replace the pages on the desk without being observant and receptive first."

I noticed how she held the attention of every person gathered on the lawn. "Another condition that takes our focus away from the heart and locks us in the future or the past or in some storm of emotion is a lack of gratitude. Why do those with so few material possessions or so few friends seem to be more satisfied with their lives? Is it that they do not know what they are missing? No, many are very aware of all that they do not have. The difference is their gratitude for what they do have. To do otherwise is to invite sorrow. How can we be happy thinking about all that is not ours and beyond our reach?

"It is not a difficult skill to learn, my friends," she continued with a smile. "It is the way we are born. It requires simply that we look at all things as new, with the wonder and fascination of a child. Our busy lives are not diminished by this focus. We do not lose any of our other senses when we utilize the senses of the heart. The heart shows the eyes a more compassionate view of the world. The heart tunes the ears to the undertones and overtones that tell what the other person really wants. And the heart makes every decision the mind has to make much easier; it chooses the path toward one's true purpose in life. There are no values of time or money or influence to cloud what is truly best for us."

Clarisse was again besieged by students after the meditation, but this time I waited until the last had thanked her and headed back toward the chateau. "I was impressed by your talk," I told her.

"Thank you," she said as we started walking back. "I am free until this evening, if you would like to go over your knowledge of Buddhism with me."

"I fear anything I could say on the subject would be . . . redundant at best," I said with an embarrassed grin.

"Ah," she replied, "you weren't paying attention during the meditation. Everything and everyone has something to teach even the most accomplished of masters."

We ate breakfast together, and I told Clarisse more about my insights into psychiatry and my experience in the Sufi community. She looked at me with both respect and full attention, and she politely interrupted to ask for an occasional clarification. I got a deep sense that she understood me.

Our discussion of philosophy, medicine and spiritual traditions continued for several hours and fueled our undeniable attraction to one another. In the haze of the mid-afternoon sun we succumbed to our desire. Despite our long periods of celibacy, our lovemaking was not frenzied, but had the subtle power of a raindrop's ripple on a deep, still lake. Clarisse's centeredness, so commanding in her speech and demeanor, was maintained in her lovemaking. She had a strong presence at all times it seemed, which made her all the more alluring to me.

Over the following weeks, Clarisse and I spent more and more time with each other at the chateau and in cafes and parks in Paris. One Saturday morning, as we were strolling along the Champs Elysees, she turned to me and said, "Carlos, I feel very fortunate to have met you. You have reminded me how important it is in maintaining one's physical health to stay in touch with life's meaning and purpose. You have provided a bridge between my teachings about heart-centeredness and the concept of the soul I had rejected as a teenager."

We stopped walking. She turned to me and continued. "I think it is time that you met my parents."

"Why now?"

"We've been romantically involved for a few weeks, and I have mentioned you to them. They want to meet you."

"I guess I have reservations because it implies a commitment I don't think I'm ready to make."

She looked at me for a minute, as if she were studying my features for an exam. "Perhaps it would be best if you moved on," she said at last.

I was taken a bit by surprise. "You don't want to see me any more?" I stammered.

"Carlos, I am not a perfect being. I think you are very handsome, and I enjoy your company greatly. I am very happy when I am with you. Yes, I would like to keep seeing you, but . . ."

"Is it someone else?" I blurted out.

"No, no," Clarisse said amid chuckles and waving arms. "Carlos, I have another meditation to teach you. Sit down here with me."

She indicated a bench on the sidewalk, and we sat down there. "From my point of view, it would seem very natural to introduce you to my parents and talk about plans for the future. But I was taught to put myself in the other person's place and look back at myself. I could see that you weren't ready to settle down and that I might seem like I was hooking you into a marriage proposal. That is not what I want from you. I will show you how I know that you need to move on. Look at my eyes.

"You must try to imagine looking out at the world through my eyes. Remember that I am younger, that I was raised here in France, that I am an anthropology student at the Sorbonne, and that I teach meditation techniques at the chateau. Try to imagine what my needs might be right now. What might I be afraid of?

"Now look out through my eyes at yourself. You sit there on the bench, your hair tousled by the wind. You're wearing gray slacks and a blue sweater. You have a look of confusion in your eyes. Your breathing is deep. Try to imagine what you look like or seem to be from my perspective.

"Then you must remember that most human actions try to increase happiness. If I were to force you into a more committed relationship, I might be happy for a while because I will have achieved one of my goals. I believe I wasn't meant to continue the solitary, celibate life of a contemplative. And you'll probably be happy at first for the same reason. You've told me you believe there is a soul-mate out there somewhere for you.

"But you'd grow unhappy realizing that our commitment was keeping you from fulfilling your greater life's purpose. Your restlessness would eventually decrease my happiness as well. If I'm grateful for the time we have spent together over the past few weeks, that can be enough.

"When I looked at you a few minutes ago, I was practicing this meditation. I realized you had needs that could not be fulfilled staying here in Paris. In fact, you risk becoming too settled if you stay here longer, am I right?"

I took her hand in mine. "I keep wondering when I'll have learned enough, experienced enough, to be ready to share it with others."

"You share what you have learned all the time, Carlos."

"I know," I said as I pulled her closer. "Sometimes I get so tired of always moving on."

Clarisse settled against my chest and put her hand on my knee. "Remember what you used to call us just after we met?"

"I'm not sure."

"You called us icebreakers," she said laughing. "And like those ships that sail icy waters, we're not stopped by the hazards and opportunities of our environments. Loneliness. Ah, that too we can break through. Our sense of meaning and purpose is our home and place of power as we move from one location to the next, or one relationship to the next."

I knew Clarisse was right, that at this time my life was my journey and I must continue along my path. But I also knew that one day there would be more, for I'd experienced a vision years ago of what a complement to my life a soulmate union would be. I wasn't interested in moving from one relationship to another, but I knew that unless I had the ultimate heart certainty, I would not settle down. I knew that it was possible to share the oneness of spirit with another human being, and I refused to settle for less. In a soulmate relationship it would be possible to focus attention entirely on the soul of the relationship instead of its interpersonal mechanics. This would create a set of values that did not exist in other relationships.

Only in such a relationship would I be able to settle down and to have children. I saw that relationships were the place where the soul works out its destiny. The soul is not concerned with making a relationship work because the soul's point of view is not an ambitious point of view. It doesn't make love a work project or a productivity project. It recognizes the mystery that is involved in the union and extension of our beingness with that of another person. I knew it was in my future and I was willing to discover it.

The next day, I decided to contact Idries Shah. Since I was in Europe, I thought it would be a convenient time to meet my longtime Sufi teacher in person. I would tell him what I had learned so far and see if he could suggest a new plan of study for me. By the following Friday, I had bidden adieu to Laurent and Clarisse and boarded a train to Calais. From there, I took a ship across the channel to England, and a train from Dover to Tumbridge Wells. At the train station in Canterbury, I was met by Shah's secretary, a young, blond Englishman named Colin, who drove me by car to the estate in Langton Green.

When we reached Shah's home, we passed through a decorative stone gate with a bronze plaque set into the left pillar that read "Langton House." Beyond the gates, a dirt driveway wove through a couple hundred feet of bright-green, closely trimmed lawn to a huge, white, English country home. A small, wooden sign at the turning circle at the house, where three other cars were parked, read "Institute for Cultural Research." Colin informed me that I would be staying in "the cottage, 'round back,'" so he told me to go in and talk to Mr. Shah while he took my suitcase and sleeping bag to my room.

I entered the front hall of the house, and immediately a small black-haired Afghani man in his forties wearing a brown corduroy jacket and a tie poked his head out a doorway to the left. "Doctor," he said with a twinkle in his dark eyes, "it is so good to finally meet you in person. Come in. Come sit down a while with me. Or perhaps you are in need of rest after your trip from Paris, eh?"

He invited me into a sitting room with an ornate fireplace and several plush, antique chairs. He took two open books off one of the chairs and sat down, offering me the chair facing it across a small, coffee table. He told me he had to leave for a symposium at the University of Geneva in two days, but that we could talk in his spare time until then and when he returned ten days later. By then, Colin had returned.

"Sayed," he said, "you have a phone call."

"Work calls," Mr. Shah told me. "Colin will show you around, but not the rose garden, Colin. I would like to lead that tour myself tomorrow."

"Yes, sir," Colin replied.

At that, Shah got up and hurried off down the hallway. "I know his first name is Idries, so why do you call him Sayed?" I asked Colin.

"It's Afghani for 'prince,'" Colin replied matter-of-factly. "Dr. Warter, if you'll follow me, I'll give you a quick tour of the main house here and then show you to the cottage. Since dinner has already been served, I can ask the cook to make up a plate for you."

"I would appreciate that," I said as I got up to follow Colin out. "He certainly doesn't look the way I imagined."

"Were you imagining the turban and jalaba?"

"Yes," I admitted. "I guess I've been so accustomed to seeing Sufi teachers wearing them."

"That's why the staff calls him Prince," Colin said with the first hint of a smile I'd seen. "When he wears the turban and jalaba, he really does look like some Afghani royal. Shah is descended from Prophet Mohammed. He is a sharif and he is royalty of Afghanistan."

At the end of our tour of the main house we were in the kitchen. Colin pointed to a door leading out to the back of the house and said, "The cottage is right out that door. I will see you tomorrow."

When I went out the back door, there was a floodlight illuminating a flagstone path over the lawn to what seemed a very large, two-story house with brick foundation and tall, cathedral-style windows. I scanned the backyard for the small, cabin I envisioned as my home for the next few weeks, but I couldn't make it out in the early evening darkness.

I went back into the house and caught up with Colin in the main hall. "I'm sorry," I said, "but I can't find the cottage."

"It's right there," he said with a scowl. "You can't miss it. Just follow the path."

"Is it behind the other house?"

"The other house is the cottage," Colin informed me. "Oh, I meant to tell you that there are two bedrooms there, but you should have the place all to yourself. The guest rooms here in the main house should suffice. We aren't expecting many visitors in the next couple of weeks. There are linens and other supplies in the bathroom closet, but if you need anything you can't find there, let me or the maid know. She will come to tidy up at 11:00 in the morning unless another time of day would be more convenient for you."

"I'm sure that will be fine," I said. "I'm not a late sleeper."

"Well then, good night, Doctor. The maid should come round in a few minutes with that plate of food."

At that, the young man went upstairs, and I wandered back out to the huge structure they called "the Cottage." I wandered around inside it admiring yet more beautiful antique furniture and rugs. After my months in Morocco, sleeping on the floor with 60 other men and having virtually no possessions, the opulence of this little cottage made it seem like Buckingham Palace.

I forgot to draw the drapes in my bedroom that night, so I awakened the next morning shortly after sunrise with the warmth of sunlight on my face. I showered, dressed and wandered into the kitchen of the main house. There, a young boy and girl were sitting at the round table arguing with each other. A short, thin, dark-haired woman frying eggs at the stove and smoking a cigarette called over her shoulders for the children to "pipe down."

"Hello," I called out.

"Oh," she said as she turned around to face me. "You must be Dr. Warter. Welcome to Langton House. I'm Shah's wife."

"Pleased to meet you," I said. "These are your children?"

She took another long puff from her cigarette, seemingly ignoring my question. "You two settle down and be patient. Your food will be ready in just a minute."

She looked up at me with her beautiful almond-shaped eyes again and exhaled smoke as she spoke. "We'll have breakfast for you and the other guests in the sitting room. It won't be ready for another half-hour yet. These two are spoiled, so they get fried eggs. You'll be having juice, tea and rolls."

"That will be fine, I'm sure," I managed to say before she continued talking to the two youngsters I had to assume were her children.

The smoke started to bother me, so I decided to go back out to the cottage for a few minutes to wait for breakfast. When I passed through the kitchen again 30 minutes later, there was no evidence that Mrs. Shah and the two children had been there except for the strong smell of tobacco smoke. I made my way to the sitting room where a table had been set up buffet-style with the promised juice, tea, rolls and marmalades. After a few minutes, Shah burst into the room and took a seat near me.

"I will be leaving for Geneva tomorrow," he said, "so I will be fairly tied up today, but perhaps we can talk tonight at dinner. I know, would you like to take a walk with me in the rose garden after breakfast?"

"I would be delighted," I said with a smile.

"Oh no," he said with mock trepidation, "being pleased would be quite enough. I always worry that I am in the process of being deified when someone says they are 'delighted to meet me' or 'delighted to be spending time with me.' I'm not a guru type. I have written over a million published words at this point in my life. I much prefer to be thought of as a writer, a storyteller. I think of myself as an importer of ideas. I'm bringing the wisdom of the Sufis to the West so that more people may be activated. And now I must go get some breakfast."

When he returned with a plateful of rolls, he began to furiously break them open, butter them and spread them with marmalade as he continued. "You are, of course, familiar with the Apostle Paul?"

"Yes."

"He wrote, 'Be in the world, not of the world.' That is the principle which I teach as well."

"I remember," I interjected. "You wrote that the objective was to become an 'invisible Sufi.'"

"Precisely. One's spirituality should blend in with the rest of one's life."

Colin appeared again. "Good morning. Sayed?"

"Don't tell me the phone calls have begun already!" Shah told Colin. Then he apologized to me. "I will return shortly, and you will see why I put up with the frantic pace here at the Institute."

Nearly an hour later, Mr. Shah reappeared, still gnawing on one of his breakfast rolls. "Come, come, before the phone rings again," he told me in conspiratorial tones.

He led me to a garden on the side of the house with several dozen rose bushes of various types. He pointed out the names of each type of rose as we strolled, and we talked about my experiences. I didn't always understand what he was saying, but I felt odd asking him to clarify since he would say, "You seem a very intelligent man, Doctor. Of course, you know what I mean." What I described as soul awareness he referred to as activating one's essence.

"We as humans have within us an essence," Shah explained, "initially tiny, shiny and precious. It does not grow as our bodies do. We must develop this essence through our own effort. Although we are responsible for developing this essence in ourselves, the development starts with the activation of the teaching. That is what the stories are for. When the mind is cultivated correctly and suitably, it becomes more stable and constant. Your consciousness is translated to a subliminal plane."

"I feel like I have been activated, as you say," I told him, "but I sometimes have difficulty maintaining that awareness. I have explored many different spiritual techniques, but no technique seems to be able to help me as consistently as the original one."

Shah stopped walking and got out a handkerchief to mop his brow. "There's a story that speaks to your dilemma: There once was a monkey that came across a tree in which long, yellow fruits hung in huge clumps. The monkey climbed the tree and picked one of the strange, new fruits. It smelled sweet, but the skin seemed a little rubbery, so he peeled the skin off and ate the softer fruit within. The monkey was overcome with joy and felt this was the most delicious fruit he had ever eaten. He called the fruit 'banana,' and went on his way. A few days later, he came across another banana tree. He climbed this tree and picked one that seemed firm and fragrant. When he peeled it and took a few bites, the monkey felt it did not live up to the exquisite taste of the first banana. It was still good, but since the second banana did not compare to the first, he decided not to try any further bananas. He would keep the memory of the first banana in his heart.

"A second monkey came across one of these strange, new banana trees. He climbed the tree and picked one of the long, yellow fruits, too. He, too, peeled the skin and was overcome with joy at the first soft, sweet bite. He gobbled up the rest of it, and he too declared this to be the most delicious fruit he had ever tasted. He picked another banana from the same tree, peeled it and took a bite. This second banana was also very good, but the monkey was disappointed that its taste was not as exquisite as his memory of the first banana. He climbed down the tree and began searching for another banana tree. When he found one, he climbed up and picked one banana after another, peeling them and taking a bite out of each. But the third, fourth, fifth and sixth bananas did not live up to the divine taste of his first banana, so he kept on searching the rest of his life for a banana that tasted as good as the first one he happened upon."

"So part of my difficulty," I concluded, "is that I keep searching for an experience like that month with Françoise back in Chile, and it was the newness that made it so special and so long-lived?"

"And part of the difficulty," Shah added as we resumed our walk, "is because society still reinforces the idea of two separate cultures, the material and the spiritual. We are entering a new age of information that will supersede the notion of two cultures. We have been learning facts. We need to learn how to learn. It is a sort of opening, making oneself available to the wisdom of the universe rather than going out to capture it. Once that information revolution occurs, there will be a consciousness revolution—the emergence of one integrated, spiritual culture.

"I come across so many seekers," Shah continued as he stopped again to study one of his roses, "who look for spirituality in places where it is not. They look at New Age thinking—reincarnation, auras, meditation, synchronicity—but this is only the fossilization of teaching, not living teaching. Everywhere I travel I find students mechanically repeating old techniques from the East or the West without the essential knowledge of those techniques. That is, what is the goal of the techniques? Have you adapted them and made them personally meaningful and relevant to your experience?

"We need to go beyond the techniques to the results they might produce. You mentioned my concept of the invisible Sufi at breakfast.

We must transform the individual so the path becomes part of daily living. No techniques or rituals can be useful over the whole of your life. It requires a new way of relating and a new ethics. Imagine an entire culture that is truly global, where our humanity and not our national or religious rituals join us—one that goes far beyond what scholars currently refer to as ecumenism."

That evening, at dinner, I was introduced to two world-renowned psychologists and a novelist who were staying at Langton House. I had seen them around on the grounds or in the bookstore—where I had spent most of the afternoon—but we hadn't been introduced. We all sat at the long table in the formal dining room and discussed what we had learned recently. Shah laughed a lot, smoked cigarettes with the same enthusiasm as his wife, and, as usual, spoke very fast. He seemed to be operating at a higher energy level than the rest of us. As I was beginning to recognize, he had a tendency to jump from one topic to the next and back again, sometimes keeping three or four thoughts going simultaneously.

After his wife excused herself from the table, Shah went on. "God is in ultimate control, and He creates the future that He wants for all of His creation. To believe that we can evolve ourselves is the ultimate arrogance. Yet, to believe that we can do nothing about our destiny is being utterly asleep."

Here he turned to me. "Religious systems have good intentions, as you have been researching them, dear Doctor, but we need to stop before the techniques and philosophies build up a false identity for ourselves instead of making us real humans. You know how many deaths have been caused by sacrificing lives for so-called religious principles. We have to be careful. These new times represent the emergence of a new culture in which what is of value in one system can be synergized with parallel values in others. Humanity is at the verge of a quantum leap of self-discovery and conscious group interaction. When we learn to interact consciously, we will activate what has been called our paranormal abilities—telepathy, clairvoyance, clairaudience.

"You said you started to experience some of these abilities in communal living in Morocco, isn't that right, Doctor? It is in these sorts of environments that the awakening is most likely to occur. All traditions speak of a time in which the ancient prophecy of unification will take place. The inner schools have set up teaching groups in carefully selected times and places with carefully selected people not to crystallize these abilities but to do a specific activation. Then the individuals become like carriers of a positive light with which they gradually affect the rest of society until the new culture of peace emerges. You must remember that you were activated in the group that you joined at the beginning of your pilgrimage in Chile, the one Horst was my deputy for. There we established a contact that enabled me to receive you here now and that created in you, like a radio transmitter, a vehicle of activation that can discriminantly search out the spiritual knowledge of this age so that later in your life you will be able to empower others and activate them spiritually.

"Do you remember this morning when you talked of not being able to remain at this higher vibration consistently, Doctor? It's as if we all have a base level of vibrational energy, and all of us will follow different paths and go to different places to gradually raise that base level higher until it is possible for you to be of service in activating others through your work, or your mere presence."

We all looked around the table at each other, and I tried to imagine all of us going out into the world so at peace that others were inspired by just seeing us.

The next day, as I approached the main house from the cottage for breakfast, I looked through the kitchen window. The beautiful Mrs. Shah was once again in the kitchen chain-smoking and cooking breakfast for her children. I thought I would try a little harder to engage her in conversation after our rather abrupt meeting the previous morning.

I entered the kitchen and greeted her. After a few moments, I said, "In living with Shah for so long, you must have had a chance to talk with a number of great thinkers."

She nodded. "He asks that I participate in some of the meals and social events held here for the guests and students."

"I was wondering whether you've developed a philosophy of your own about where we're all headed," I said. "What do you think is the goal of evolution?"

Mrs. Shah scooped the fried eggs out of the frying pan and onto plates she set in front of the two children. "You will have to ask Shah," she said bluntly. "My focus is clear. I only take care of Shah, his children and his home."

I felt a bit embarrassed. In Morocco, I had often engaged the wives of the sheik in discussions about spiritual matters. I wasn't sure if she really had no interest in such things or whether I might have touched on a source of past arguments between the two of them.

So when Shah was gone to Switzerland for ten days, I contented myself with reading his books—*The Sufis, Tales of the Dervishes, Thinkers of the East, The Dervish Probe*—and the other books in the bookstore on sociology, anthropology, religion and philosophy. It was awe-inspiring to realize that books had made his teaching available to millions of people. Even though I was a guest in his home, I experienced a knowledge from the books similar to the initiations and other training I had undertaken in Chile and the United States. This written information contained the same activating factors for the awakening of consciousness. When I grew tired of reading, I took walks in his rose garden, thinking about what would be next for my life.

When Shah returned, we took a few more walks together in his rose garden. He told me about his fascination with electronics and pumped me for what I knew of their use in medical research. I told him about the methods I used in my clinical practice, and he discussed them quite knowledgeably, occasionally offering new techniques or models. Shah questioned the time-frames of history, insisting that the Church had ignored the first half of humanity's 10,000 years of development on earth. He also talked of how the world's dependency on money had skewed our sense of what had value.

During one of these walks together, Mr. Shah took a deep breath, turned to me and said, "Your stay here is complete, I think. It is time for you to take what you have learned and share it with others."

"But how shall I do this," I asked him.

"You can go back to America and become a guru. There are many people there who need spiritual guidance."

"I have seen the gurus in America," I told him. "I think they sometimes lose their essence because of their concern with techniques.

Besides, that would not incorporate all I have learned. It is not the whole existence that I feel drawn to. It is so separated from the world."

"If it is the world you seek, then go into business. That is another area that could use enlightened men."

"But it is not spiritual. If I was to throw myself into business, I would be as one-sided as a guru."

"Then you must take your concept of spirituality and share it with others. You are a psychiatrist, and from what you have told me you feel a vocation to service. Incorporate the two, for you know they are connected. I notice you read when you are not actively studying. If you have so much faith in books, why don't you write one that incorporates spirituality into psychology. You have seen the healing power of the spirit. You should share this knowledge with others."

The Healing
Power of
the Soul

I considered going back to Paris and I called Clarisse to see how she was doing. I told her I was thinking about visiting a psychiatric colleague and friend from Chile whom I heard was living in Miami, Florida. She said that she would be glad to see me again, but if I were to go to the United States, I should be sure to look up the French obstetrician Frederick Leboyer, an expert on childbirth without violence. She gave me his address and phone number.

I then found out the phone number of my Chilean friend from information and called. Ramon was glad to hear from me after two years and invited me to come visit for a while.

Two days later, Colin drove me to Heathrow Airport, just outside London, and I boarded a plane to Miami. When I arrived it was

165

Monday afternoon in sunny south Florida. Ramon and his wife Selina met me at the airport. I could tell the city agreed with both of them. Ramon told me the weather was ideal for two of his favorite pursuits: tennis and boating. I could tell he was spending a lot of his time outside because he was very trim and, being Sephardic, his always dark skin was darker than I had ever seen it. Selina was in very good shape herself, and could have passed for a model with her long blond hair and long legs. She was a nurse at the same hospital where Ramon worked, and he told me she was one of the most caring people he knew in the medical field.

"Some patients got well just because Selina is so nice to them," Ramon said on the way to their home. Though Selina blushed at this statement, her brightness and attentiveness when dealing with others made me believe it was true.

They took me to their house which was just a few blocks from the beach. A huge palm tree dominated the rather small front yard. They showed me to a guest room they had made in the attic, and although I had to duck under diagonal beams to get to a couple of areas of the room, it was pretty spacious and I had my own half-bath.

Ramon and Selina took me to a Cuban restaurant that night for dinner, which included fried plantains, black beans and rice, and cafe Cubano. Selina was anxious to make sure I had a good time there, so she told me a lot about the tourist attractions in Miami.

"If I know Carlos," my friend Ramon interrupted, "he will want to tour the clubs and meet some of the beautiful young women of Miami."

Ramon laughed, but I did not. "Do you want us to introduce you to someone?" Selina asked.

"I don't think I'm ready to start dating again," I admitted.

"Well, if you were dating," Selina said, "what would you be looking for in a woman?"

"I thought about that for a moment. "Someone serene, non-neurotic and spiritual."

"I have a friend who works with me at the hospital whom you might want to meet then," Selina said. "She is also a nurse. I could give you her number. I know she's not involved with anyone right now. And she's very pretty."

"Are you talking about Maggie?" Ramon asked. Selina nodded. "Yeah, she seems very nice and she is quite beautiful."

The next day, I called the number Selina had given me. I talked to a woman who seemed pleasant and friendly, and I suggested we might go out dancing that Friday night. She agreed and gave me her address. I then called Frederick Leboyer. He was pleasant on the phone and asked about Clarisse. He also invited me to a seminar he was giving on Thursday.

I arrived at the hospital on Thursday morning and made my way to the lecture room where Dr. Leboyer's workshop was being held. There were a number of doctors in white coats gathered there talking among themselves, and I felt somewhat out of place. When Dr. Leboyer entered the room the other doctors sat down and grew quiet. Leboyer was not a tall man, but he was distinguished looking and obviously held the respect of the other people in the room. He spoke with a slight accent when he began to explain that he had learned much of his method in India. The idea behind his work was that the birth process does not have to be traumatic, that it can be done without the violence so often seen in the delivery room. Dr. Leboyer had recently finished his book Loving Hands: The Traditional Art of Baby Massaging, and he included these techniques in his presentation.

After the seminar I introduced myself to Dr. Leboyer.

"Seeing you here among all these white coats I figured you must be Dr. Warter. I called Clarisse after we spoke on the phone. She had many wonderful things to say about you," he said with a wink.

I talked to him for some time about his methods and his studies in India. I also explained some of the work I had done incorporating other Eastern traditions into medical practice.

On Friday night I arrived at Maggie's house and was pleasantly surprised by the young woman that answered the door. She reminded me of a cherub with her long golden hair her small, round figure. There was also a glow to her cheeks when she let me in, asking me if I would like to sit and talk for a bit before going out. I told her that would be fine, and she showed me into her living room and offered me something to drink. As she went off to the kitchen to get us some iced tea, I surveyed the room. Maggie had decorated the walls with paintings and tapestries. There was a large Persian rug, an ornate incense burner, a crystal chandelier and several bookshelves filled with books. There was something very peaceful and comfortable about this place, I thought. When she came back with our drinks, I commented that her home seemed very peaceful.

"That's because I have an Indian teacher who has helped me center my mind," Maggie said. "He says the outer environment and inner environment tend to mirror each other."

Inside, I laughed. There was no escaping soul awareness. I just wanted to meet someone and have a good time, I thought to myself. Here I am again with another spiritual seeker.

We ended up staying there and talking for many hours, and then we decided not to go out. The spiritual energy was so comforting and so peaceful that we actually fell asleep in each others' arms. It was warm, brotherly and sisterly affection.

When dawn came, I said farewell to Maggie and returned back to Ramon and Selina's home. I called Maggie later in the day and she agreed to meet me for dinner on Sunday.

Ramon and Selina let me borrow their car Sunday night, and I picked Maggie up at her house around six o'clock. "Would you mind stopping by the hospital on the way to the restaurant?" she asked me as she got into the car. "It's only a few blocks away, and I left a book there yesterday that I'd wanted to show to you."

"We have plenty of time," I told her. "I don't mind. Which hospital is it?"

"Jackson Memorial Hospital," she replied. "Just go to that next stop sign and make a left."

We drove through a neighborhood that looked like a war zone. All the buildings were painted green and brown, and many of the windows were broken. We passed burned-out car bodies with no wheels and even one burned-out school bus. At one intersection, we came to a stop and watched a rat the size of a small dog cross the street. "Welcome to Overtown," Maggie said ironically.

When we got to the hospital, Maggie got out and told me she would only be a minute. As I waited, I observed a nurse waiting at a bus stop. She pulled a handgun out of her purse, checked to see if it was loaded and put it back in her purse. When Maggie returned, I asked her, "Is it common for the nurses here to carry guns?"

"There's a lot of crime in this neighborhood," she said calmly.

"How do you get to work?" I asked her. "You don't have a car."

"I usually ride my bike."

"Aren't you afraid of being attacked?"

"I've never been attacked. I don't let that possibility into my consciousness, and I've been fine for the two years I've worked here."

Over dinner, she told me how she had recycled most of her waste long before any of her neighbors had heard of it. She got out into nature at least once a week, because she thought it was as important to health as a good diet. She sat in raja yoga meditation—an ancient harmonizing technique from India—for an hour every morning and every night. The meditation activated what she called the divine holy name; allowed her to experience the light, the inner light and the sound; and nourished her with her own divine nectar.

"Do you think you might stay in Florida?" Maggie asked at one point.

"I don't know. I had just planned to visit for a couple of weeks."

"What were you planning to do after this trip then?"

"I'm not sure," I admitted. "I've been thinking about going back to Chile, but I'd go anywhere I could practice psychiatry and not be ostracized for acknowledging my patients' spiritual needs."

"I know this pediatrician who also studied with my yoga teacher for a while. He moved to the Rockies. There is this group there starting a more holistic clinic. Do you want to talk to him?"

"Why not?" I replied.

Maggie gave me the number of the pediatrician living in the Rockies. I had no definite plans to call him, but then I had an experience that convinced me to move on with my life. I was running along the beach the following morning when I heard a voice calling, "Young man, young man, come here" I looked around and finally saw an old woman sitting in a chair next to one of the beach hotels. I ran over to her and asked if she need some help.

She held out a bottle in her twisted, wrinkled hands and said, "Can you please go down to the ocean and get me some saltwater?"

"It would be my pleasure," I told her as I took the jar and ran down to the water. I returned to the women and handed her the jar full of saltwater. She smiled broadly and asked me to sit down and talk to her.

"You know I worked my whole life so I could retire to Miami and enjoy life. I knew Florida was where I wanted to be, so I planned to move down here when I reached that magic sixty-five. I worked over-time, I worked weekends, I did everything I could to save my money. I never did like my work, I was a seamstress in a dress shop, but I knew that one day I could retire and come down here to Miami. It was the only thing that got me through some days. Then one day my retire-ment came, and I moved down here. The trouble is, now I don't walk so good so I have to keep off the beach for fear of falling down and not being able to get up. My heart's not so good either, so I spend most of my days inside where it's air-conditioned. You know I saved all my life to come down here, it was the one thing I wanted out of life. Now I'm here and I'm too old to enjoy it."

As I was finishing my run I thought about what this old woman said. She knew what she wanted out of life when she was young, but she didn't think she could have it then. She thought she had to post-pone the longing of her heart until later when she was ready to retire. It made me think about what I was doing in Miami, and whether I might not be better served by following my own heart.

I called the pediatrician a couple of days later, and the man was very nice and seemed happy to hear I was a psychiatrist. He said the clinic he worked at needed a psychiatrist, and asked if I would be will-ing to come out and visit. Having no other plans and intrigued by a clinic that he reported started its meetings with group meditations, I agreed to visit the following week.

The clinic was a large, Victorian house with a white, picket fence in a tree-lined neighborhood not far from the downtown area. It was not yet open for business. There were boxes everywhere and painters were still at work in a couple of the rooms. I was introduced over the next two days to most of the other clinicians, which included a physical therapist, a health-awareness teacher, a yoga teacher, a nutritionist, an acupuncturist, a massage therapist, a cardiologist, a midwife and other therapists.

I sat in on a clinical meeting. It started with a meditation, and the discussion afterward focused on the healing value of spiritual understanding and on the psychology of hope. I was convinced this was where I needed to be.

"So do you think you might be interested in serving with us?" the pediatrician asked at the end of that meeting on the second day.

"Definitely," I said. "When are you planning on opening?"

"Not until next week," he said. "You'll have plenty of time to move your things out here, if you want."

"I have all my possessions with me," I said smiling. "Where would I be working?" I was a little concerned that my office would be one of the narrow rooms on the first floor.

"This was the library," he said as he showed me a large room on the second floor with bookshelves covering two walls. French doors at the far end of the room led onto a balcony overlooking the backyard. "We were going to let whomever took the psychiatrist position choose his or her own furniture. That's why there's nothing in here now."

"It's perfect," I said.

One of my first clients at the clinic was a 62-year-old woman who was very unhappy. She felt lonely and bitter since her husband had died four years before, she no longer had contact with her children, and none of a half-dozen therapists she had visited were able to make her feel any better. In our first session she declared how little faith she had that I could help her. I put up with her demanding, negative, even obnoxious behavior for about a month. At that point, I told her she was wasting her time and money, "I don't see how I can help you. I don't feel any affinity toward you."

The woman stared at me blankly for a moment, and then tears formed in her eyes. "I've seen every shrink in town, and finally there's one honest enough to tell me how he feels about me. I like that. Maybe you can help me after all."

"All right," I said, "let's give ourselves another chance."

That shift in our therapeutic relationship made all the difference. She wasn't fighting me any more. She honestly faced some things in herself she had been denying for years. As a result, she started volunteering her time at the local hospital, and dating a man close to her age. She got a job at a fabric store, moved to a new apartment and started eating better and generally taking better care of herself. She described her renaissance as waking up to her true self—at 60 years of age. A true spiritual healing had taken place in which her identity had been moved from a neglected, mishandled daily lifecycle pathology, to a healthy thought process that recognized her usefulness at any age.

I realized I had been effective in turning this woman's life around because I was coming from the heart, and I had spoken the truth. I was being honest without trying to hurt her. I now tell people that coming from the heart doesn't always mean playing nice. I have watched too many colleagues drop their fake smile and start complaining about the patient they just saw. Healing occurs when the connection between the healer and the patient is clear. When the relationship is clear, both parties can make more informed, and potentially more healthy choices.

I started developing a process for dealing with new therapeutic relationships. The first step is to consciously and honestly describe the present status of events. When we lie to others or to ourselves, we become unable to tackle a project. All possible choices are unconsciously floating without description. When we consciously state the truth, we can get to the second step—making a choice. Step three involves making a clear commitment, to ourselves or others. This reinforces a state of connection between a doctor and a patient through communication and cooperation, so that whatever gets created is a complete, mutually enhancing, life-affirming situation. At the quantum level, we are all connected, and there is a hidden physiology that keeps us together the same way a planet and its moon or the protons in a water molecule are joined. Honoring this connectedness deepens our interactions with others and delves beneath the masks that our roles or functions represent.

The traditional problem-solving process for doctors involves asking, "What is your problem?" or "What has happened?" With the more holistic process I was developing, the first question becomes "Why is this happening?" In order to diagnose the depths of the intimate self, this process responds only after we let go of our social, professional, or chronological identification or the subjective feeling of waste or success. We will often find a similar state, in which the quietness of the answer leads us to the reconnection of the eternal youth within. We create many circumstances of success and failure to be able to return, to nourish ourselves in the silence of our souls.

Another early client at the clinic was a man named Barry. He was completely identified with his addiction. He had gone through many programs in which being an addict was his identity. Although Barry had not taken any drugs or alcohol for a long time, I noticed he had forgotten his soul. And by forgetting his soul, his way of connecting with the world was then his statement, "I am an addict."

So one day, I talked with him in a regular therapy session and asked him about his plans for the future.

"I can't think about the future," Barry replied. "I'm an addict. I have to take each day as it comes. I am really stuck. It doesn't matter how many years I'm clean and sober."

"Maybe you're not an addict any more," I suggested.

Barry's face got very red with anger, and he shouted back at me, "Then you're not a doctor!"

I immediately stood up and took off my white lab coat and said, "Okay, I'm a human being. What are you?"

"I'm a human being too!"

With that statement, Barry made a breakthrough. He reidentified with his essential self and let go of the "addict" identification that had helped him through the crisis of withdrawal early in his recovery. I noticed how much of the recovery process focused on first identifying with the individual's addiction: "I am Jane and I am an alcoholic." While this identification is useful initially it tends to localize the problem. Moreover, it creates a secondary problem when the soul identity of the individual is linked with this label for years. A better solution is to have the individual look heavenward and know that his or her eternal soul is expressing the condition from which he or she needs to recover.

About the same time Barry came to this revelation, I started looking for new methods to help clients reconnect with their soul. Some clients were not able to benefit from less structured techniques like meditation. I finally hit upon a process that worked not only in contacting one's own soul, but worked well with relationship problems because it also identifies the soul in someone else. I call it the "Love Letter" process.

I was seeing a young married couple having severe problems with trust and communication. Both husband and wife had been unfaithful to the other. They had trouble being civil to each other. They were constantly hurting each other. I tried getting them to talk about their anger and frustrations, but it always turned into a vicious fight where one or both of them would stop talking completely.

I finally gave each of them a pad of paper and a pencil and told them to write a very long letter to each other. The first portion talked about their resentment and anger for the other person. After a few minutes of writing, I stopped them and asked them why they were so angry with this person. "If you were really that angry with the other person," I said, "your relationship wouldn't mean anything. There would be no reason for you to be together."

They said they were angry because they had been hurt. "Okay," I told them, "now write down what is hurting you."

The two of them took to this next section of the letter with much energy and fervor. "I'm hurt because you did . . ." started a series of accusations from neglect to lies to disrespect.

"Why did this hurt you?" I asked next. "Why couldn't you accept these actions of your partner?"

"I don't know," the husband said.

"How do you feel after listing all these ways that you were hurt?" I asked.

"Sad," they said in unison as they finally looked at each other for the first time during the session.

"So write this down," I instructed. "I am sad because . . ."

"I had expected you to . . ." the wife blurted out.

"Write it down," I reminded her, and they proceeded to write how each of them had failed to live up to the other's expectations.

"Now what?" the husband asked when he'd finished writing this section of the letter.

"Did either of you write that you had expected more love from the other?" I asked.

They both said they had. "So now you are going to write that you forgive the other person, how much you love him or her, and why you love him or her. This section needs to be longer than the other three, so take your time and see how much you can write here."

When the two of them finished writing minutes later, each of them had used up several pages from their pads. I told them to tear out the sheets with the letter on them and give them to the other to read. Looks of horror appeared on both faces as they looked first at me and then the other spouse in disbelief. Tentatively, they exchanged their letters. I stopped them as they began reading the other's letter. "I want you to read the letter out loud."

"Read his letter out loud?" the wife asked.

"And act it out, dramatize it," I added.

By the time each of them had finished, they were in tears. They had been exposed to a deeper, more intimate part of their spouse than they had ever known before. They hugged and declared that they were going to try harder to be nicer to each other.

I also used writing with older clients. I had them write creatively about how their lives would be different, if they had them to live differently. It seemed to really boost their self-esteem when they realized that some of the things they would have changed earlier in life were still possible to change.

One patient with whom I used this technique was a 65-year-old woman named Barbara. She suffered from severe depression. During a session I asked her to reimagine her life. The next time I saw her, she said she was having difficulty imagining a different life for herself.

I got a call from a resident at the local hospital three days later. Barbara had been admitted the day before for a heart attack. She was diagnosed with angina, and she was in the intensive-care unit not expected to live long.

I visited Barbara in the hospital that night. She was weak and kept fading in and out of consciousness. She had two I.V. tubes in her arm and an oxygen tube attached to her nose.

"It's Dr. Warter," I explained to Barbara as I entered the small room. "How are you feeling?"

"Scared," she whispered.

"What are you scared of?"

She coughed and then responded, "I think I'm going to die here."

I had no idea how close to death she was, but I suggested she might want to process her fear of death. She agreed.

"Where is the fear located?"

"In my chest."

"What does it look like? How much does it weigh?"

"It feels like a . . . like a stone, about 10 pounds."

We went on to explore all the aspects, concepts, emotions and sensations that came with her fear. I asked, "What feelings are around this fear? When do you remember a fear like this before?"

At this last question, she went back to a time when she was an infant, less than a year old, and she had a high fever from some disease. She started gasping again as she relived that experience. I tried to calm her down, and she slowed her breathing and fell asleep.

After a couple of minutes, I told her to wake up. I was a little worried that I would be called on to help with her dying, but I asked anyway. "Have you made any decisions?"

"I don't think I'm worthy of living," she whispered.

After spending over four hours with her in deep, silent prayer, trying to bring together everything I had learned in my spiritual investigations to bear on this situation, I went home. The next day I was worried about her and had some time before my first afternoon clients, so I went back to check on her. Barbara's bed was stripped and empty. I thought back to a female patient I had tried so hard to keep alive while in medical school. I even went on the radio to find more blood donors for this patient, and when I returned, her bed was empty.

Now the old fear rose in me again. I went to the nurses' station expecting the worst. "Did Barbara die last night?"

"No, no," the young nurse said with a giggle, "she's just been moved down to intermediate care. She's in room 224, Doctor. The resident checked her this morning and said she was doing much better, and she didn't need to be in ICU. This morning's labwork showed no enzymes."

I went downstairs to room 224. Inside was Barbara, with no more oxygen or I.V. tubes, sitting up in bed reading a book. "Hello, Barbara. This is a much nicer room. I think you made a good choice in coming here."

Barbara laughed. "You came to visit me last night, didn't you?"

"Yes, I did. You weren't feeling very well. How are you now?"

She showed me the book she was reading. It was called *Life After Life*. "One of the nurses got this for me from the book cart," Barbara reported. "I think I had a near-death experience last night."

"What happened?"

"When you were talking to me and I fell asleep, I was deathly ill. I was shaking. I was afraid. And when you asked me those questions, I got even more afraid. I felt an incredible pain. It was like my whole body was exploding. When you told me to think back to that earlier time when I felt the same fear, I felt like I was leaving my body. I was in some sort of tunnel with cloud-like walls I could see through partially. I thought I felt wind brushing against my ears, but I realized I didn't have any ears. I realized I could hear you ask me the question about whether I'd made a decision."

"You said you weren't worthy of living," I said.

"When I said that," Barbara continued, "there was some presence there . . . and a bright light."

I remembered my grandfather talking about some presence and a light guiding him to the afterlife, and I was quite relieved Barbara hadn't died. I would have felt responsible, even though that hadn't been my intention.

"The presence seemed very wise," she told me, "and it told me to go back to the world, because it loved me and knew I was worthy of living after all. I started to see that what I was doing to my body was something that didn't just come from my physical condition. It came because I didn't forgive myself for that feeling I had as a baby, that I was unworthy."

My throat started tightening. She concluded, "I knew that I was more than that body. There's a soul that's really me, and it's always with me."

I started to cry. I had dedicated my life to seeing this soul awareness, and I had traveled east, west, north, and south, to shamans and Sufi teachers just to recapture this same sense of the soul Barbara was realizing now and that I had felt in my childhood.

People who have near-death experiences outwardly seem to die: their hearts and lungs cease. Inwardly, however, they are very awake and alert. They travel down a long tunnel, hear a distinctive sort of celestial music, are greeted and guided by the spirits of previously deceased relatives, saints or Christ and encounter a being of light that is unconditionally loving and accepting. Their lives are often unjudgmentally reviewed in detail in a flash and they may be given the choice to return to life or be told it is not yet their time to pass over to the spirit world. Then they awaken again in the spiritual body. This is what happened to Barbara.

Near-death experiences are profoundly transformative. They remove all fear of death, awaken beliefs in survival of the spirit and reincarnation, and lead people to more spiritual awareness on a personal basis. This experience meant a tremendous healing for Barbara.

A few months later, I went to a training seminar in Washington, D.C., that had been recommended by one of the other clinicians. There I heard several theorists and researchers talk about the value of extremely high doses of various vitamins and minerals, special diets and regular exercise to bring about a physiological and healing change in the brain. The emerging field was called ortho-molecular psychiatry.

When I returned to the West one of the other therapists at the clinic knocked on my door to warn me that she was sending down one of her clients, a man named Stan. He had been seeing her for depression for several weeks when he asked her to get him on antidepressant medication. I agreed to see him, and a couple of minutes later, Stan was knocking on my office door. I asked him what I could do for him.

"I want Valium," the man in his mid-twenties said.

I decided to take him seriously and try out my new knowledge at the same time. "I'm an ortho-molecular psychiatrist," I announced, "so I am not going to prescribe any drugs for you. I am willing to work with you if you stay off tranquilizers and antidepressants."

"I just want something to calm me," he begged. "I feel nervous and jumpy all the time."

I found out that Stan was 28 and had just lost his job as an engineer. Now he was driving a cab to pay his bills. He seemed very anxious and he didn't have any definite direction in his life, no purpose. "Well," I said, "I'm willing to give you some biochemical support, but it will be mega-doses of vitamins and minerals, if you decide to enter psychotherapy with me."

"Okay, I'll try it," Stan said reluctantly.

For weeks, I saw Stan, and the same cycle kept occurring. I would conduct a variety of approaches with him, he would feel better for a few days, but by the time I saw him the next week, the same anxious feelings and depression had returned. I started to feel like it was the therapy that was actually holding him back from feeling better all the time. I couldn't tell what it might be in our sessions that was producing this weekly regression in his progress.

At one session, I resolved to do something radically different to shock Stan out of this cycle he was in. When he entered and settled in the chair where he usually sat, I started reciting one of the Sufi prayers I'd learned in Arabic. I focused my mind on empowering this young man while I repeated the prayer.

He looked at me like I had lost my grip on reality. I suddenly stood up and told him, "Follow me!"

Stan shrugged his shoulders, mumbled an unenthusiastic, "Well, okay," and did as I asked.

For the next hour, I walked very energetically all over town with Stan following silently a few steps behind. I led him back to the clinic and into my office, and we sat down again. His appearance had changed noticeably. His circulation seemed better because his face was no longer so pale.

"The session is over," I told him. "I'll see you next week."

The following week, he came back for his therapy session and he couldn't come up with any symptoms to report. The week had gone fine, he said. He reported that he didn't feel so tired and depressed any more. His energy level was up. "I can hardly believe how much I've gotten done this week," he said. "I got all sorts of housework and yardwork done, I took the kids out to the park several times, and I made phone calls and sent out a dozen resumes to get a new job."

I realized over the next few sessions that Stan had been "preparing" for his therapy sessions by manufacturing symptoms and stories to report. When I changed the format of the therapy session that one week with the Arabic chant and the silent walk around town, he didn't know what to expect the following week, and he couldn't "prepare."

Stan now felt so much energy and enthusiasm for life I spent several sessions teaching him how to handle and channel all of it. He remarked that it was a shame I was sharing these techniques one person at a time and suggested I start working in groups.

I took his suggestion and started conducting workshops in the area on soul awareness. A psychiatrist who attended one of my workshops invited me to give workshops at a center he ran in Venezuela, because he had been searching for new soul-centered approaches to health and healing. During this time, I also wrote a children's story book on personality types based on my research into the enneagram called *United in Freedom.*

And I had another meeting with Clarisse. She came to the city I was living in to study with the Buddhist master Chogyam Trungpa for a few days. When I saw her, it was clear to me that the romance was over. We were still friends, but only that.

While in the Rockies I also had an unusual encounter with a Native American named Wallace Black Elk, a member of the Sioux Lakota tribe. He invited me to participate in several Sioux ceremonies. In one particular ritual, conducted high on a mountain just west of Evergreen, I sat in a circle with a group of participants. It was a late, moonless night so the sky was very dark. The air around me was disturbed and I heard a flapping of wings. Those sitting next to me also reacted to the flapping and the dust raised in the air. Suddenly, I felt the weight of a large bird landing on my shoulder. I couldn't see it, but Black Elk told me it was an eagle. Though I experienced the eagle's presence physically, this was not a physical eagle but an ethereal one. Black Elk said that in the tradition of his people an eagle coming to a man was an initiation into becoming a healer. This once again confirmed I had been given the blessing of healing.

My experiences with Black Elk and Native American traditions assisted me with a client I had named Jim. At 50 years of age, Jim was a lonely man who never fully lived his life or established strong relationships. Originally from Arkansas, Jim had a lifelong affinity for Native American traditions and felt compelled to serve the people. For six years, he worked on a reservation teaching the Navajo French and Spanish. Despite his time there, Jim never felt accepted by the Navajo, but stayed because he felt there was a large debt that he owed them.

When he was a child, Jim told me was strongly attracted to a cave in Hot Springs. When he went into it he entered a trance-like state and saw himself as a Cherokee woman living in what appeared to be the eighteen hundreds. She had fallen in love with a white man, a captain in the cavalry. They would secretly rendezvous in this cave for, at the time, interracial romances were taboo. When the captain's commanding officers found out about the love affair and secret meeting place, soldiers were sent to the cave where they killed the soldier and his lover.

"Dr. Warter," Jim told me, "I know this sounds crazy, but I feel like this Cherokee woman's spirit is with me all the time. Even though I haven't been in Arkansas for years, I have very vivid dreams about the cave and this young couple. The dream always ends the same, with the murder."

I asked Jim, "Do you remember the first time you entered the cave and felt this woman's presence?"

"Yes, when I was quite young, but my memories are somewhat sketchy," he answered.

"What I'd like to do Jim, with your permission of course, is to hypnotize you and take you back to the time when you visited the cave. I think its quite possible that this woman's spirit is still with you."

Jim agreed to this approach and we did a couple of hypnotic regressions taking him back to the time early in his life when he had, indeed, allowed the spirit of the Cherokee woman to enter him. This had bound him to being a servant of the Native Americans, thus his affinity for them and their way of life. It was also the reason Jim had been so inexplicably unhappy all his life.

I had discovered an ancient exorcism technique used by Black Elk and the Sioux Indians that I employed here. I released the Cherokee woman's spirit from Jim's system, and freed him to embrace his own sacred identity and his own life. Afterward, Jim experienced a joy for life he hadn't felt since he was a small child. This interesting case history was very important because I could see that spiritual possession was often the cause of certain pathologies such as ulcers, and clinical disorders such as alcoholism, drug abuse, and depression.

After three-and-a-half years working at the clinic in the Rockies, I started gaining a reputation for my approach to psychiatry. I received an invitation to return to Rome for a two-week international conference. I was one of about twenty thousand participants who listened to speakers share their experiences with meditation and their inner lives. As I heard the presentations and participated in the group meditations and prayers at this conference, I developed an awareness that the world must be changing if twenty-thousand people will come to Rome for a conference like this one. My dream and the forecasts of a new era of spiritual consciousness was finally coming true.

Among the other conference-goers were a great many physicians and therapists. One, a Swiss veterinarian who introduced himself to me as Jonah, said he was living in Israel helping the government manage its honey production.

"So you're helping with the honey part of the land of milk and honey," I joked.

"I guess you could say that," Jonah agreed. "Have you ever been to Israel?"

"No, I haven't. But it was my grandfather's ultimate wish and I'd like to honor his memory by taking a trip to the Holy Land sometime."

"I think you'd find it very interesting," Jonah offered.

"Well, maybe some day I'll come visit you," I told him.

"Please do," he told me as he handed me his business card.

Two days later, I was walking near the ruins of the Coliseum, and I passed by an American Express office. I saw a poster in the window advertising trips to Israel, so I decided on the spur of the moment to go in and ask about the next flight to Israel.

"Well, the next El Al flight," the ticket agent explained, "is in two-and-a-half hours. You would never make it to the airport in time. Let me look at flights leaving tomorrow."

"I want to buy a ticket on today's flight," I insisted.

"You won't make it in time," the agent repeated.

"That will be my responsibility."

I rushed to my hotel and made it to the airport in time to telephone Jonah before getting on the plane. "My plane arrives at six o'clock this evening at Ben Gurion airport."

Jonah was both excited and happy to hear from me. He felt it was some kind of a cosmic destiny that I so quickly responded to his invitation. He said he would be at the airport when I arrived and that I could stay with him at his beach house.

The Mystical
Holy Land

9

$\mathbb{A}$ deep feeling of reverence filled me as my plane touched down and I saw the brilliant white flag with the blue Star of David waving in the desert sun. My arrival in the Holy Land felt like landing in sacred territory. Jonah and his wife Rachel, both Swiss and in their sixties, met my flight at the airport. Jonah was very active and well-preserved, and he retained a boyish type of charm in the way his uncombed white hair stood up from his head and his big square glasses sat on his face. His wife was not so active, but she was a woman of good health with short curly hair and a kind demeanor.

They had driven to Tel Aviv from their home just outside the city on the beach of the Mediterranean Sea. They both welcomed me with heartfelt embraces, as if they were my closest relatives. I felt totally at home. They loaded my bags in their Jeep for me. As we drove southeast toward Jerusalem, Jonah asked me how my flight was.

"Pleasant," I told him. "The two-and-a-half hours passed more quickly than I expected. I sat next to a French nun in her seventies, and we talked for most of the trip. I could tell by the habit she wore that she was an Ursuline nun. That order was common in Chile when I was growing up and they were very active in the hospitals and service. She told me she was the head of the Ursuline order and that after 55 years of service as an administrator, she was finally on her first trip to the Holy Land. Her duties, apparently, had made it impossible for her to make such a pilgrimage until now.

"She was inspired by my pilgrimages and she told me about her vocation of spirit and service, and her love for the poor. She was a true vocational Christian, a wonderful human being. When I told her I discovered my purpose in life, she told me she had been overwhelmed by her service and her duties in the order and that most of her life was spent in management. She was very, very happy that this was a time in her life when she could reconnect to the Holy Land as a source of inspiration, to the Jewish roots of the Christian tradition and to the vocation of spirit."

"She sounds like a wonderful woman," Rachel smiled.

"She was fascinating. I told her about my travels and all I had learned, and she congratulated me. 'You were awakened fast,' she told me. She said it had taken her most of her life to truly open to the life of the spirit."

"It sounds like you received much more during your two-hour flight than mere passage to the Holy Land," Jonah mused. "Knowing how much you like to talk with people, you will be happy to know that many Israelis speak English. You should get by okay if you decide to wander off by yourself, which I'm sure you will."

"You know me too well my friend," I said laughing. "But I do know some Hebrew."

"How do you know Hebrew?" Rachel asked.

"It is in my genes," I answered.

"I never would have guessed it," Rachel said in wonder as she examined my blond hair and blue eyes.

"My grandfather, in particular, passed down to me the essence of the Hebrew tradition. However, I have spent the last few years studying other religious traditions."

"Anything you know of Hebrew will certainly make your stay here easier. Now," Jonah announced spreading his arms, "I promised you that when you came to this country, our home, you would also feel at home. You are our guest. The moment I knew you were coming I arranged my schedule so that I could take you to our sacred places and give you a tour of the sacred geometry of the Holy Land."

"If it isn't too much trouble . . ."

"No," Jonah responded, "no trouble at all. It is my pleasure to show you around."

Since it was nighttime when we reached Jonah's home near the beach outside of Tel Aviv, we decided to go to bed early. I fell asleep on the cot in their living room that night dreaming happily of all the people I would meet and all the sights I would see.

But when I awakened in the morning we did not immediately begin our exploration. We ate a leisurely breakfast and then Rachel set about doing household chores while Jonah sat down to read. I decided to take a walk around the neighborhood while the two of them got ready for the tour I was promised.

I walked down to the beach, and as I lay down on the sand, I was filled by the spirit of what the Mediterranean was. I could see in my mind's eye the history of the land of the Canaanites, of the Hebrews, of the Israelites, of the Jews, of the Philistines. I pulled up memories of biblical history and saw the invasions from foreign countries. I was totally overwhelmed by being in this Holy Land. Judaism, Christianity and Islam: the monotheistic basis of our whole culture was breathing in the stones and in the air of this wonderful place. I had not seen anything of the old city of Jerusalem, so I was still trying to imagine all I'd heard or read about Jerusalem: the Church of the Holy Sepulchre, the Dome of the Rock, the Wailing Wall.

When I arrived home from my walk, Jonah asked me if I would mind having soup for lunch. I was rather anxious to get going, and was a bit disappointed to learn we probably wouldn't start our tour until after we ate. Still, I thought, our meal couldn't delay us more than an hour. But after lunch, Jonah got up from the table and went back to his reading.

"Aren't we going into the city today?" I asked.

"Patience, Carlos," Jonah told me. "Relax today. You will see Jerusalem tomorrow."

The next day, we loaded the Jeep with some supplies and records Jonah needed and drove off toward the old city just after ten o'clock in the morning. He said he had an appointment in the morning, but he would show me the city in the afternoon. We turned off the highway onto an unpaved road.

"Where are we going?" I asked carefully.

"To Jerusalem," Jonah replied.

"You just turned off the highway leading into the city, though."

"This road also leads to the city. Remember to have patience, Carlos," the older man said with a bit more of his Swiss accent coming through. "Some things are worth waiting for."

The road we took raised a plume of dust behind us that caught up to us when we stopped to let a man and his goats cross the road. We both coughed a bit. "I'm sorry about that," Jonah said, "but I want to have the top off the car when we approach the city."

"What road is this?"

"Have you heard of the Road of King Solomon?" Jonah asked me. I nodded. "This is it. Some people call it King Solomon's Road but it was really David's road when Samuel brought him to meet Saul as a young musician."

The Bible was in front of me. The readings of my grandfather were coming out in every single edge of the landscape.

After the goats had passed, we drove up a gradual hill beyond which I could see only the blue sky. As we neared the top of the hill, I glimpsed the top of a silver dome of pure energy. As we climbed higher, a golden dome seemed to sprout on top of the silver dome, and the rest of the city started coming into view. I looked up and the sky was filled with clouds that looked like angels, or angels that were patrolling the clouds. I knew the city was an anchor point for the world. I remembered a song I'd learned as a child that went something like "I saw Jerusalem of silver, and I saw Jerusalem of gold . . ."

Jonah stopped the Jeep at the top of the hill, and we got out and looked down on the city so many people had fought to possess. I felt the vortex of energy that this place represented, and I was overwhelmed. Tears streamed down my cheeks. Touched by strong emotions, I could fathom why there had been so many wars fought over this city. I sensed this sacred place was an anchor for the world; it was the navel of peace, as it has been described.

The highway from Tel Aviv to Jerusalem, which is a brief but significant route, is more than a road, it is a road heavily annotated, a road turned scripture. First, we passed a Trappist monastery. Then a British garrison fort, still trim and intact. Then, less pristine, a Crusader castle. Amid eucalyptus trees planted on a steep hillside by Jewish settlers in the last century we saw more recent wreckage: burned out tanks, rusted vehicles and the skewed limbs of derelict artillery. They were not mere eyesores but studied relics of the Israeli and Arab claims on Jerusalem. It was obvious we were nearing a dearly disputed place. It was only ten years since Israel had won the Six-Day War in 1967.

"The harbingers of Jerusalem's hills were designed for a pilgrim's first visit," said Jonah.

I nodded my head in agreement. "If you arrive as I have, with no more than a childhood-bred vision, Jerusalem is entirely gratifying. It's golden," I said.

When we entered the city Jonah left for his appointment and I wandered through the city. As I was admiring the architecture of a government building an old man approached me. He had a lined face and was bent over the cane with which he walked.

"You do not look like an ordinary tourist," the man said to me in English, though colored by the familiar sound of Hebrew. "There is something about you that I sense is different."

"I am not really a tourist," I replied to the man. "I am more of a pilgrim, though not of any one faith. I am here to experience for myself the spiritual energy that resides in Jerusalem."

"Then you will need a guide," the old man said with a smile. "My name is Isaac and I am a bit of an amateur historian of the city. If you would like I will show you the sights. You see, I too am a student of the spirit."

"I do not want to inconvenience you," I told Isaac, looking at his cane. "I intended to walk through the city."

"That is not a problem for me," he said. "This cane is just for company."

"Alright then, lead on my friend."

Isaac's history lesson commenced. "According to the history books the British military governor of the city in 1917 wanted a radiant focus for those descending from these hills. He must have heard the hymns of heavenly Jerusalem echoing in his mind when he decreed that all new buildings be constructed of stone mined from local quarries. Even the most brutal high-rise hotel is clad with this pink to amber stone. Well, you can see the effect, the city glows."

We walked into Old Jerusalem as the pilgrims traditionally do: through the Jaffa Gate. Inside an hour I realized that the hymns I'd learned in my life had not properly prepared me. The topography of green hills and city walls was, not surprisingly, all wrong. Aesthetic sensibility was nowhere evident in the sort of gospel theme park that had been created there. A 19th century world in which, having run the gauntlet of hawkers to reach the Church of the Holy Sepulchre, there was no sanctuary. Calgary is a palace of gaudy altars, stone cisterns and grottos where the presence of six separate Christian factions simultaneously compete for the pilgrim "customers." We suffered as two rival guides bartered their prices for the Via Dolorosa before we made our own sad way. Some dignity and loveliness were retained by the Mount of Olives. Yet the verdict must be that Christian Jerusalem was not so much golden as brass.

The Christian guides admitted the Dome was an outstanding example of Islamic design. Together with the nearby Al Aqsa mosque it offered a marvelous panorama where we went to pray and do our self-practice. We also prayed on Mt. Zion itself a few minutes away. I saw how everything spiritual merged in this city, a holy place for Christians, Moslems and Jews. Everybody wanted it to be theirs. I was awestruck.

"Carlos, do you know what makes a place sacred?" Isaac asked me as we continued our walk through the city.

"There are probably as many answers to that question as there are people who think about it," I answered.

"That is true, but do you know that all seem in agreement on one point: the sacred in Jerusalem is manifest in meeting places between heaven and earth, where the divine touches and enters the human world."

"I've always heard life in the holy city described as being of a different nature and quality from the profane world surrounding it," I told Isaac. "When Moses encountered the divine in the midst of the burning bush he was told, 'Put off thy shoes from thy feet, for the place whereon thou standeth is holy ground.' This was in the Bible. But what does this mean for us today? What does it mean when I arrive in the city and the divine now seems to hide its face, and all that remains of its presence are monuments commemorating the sites of former glories? I hope that the sacred is alive and still to be found."

"Look around us Carlos, and tell me what you see."

"I see pilgrims and visitors, much like myself."

"Yes, and they all come here with expectations that they bring to no other sacred place on earth. For Jerusalem is not just a city of the past; it is here that the divine presence has promised that it will one day renew its ties with men, bringing them eternal salvation and re-establishing God's kingdom on earth. Each person, consciously or unconsciously, is here seeking a confirmation of this promise."

I had to admit that I was also so moved. Even the most rational part of me hoped to find here some indication that would bridge the gap between the outer material world and the world of the deep, inner beliefs and hopes. I somehow secretly knew I was going to have, in this trip to the Holy Land, a real and new contact with another level of being.

"But where is God when I look around here in the city?" I demanded of Isaac. "I see monks hawking tombs of saints like a freak show. They remind me of the money changers Jesus threw out of the temple."

"It is true Jerusalem is a place where the divine no longer lives openly," Isaac said sighing. "Theories behind the cause of this run the entire spectrum from the excesses of religious emotion to the coldness of pure intellectual speculation. All contain a fragment of truth. But look at that woman there," he said pointing to an elderly woman kneeling before the tomb of King David. "Do you doubt that she believes the divine is present?"

Watching the woman, overcome with emotion, I could not doubt her sincerity. "She certainly seems to feel the presence of God. But I am not completely surprised, she is praying at the tomb of David."

"And what if I told you this was not the real site of David's tomb, and the tradition here was Christian in origin. Would you then be forced to question the nature of the experience. The same is true of the places of devotion along the Via Dolorosa, which we know is not the real route taken by Jesus, nor the one commemorated in the first 11 centuries of Christianity. But do you doubt that woman is in touch with something holy?"

I looked again at the woman. There was no doubt in my mind that the spirit was in the air. It was in the stones. It was in the rocks.

As Isaac and I walked through the city I noted the way the buildings seemed to grow in all directions, often on top of or around each other.

"Some contend that sacred buildings and sites arise from the earth in places where vortexes of energy are especially strong," Isaac explained. "It has been claimed that Jerusalem, especially the area of the temple mount, is such a vortex. While this may be true, and there may be people who are sensitive to that force, many visitors think of it as just a theory. A visitor may choose to believe in this theory intellectually, but it is far from the real context he seeks, which is faith.

"So what do you think Carlos?" Isaac asked. "Do you see any order in all this chaos? Or do you just see a random sprouting of structures?"

"I can see a vague, underlying order," I admitted. "Something in the way this building is in line with the one there and another further down that hill. But I can't really make much sense of it."

"The streets we are walking through right now," Isaac told me, "are all on sacred ground. The construction of the sacred geometry of pyramids and stone circles, and the orientation of certain churches and ancient temples have been shown to be intimately related to the recording of astrological phenomena."

"I know that the ancients were capable of measuring both the Earth's surface and the heavens with incredible accuracy," I commented. "You know, in school I was taught that ancient cultures were primitive, but after my journeys with shamans, Sufis and Native Americans I know that these cultures were very advanced in some ways. But I don't know if I understand how these buildings could represent the heavens and the earth, and the rest of God's creation."

"These sites are believed to lie along a vertical line of descent, which connects the heavenly world above with the earthly world below," Isaac said. "Consequently, they're centers for the divine manifesting itself in earthly form and from which, under favorable conditions, its influence can spread outward to the profane world.

"The divine is seen as a well-defined world of order, while the profane is an endless ocean of chaos," Isaac continued. "Modern physics demonstrates the organization of the profane is chaos theory. The form taken by the sacred, which is an earthly material reflection of the divine world above, manifests aspects of the heavenly order. The simplest of forms reflect the outer physical order of the heavens and are astronomical in nature. But there are others which reflect some aspects of the inner nature of the divine order of the universe. Jerusalem is a sacred place. The city's monuments consistently demonstrate the laws concerning man's relation to the cosmos, from his fall from grace to the inner spiritual evolution that leads to eventual salvation and return. What is remarkable is that no one building or sacred site in Jerusalem contains all this great knowledge. Rather, different places combine with certain of the city's traditions, legends, histories, religions. Jerusalem itself is a living being, as is our whole earth."

"Then tell me Isaac. What is the sacred?"

"Carlos, Jerusalem is a city with more than 100 names. Does that make any sense to you."

"It reminds me of the hundred names of Allah in the Sufi tradition," I told him.

"That's very good," Isaac continued. "The rabbis of old claimed that the city had 70 names which were equivalent in number to the names of God."

"I've done some research on the city," I said, "and I know the Hebrew word for Jerusalem itself appears 656 times in the Old Testament in a singular form, Jerusalem. Only three times in the plural. The earliest historical record is in an Egyptian text from the eighteenth or nineteenth century B.C. where it is mentioned as a Canaanite city-state called Eshelmus. In the latter Kalalamana Letters it is called Rushalim, while in a Syrian inscription it is called Hierosolyma. The Greeks called it Jerus Salim, holy. The Christians called in Jerosalem. And from that derives Jerusalem."

"Do you also know that it's considered the navel of the world?" asked Isaac. "It is believed to be the place where Melchizedek, the king of salem, the king of peace, was tithed to by Abraham. And this Melchizedek, without father or mother, without descendants, having neither the beginning of days nor the end of life, became the son of God. The Jewish tradition established that it was at Shalem that Melchizedek founded an academy or school to instruct the people of the world in the ways of God.

"This picture of an immortal priest who rules the city of perfect peace and instructs the nations of the world is reminiscent of Isaiah's prophecy for the end of time, for the time I felt we were living now. 'And it shall come to pass in the last days that the mountain of the Lord's house shall be established on the top of the mountains and shall be exalted above the hills.'"

Though it was many years before this knowledge became active in my consciousness, the seeds of the Melchizedek priesthood entered my heart at this time.

The old man continued this tour of the city, telling me its history and legends. Yes, being in Jerusalem with the Church of the Holy Sepulchre, the Dome of the Rock and the Wailing Wall was a rebirth for my spiritual journey.

Eventually I finished my walking tour with Isaac and said good-bye to this warm old man. I returned to the place Jonah had parked the jeep, and he was waiting patiently for me.

"You just can't stand to wait around and do nothing, can you?"

"Not when there is so much to see, and so many people to meet," I said with a smile.

Over the next three days, Jonah drove into the old city each day and dropped me off so I could wander around while he took care of his business with the Israeli government. When he wasn't busy he walked with me. Sometimes we sat in small corner cafes in view of the Tower of David and the walls where I had walked. As I strolled the ancient streets, I felt transported to another time. Many times I saw myself in different past lives wearing the same clothes as the people were wearing today, jalabas. It could have been anywhere from 500 to 2,000 years in the past, I couldn't tell for sure, but it definitely seemed a very long time ago.

I went to the Wailing Wall, with its many slips of prayer-inscribed paper sticking out of every conceivable crack and hole in the wall. I met some of the traditional Jews who were there praying, and I prayed with them. They told each other Hasidic teaching stories in Hebrew just like the one's I had learned among the Islamic Sufis. The characters were almost exactly the same and the outcome was always similar. I was again struck by the similarities between the world's spiritual traditions, knowing they must have all sprung from one root.

I went to the tomb of King David, and as I stared at the monument, I felt my consciousness changing. There was something about this holy place that gave me a sense of completion. I felt I had somehow just integrated all the travels and teachings I had experienced in the previous seven years and was ready to move onto the next phase of my life, but I had no idea what that was yet.

Jonah volunteered to meet me at the Church of the Holy Sepulchre on the third day. "I have something I'd like to show you," he told me.

At noon I waited for Jonah at the huge entrance gates to the church where the remains of Jesus were buried. Priests and monks tried to draw passers-by into the church in the style of carnival sideshow hawkers. I was approached several times in the few minutes I waited for Jonah to arrive.

"There you are!" Jonah said as he approached me and patted me on the shoulder. "I was waiting for you on the other side of the church. My apologies."

We entered the huge gateway which opened into an inner courtyard. Ahead of us, through crowds of tourists, lay a series of doorways and archways. The openings were covered with symbols and words in various languages. Beyond lay hallways and passages leading somewhere deeper into the church. As we walked to the right, we could see even more doorways. And at most of the passage entrances, priests and monks of various Christian sects like those outside the church were beckoning the crowds of tourists down their particular passage. Each of them claimed that their passage was the true entrance to the Holy Sepulchre. There were dozens and dozens of these entryways. We finally followed one of the passages into the tomb. Ornate lamps illuminating the shadowy corridor enough to see various shrines set into the walls.

The passageway eventually opened into a fairly large chamber where all the passageways seemed to converge. We made our way through the throngs of other tourists to a roped-off area in the center of the chamber. There we saw a large flat stone surrounded by signs in over a dozen languages describing this as the burial place of Jesus.

Jonah must have seen the frustrated look on my face as I was jostled by other tourists and once again assaulted by the various proselytizers and mendicants. "It is really quite a sacred place," he said to me as he pulled me aside, "but it is difficult to appreciate here. Let me take you to a non-commercial part of the church."

We took a different passage out of the chamber, a Greek Orthodox passage, I believe. In the courtyard near the huge doors through which we had entered, Jonah pulled open a door and motioned for me to go through it. It was a dark, narrow stairway leading up. After climbing several flights, the stairway ended at a narrow hallway. At the end was a door around which bright sunlight shone. I stepped out onto what must have been the roof of the church. The city stretched for miles in all directions, and most of the buildings and streets looked hundreds if not thousands of years old.

"Over here," Jonah said as he guided me toward the other end of the roof.

There, in front of a cave-like shack, were four elderly, bearded, black men in robes and sandals. Each wore a large cross made of wood around his neck. None of them said a word, but they put their hands together and smiled at us as we approached.

"Sit here," Jonah instructed as he pointed to an area of the roof a few feet from the monks.

My older companion sat down next to me on the roof facing the four monks. They acknowledged our presence, but they did not approach us or speak to us. I felt myself relaxing and breathing more deeply and slowly. Over the next 90 minutes or so, I sat on the roof of this sacred building with Jonah and the monk, none of us saying a word. I looked out at the spectacular view and observed these simple, peaceful men living up here. I could feel my body becoming lighter. Joy and peace washed over me. I was so content. Nothing else in the world mattered.

It was Jonah who got up finally and said, "I need to be getting back to work."

I joined Jonah and followed him back down the steps into the church. He explained as we descended that these monks were from Ethiopia, and that they lived on the roof of the Church of the Holy Sepulchre and prayed without uttering a word. Their order had occupied this unlikely spot for centuries.

Over the following two weeks, Jonah and I went to various cities around the country during the day and returned to his home just outside Tel Aviv at night. One of the first stops we made after our time in Jerusalem was a kibbutz on the outskirts of Tel Aviv. Jonah was there to check on the honey production for the government. While I was waiting outside the kibbutz for Jonah to finish his business, I noticed groups of Israelis and Arabs milling around.

I felt myself drifting into an altered state of consciousness. Just as I had on my first day in Jerusalem, I was transported back to a time centuries past. I wore the same long caftan and sandals as before, but I saw more clearly now that I was a healer in this time—a faith healer. I cured the sick by invoking the power of God and directing it with a touch of my healing hands.

I suddenly had the urge to shout out some Arabic prayers I learned in Morocco at the Sufi community. The people nearby stopped and looked at me with wonder. I then changed to some Hebrew prayers I learned as a child. The onlookers became quieter and drew closer.

Suddenly, I found myself uttering prayers in some language I had never heard before, and the crowd became silent.

"Who are you?" a very old Israeli woman shouted.

"I am a healer," I replied.

"Can you stop the pain in my back?" another older Hebrew woman shouted.

I stepped toward the woman and looked at the way she stood bent forward with her shoulders almost touching the sides of her face. "If God wills it," I said.

I stood behind the woman and placed my hands on her shoulders. I started chanting one of the Hebrew prayers again, and I started to feel my hands becoming warmer. The woman's shoulders started to drop and fall back. I moved my hands down to her lower back and touched it with my fingertips. "Refua!" the woman cried as she straightened her posture slightly. "The pain in my back is gone!"

I learned from one in the crowd that now surrounded this woman that she had not stood upright like that in over ten years. Her cry of "Refua!" meant that she believed the power of God working through me had alleviated her pain and stiffness.

An older Arab man and his teenage son came up to me then. "Could you see if you could help my daughter?" the man said quietly. "She hasn't risen from her bed in weeks, and we fear she may be dying."

I followed the man and his son to a fairly large house that lay 20 minutes by foot from the kibbutz. Once inside, the man took me into the bedroom of his daughter, a thin girl in her teens whose large, brown eyes stared blankly across the room from her cot. I knelt on the floor next to her and placed my hand on her forehead, hot with fever. I moved my hand to the top of her head and began chanting one of the Arab zhikrs Hassan had taught me. After a couple of minutes, the girl's eyes started to blink and scan about the room. I told her to sit up in bed, and she slowly worked her way up to her elbows and then to a sitting position. The man called for his wife to come see. When she arrived, their daughter was putting her feet on the floor and standing up.

The mother ran up to her and embraced her. "Praise be to Allah!" she cried. She felt the girl's forehead. "The fever has gone," she announced.

The man looked at the now-smiling face of his daughter and said to me, "I don't know how we can repay you for your help," he said, "but I have some fruit from our orchard I would like you to have."

He left for a moment and brought back a burlap bag of oranges, grapefruit and lemons. I accepted the bag, wished them much peace and joy, and left. I walked back toward the kibbutz. There were still a dozen or more people near the front gate. I set the bag down on the roadside and said, "I have a gift for you. Take as much as you like."

Most of those nearby took several pieces of fruit each, but when I looked in the bag, there were still about eight pieces left. "I will leave the bag here," I told them. "Please take the rest of the fruit before it spoils."

And that was what I did at our other stops over those two weeks. Jonah would drive us to some city where he needed to check on the honey production. While he was off inspecting the bees, I wandered around performing other healings by laying on of hands. Whatever gifts I received—fruit, chocolate, wine, perfumes—I immediately distributed to the next people I met. In this way, we visited Caphernaum, Tiberias, Safed and settlements along the Sea of Galilee.

We arrived in Caphernaum on a Friday night and, since we were unlikely to get back to Jerusalem before sundown, the couple Jonah worked with during the day insisted that the two of us stay with them during the shabat, the Jewish holy day.

The shabat is a celebration of time more than space. For six days people live under the tyranny of things of space. In shabat we become one with the sacredness of time. Jewish faith is not a map outside of this world, but a way of living in the super-consciousness in this world. It is not rejecting or detaching from civilization, but going above civilization. Shabat is the day that people learn the art of timelessness. Shabat is more than an armistice. It is the profound harmony between man and the universe, the affinity of all things and the participation of spirit that unites that existing above with that below.

We think generally of the earth as our mother. In our mother's civilization, time is money and success is our companion. The seventh day reminds us that God is our father, that time is light and that spirit is our companion. We have combined in our culture a romantic conception of adoration and love that combines myth and passion so that it dominates man, and has produced the weak spirit of Western man. The Jewish contribution to the idea of love is the conception of love of shabat. The love of the day, the spirit in time. This was taught by Jonah's friend in Caphernaum, which was also the place where Jesus preached in the synagogue in his early days.

In Safed, one of the kabbalistic cities in the north, we also stayed overnight with some friends of Jonah's. Since Jonah did not have to work the next morning, he took me to a large temple in the middle of the city. There, we met with the rabbi, a bearded, Hasidic man in his seventies.

The rabbi spoke to me in English, and after relatively little introduction, he asked me, "Do you know daven?" I didn't answer him right away because I was transfixed by how much he reminded me of my grandfather. Looking at and hearing the rabbi took me back to a time when I saw my grandfather praying.

"The daven?" I said, searching through my memory for the many prayers my grandfather had taught me.

Jonah explained the rabbi was talking about a type of prayer that involves the shaking or vibration of the body. "Ah, yes," I replied.

"I learned a similar Sufi meditation performed in a circle called the hadzrat."

"The daven is also performed in a circle," the rabbi smiled broadly.

"We repeated a prayer or mantra over and over during the hadzrat," I said. "Do you have something like that?"

The rabbi asked Jonah for a clarification of the word "mantra" and, upon hearing Jonah's explanation in Hebrew, he broke into a quiet laugh.

"Yes," the rabbi said. "The daven is not practiced very much any more, so there are few who know the chant that goes with it to bring the Holy Spirit into the body. We say 'Ribbono Shel Olam.'"

I didn't understand the phrase immediately. When I asked Jonah about it later on the drive back down to Jerusalem, he explained that the pronunciation was Hasidic and pronounced it for me in standard Hebrew. Then I understood that the translation was similar to one of the Sufi zhikrs I often used: "Master of the Universe."

"Rabbi," I asked, "can you tell me the basis of your tradition? I have studied Sufism and you seem to incorporate many of the same rituals."

"I'm always happy to share our history with a seeker," the rabbi responded. "The philosophers can only surmise what exists in the metaphysical realm, while the kabbalist can actually see it. The most important system we utilize involves the pronunciation of the divine name." I was amazed at the similarities of the Sufis and this esoteric Hebrew tradition.

"Safed is a famous kabbala academy city," the rabbi continued. "It has been so since the 15th century. Before that time kabbalistic traditions existed but they were not very powerful. Three events in the late fourteen hundreds gave rise to its influence. The first was the printing of the Gutenberg Bible, and by 1475 the printing of the first Hebrew book. The second was the discovery of America by Columbus. This discovery changed man's view of the world, and as a result many earlier philosophies had to be re-examined causing the philosophical schools that had opposed the kabbalistic knowledge to be significantly weakened. The third was the Spanish Inquisition which brought the Jews out of Spain and made them migrate to Safed, bringing the synthesis of the Islamic, the Christian and the Jewish knowledge to this town. It was a renaissance, exactly half a millennium ago. A radical transformation occurred, a reconnection of the soul. We live in the time of a similar shift in spiritual awakening on the planet. Yet there is a difference: it is now on a massive scale."

The last thing the rabbi said to me was, "All religions come from basic spiritual experiences that turn into ritual to maintain the experience, but then end up an ideological belief system that is removed from the experience. I am Jewish but I am not dogmatic. I know there are many things to be learned from other traditions. A man who truly reaches enlightenment, regardless of the path he follows, will discover that there are other roads leading to the place of God. It is the followers that desecrate the experience through fundamentalism."

I thought about what the rabbi said in terms of world crises. Because there is such a strong need for community, people are becoming xenophobic. Because there is such a strong need for spirituality people become fundamentalist and fanatics. Because there is so much need for stability there is a threat of authoritarianism. There is a fine line between authority of the soul that gives stability to an individual and authoritarianism which leads to tyranny. Just as freedom of thought and democracy go hand-in-hand, so too freedom of spiritual expression and experience goes hand-in-hand with holistic living. We are not Jews or Christians or Sufis or Muslims, we are human beings with a divine connection. These labels are merely the traditions that we follow, and these traditions come to the same conclusion: the sacredness is in all; God is in all.

One Friday Jonah and I were in Nazareth, the birthplace of Jesus. Jonah again had some work to do while we were there, but he said that it should only take half the day and then he would show me around. Jonah suggested that I explore the area while he was at work so that when he had finished with his work we could go back to anything I wanted to investigate in depth.

I had set out on my own to find a church supposedly built on the site where Jesus was born. I was in an Arab neighborhood of the city headed toward the church when I had a vision of a man with long hair in white robes walking along the street ahead of me. The vision was so clear I thought not only that it was a real person, but that it was definitely Jesus. My heart burst wide open and I felt connected to him by a ray of light coming from his chest.

At first we stood face-to-face then he turned and I followed him down the street, trying to get his attention. It was all very vivid, like going into a parallel universe in which the street was there but I was also in another dimension walking after him. He turned right down a narrow alley, and I followed after him. As I turned the corner into the alley, I saw the figure was getting too far away, and I shouted out, "Rabbi!" to get his attention. He disappeared down another alley to the left.

When I turned and looked to the left down this darker, narrower alley, the white-robed figure was gone. There was a young boy sitting in a doorway on the left, however.

As I approached the boy, he called to me in English, "You're looking for him? He went that way." He pointed further down the alley.

I continued down the alley until it came to a dead end. At the end was a small, old, wooden door. I stood there a moment considering what to do. Just then, a woman came out the door and shouted at me in English, "Get out! This is private property!"

I pointed back down the alley where I had spoken with the young boy. "Excuse me, but the child over there told me that a man in white robes had come this way, and I was trying to find him."

"You're lying!" the woman shouted. "That boy doesn't speak any English."

I apologized for disturbing her and headed back down the alley. I felt certain I had been here before, but it was many years later before I found out where I had been.

As I came upon the young boy again, I said, "The woman at the end of the alley told me I couldn't go in."

The boy looked up at me with a puzzled expression and said something to me in Arabic that I couldn't understand. I walked away bewildered, knowing something profound had happened but not knowing exactly what it was.

For my last days in Israel before returning to the United States, I ventured alone into Jerusalem. I had heard of a famous Jewish school or yeshiva there where students were preparing for the coming of the messiah. I had wondered how similar this messianic consciousness was to the prophecies of the South American Indians I had encountered earlier.

When I got to the yeshiva, there were many orthodox Jewish men of various ages scurrying about with huge books and scrolls under their arms. An older bald man wearing a white yarmulke and thick glasses was sitting at a desk facing the front door, so I went up to him and asked if I could see the head rabbi.

"I'm sorry," the man at the desk said, "but Rabbi Cook-ha-Cohen does not speak to anyone other than the fourth-year students enrolled here. Perhaps I could find one of the other rabbis to answer your questions . . ."

"I think the rabbi might be interested in meeting me," I said. "I've been studying . . ."

"Rabbi Cook-ha-Cohen is the son of Rabbi Cook. Rabbi Cook was the head rabbi of Jerusalem. Our rabbi does not even receive heads of state."

"Would you just tell him that a doctor from Chile is here and would like to find out more about his preparations for the coming of the messiah?"

The man at the desk stared at me for a minute. With a raised eyebrow, he got up from his desk and said, "I will tell the rabbi you're here, but he won't have time to see you."

He trudged off down the hallway and through the double doors at the end. Two minutes later, he returned with his mouth hanging open a bit. "The rabbi will see you," he said as he motioned for me to go down to the room at the end of the hall.

When I entered the room, I made my way through a small, staring crowd of men about my age near the door. At the opposite end of the room on a raised platform sat a man in his late eighties. His peaceful and joyful gaze and long white beard reminded me of the descriptions I had read of the Bal Shemtov, the father of Hasidism.

When our eyes met, the elderly rabbi rose from his chair and embraced me. He looked into my eyes again and said, "Ahavah," the Hebrew word for love. He grabbed my hands and started dancing with me around the room singing the word "ahavah" over and over.

After a couple of minutes of this, the rabbi sat down in the chair again to catch his breath. One of his students who had been watching this unusual display came up to me and asked me in English, "The rabbi sleeps and eats and teaches in this room. He does not speak except to lead the prayers. How come he is so happy and dancing?"

"I don't know," I said honestly.

The rabbi called to one of his students and briefly said something to him that I couldn't hear. The rabbi beckoned me to come closer, so I did. He whispered something else to the young man, who then turned to me and said, "The rabbi says that he has something to teach that he is sure will benefit you." With this student translating into English, I heard the following from the rabbi:

"When a person sets his mind on something, its essence returns to him. Therefore, if you wish to pray or to grasp the true nature of an idea, do the following. Imagine that you yourself are light and that all of your surroundings on every side are also light. And in the middle of this light is a throne of light. Above the throne is a light called 'the Glow.' And facing this is another throne. Above the second throne is a light called 'the Good.' You are standing between the two. If you wish to take revenge, turn to the Glow. If you wish to seek mercy, turn to the Good. The words that you speak should be directed toward the light of mercy if you wish to heal.

"Now turn yourself to the right, and there you will find another light. And that's a brilliant, almost blinding light. To your left you will see another light called 'Zohar,' the radiant light. Above these two, between them, is a light called 'Glory.' And around it is a light called 'Chaim,' or life."

I remembered at just that moment the Hebrew name I'd been given as a young child was "Chaim."

"Above it," the student went on translating for the rabbi, "is the Crown. This is the light that crowns the desires of the mind and illuminates the path of the imagination, enhancing the Zohar, the radiance of the vision. This light has no end. It cannot be fathomed. From the glory of its perfection comes desire, blessing, peace, life and all good to those who keep the way of its unification.

"This light is hidden from those who stray from the path of this light and are transformed into its exact opposite. The true path is straight."

This is the first verse of the Koran, I thought. How unexpected to hear it coming from a Talmudic rabbi.

I suddenly remembered, several years before, lying in a field in Chile just after one of my drumming sessions with Don Eduardo, my shaman. The thrones of light Rabbi Cook-ha-Cohen had just described were in one of my visions at that time! I had chosen at that particular point to devote my life to service.

"Separate your soul from your body. Then your soul can be clothed in the thought that is contained in the words you pronounce, your prayer. You will then be able to perceive many universes on high.

"You have many powers. One acquired for one universe, and another for the next. When your soul ascends to all the worlds that you must elevate to, it is examined in each universe to see if it is fit to go higher.

The power of concentration is vital and total attention is needed. When an extraneous thought comes to you, that is a sign that you can be cast out, but if you are wise you can use that thought itself to bind yourself to God all the more.

"Your thought consists of ladders that are part of the divine presence's body, but they fell as a result of your incarnation. You must understand the idea that you can elevate the thought that falls into your mind. The thought comes from a divine universe: if it involves desire or lust, it has fallen from the universe of love; if it is a debilitating phobia, it is from the universe of fear; if it involves pride, it is from the universe of beauty. You must use the thought to enter the divine universe from which it came. The same is true of all other such thoughts; the attributes that can be used one way can also be transmuted into its opposite."

The metaphysical process of transmutation was becoming clear. I understood the importance of the power of not having remorse for the negative, but to instead transform it. This was just like what Otis Jefferson had told me when clearing the past: take all those negative traits that the little child, the inner child has inherited, and transmute them into the positive, into the attribute, into the virtue.

"The same ladder," said the Rabbi, reminding me of the Sufi mystic Rumi, "that you have used to leave this world is the ladder that you can use to enter another.

"It depends on the concentration of the individual. He must know how to concentrate on this truth with a combination of thought and desire derived from the real power. And according to the strength of his concentration, he will then transmit power through his desire, desire through his knowledge, imagination through his thoughts, strength through his effort, and fortitude into the infinite contemplation."

As Jonah drove me back to the airport in Tel Aviv the next morning, I described for him this meeting with Rabbi Cook-ha-Cohen. He listened quietly as he drove, responding only with nods of his head. When I had finished, he asked me, "Carlos, you have seen much of the Holy Land. Is there anything you think I missed?"

"No," I answered, "you have been a wonderful guide."

"You never told me what happened in Nazareth on Friday. What did you do for the three hours you were on your own?"

"I was just walking around," I said.

Jonah must have decided to let it pass because he didn't ask me further about what happened. I was relieved because I didn't feel like discussing it. Although I felt fairly comfortable with this Swiss bee expert, I wasn't sure how accepting he would be of what I encountered in Nazareth.

The Healing Journey: A Return

I said my goodbyes to Jonah at the airport in Tel Aviv. Several hours later I was changing planes in New York City on my way back to the Rockies. Though I didn't have much time between flights, I phoned my mother in Chile to tell her I was on this side of the Atlantic again.

"How are you doing?" I asked her.

I could hear her over the phone line taking a deep breath. "I have had a mastectomy, Carlos. They found cancer."

I was shocked. Only two weeks before I had been at the Wailing Wall in Jerusalem praying for my father's well-being and my mother's health. Now this. I explained that I only had a few minutes to change planes, but I would call her again from my next stop.

In Chicago, where I had one more change of planes to make, I had a little more time and called my mother back. She explained everything that had happened since I had spoken with her a month before. She had noticed pain in her left breast when she woke up in the mornings, so she went to our family doctor for an examination. They had found a tumor in the breast and, since at that time they did not do lumpectomies, they advised her to have the breast removed by mastectomy to keep the cancer from spreading to the rest of her body.

"I am sorry I told you the news so abruptly when you called a few hours ago," my mother said, "but I knew you had the strength of spirit to handle it."

Because of the seriousness of my mother's condition I decided that I would engage in no service other than easing her pain. The reminders I had while in Israel of my dedication to service made it easier for me to go back to the clinic in the Rockies and tell my colleagues I was leaving.

When I arrived in Santiago a couple of days later, both my parents met me at the airport. I hadn't seen them since we travelled to Rome together seven months earlier, when we took a wonderful driving tour through France, Switzerland, Austria and England. Now at the airport my father was smiling at me, but there was definitely pain in his expression as well. My mother was only 65, but she looked thinner and had aged considerably in half a year. I could see the pain in her face as well. We hugged and cried, and I felt a love between us that was broader than our mother-son roles. I was deeply saddened by my mother's disease. All her life she had been afraid of breast cancer and now this self-fulfilling prophecy had come to pass.

Over the next three months I lived with my parents and devoted the majority of my time to working with my mother. I applied the techniques of creative visualization I had learned to my mother's case because they had been successfully used with my patients to combat cancer. These techniques were based on the Tibetan model of visualization. I told her to imagine the "good" cells eating up the mutated, cancer cells. I had her imagine the best possible outcome for her life and keep all her actions focused on that goal. With my suggestion, she started keeping a daily journal. In her journal and in separate writing exercises, I asked her to write down dialogues between the negative, angry part of herself and the positive, life-enhancing part.

I found that she felt in some way that she had caused her illness, that she had allowed the cancer in, so we spent quite a bit of time talking about her feelings of shame. Somewhere in her consciousness she knew energy followed thought and matter followed energy, and that the manifestation of her disease at some level was self-created. But even so, I had to work with her to see whether there were other unknown factors involved. I knew that the easy New Age approach of, "You created it, you are responsible, you can cure it" was not the most appropriate one for my mother.

I showed her my model of medicine which had evolved along with my spirit. This model can be thought of as a four-tiered pyramid starting at a base of therapies that work at the same basice level of matter-energy: allopathic, naturopathic, homeopathic, acupuncture and energy medicine. The next tier is responsibility, which involves the mind. Then comes love, or the heart. Finally, at the pinnacle, is the soul. As one moves further up the pyramid the healing becomes stronger and more permanent.

The first level of healing utilized in treating my mother's cancer was allopathic medicine: she had surgery. She also used energy therapy, homeopathic medicine, acupuncture and faith-healing to alleviate the symptoms and the pain. The next step was to guide her through a phase of taking responsibility for her situation. From this she went to a third level of love, compassion and self-understanding. This kept the shame and the guilt that were associated with the causation, with the responsibility, from overburdening her in the emotional realm.

The next level was meditation: from love and understanding, there comes surrender, and it is only through surrender that one reaches one's soul identity. I applied the techniques of the Holy Names, of zhikrs and of prayer so there would be a complete understanding that no matter how much the disease was self-inflicted or biologically-inflicted, there was a higher level of surrender to the real identity which depended on God. This God-healing was what I was calling forward as the philosopher and physician Maimonides had taught.

Feelings of shame and guilt seemed to be part of my father's experience as well. He too felt there was something he could have done to keep his wife from getting sick, that there was something more he should be doing to make her feel better. He actually felt guilty about leaving for work every day because he thought he should be with her.

We talked on occasion about his feelings. The most difficult emotion for him to acknowledge was the anxiety produced by his belief that he was supposed to be in control and take care of his family because he was a man. He acted in a very integrated manly way of supporting my mother and opening up his own sensitivity. It was a very powerful example for me—seeing how strong he was and how easily he could give support and camaraderie. My mother and I both told him what a good husband and father he had been and how much love he had shown my mother and continued to show. He finally started to let my care and attention for his wife be enough.

I rarely stopped thinking of ways I could help my mother in her healing process. I occasionally took breaks from caring for her, though she remained ever on my mind. I would swim or lie in the sun at the beach or the nearby swimming pool. Otherwise, I never left my parents' house during this time.

Observing my mother during her healing process gave me solid proof that it was possible to create a process of recovering the sacred out of illness. In our society there's a great deal of sympathy for having a life-threatening illness, but there is not much support for finding meaning and growth in a positive direction from this experience. Yet there is no future in sympathy for the patient: there is no joy or satisfaction in it. Sympathy really serves to make those around the patient feel better. The experience and mindset of victimization has to be reversed or transcended by de-diagnosis, even if the diagnosis is accurate, in order to generate personal growth and personal renewal.

Seven years before my mother was diagnosed with cancer, I wrote my medical thesis in Chile on the pioneering field of psychoneuroimmunology. I had done research on a family of psychotics and observed that there was a direct relationship between immunoglobulin and the psychotic brain. My professors accepted this thesis 25 years ago because I had been a good medical student, not because I was a pioneer. The established doctors thought the way I was trying to combine basic sciences with clinical work was outrageous and therefore meaningless. But by the time my mother was sick, psycho-neuroimmunology was already gaining some measure of recognition—at least enough to get it out of the incubation stage and into diapers. It was very clear from the research being done during my mother's illness that a patient's attitude, sense of humor, social support, stress and emotions did effect the immune system and there was a relationship between these factors and cancer.

A partnership with mind, body and spirit was essential. Neither in medical school nor in the practicing world of high-technology medicine did I learn to consider spirit. But all my lessons learned with kabalists, Sufis and the shamans had considered spirit, so it was easy for me to affect a change in my mother's attitude about being sick in order to reduce stress. Social support did not just mean having people around, but having people in holy company. My mother needed people who would find ways to work from the vital identity by considering that she was a soul. The soul was not sick, the body had become sick. By establishing another perspective, by placing the illness in a higher context, the divine could be brought into the healing process.

Change must begin in ourselves. The path of our lives is something we dream of and create. It is the possibility of imagining something and having it become reality. Personal development is not the only work of the recovery of the sacred, nor is it the most important. The heart is most vigilant when it works to help all, especially when we crystallize our perceptions of why we are where we are in life. This involves directing our steps with optimism and vital force to create a brighter tomorrow.

This idea led me to create a nourishing circle similar to the healing circles I helped establish first in medical school and then in the Rockies. My mother needed a nourishing circle to come home to and heal in. To create this nourishing circle I knew we needed to develop relationships and situations that would not drain her and would not be toxic. Many times just going to the doctor's office for a visit would be very draining because it was like being on death row. I saw that personal relationships either give energy or take energy. Those which are emotionally supportive keep energy in motion. They help the person become hopeful and are thus nourishing.

I started educating my mother to select her friends from those people she knew who would not see her as a label. She needed people around her who would see her as a human with possibilities for growth and would love her accordingly, even if she had feelings that she hated.

One of these feelings was anger, which many people with cancer experience. The person holding on to anger is like a man grasping a hot coal and attempting to throw it at another person. The man holding onto the coal is the one getting burned. In my mother's recovery we made the distinction that feeling anger was normal but hating was not. The behaviors of anger were just concentrated energy that could be channelled for other purposes.

I was motivated by this idea over the next year because my mother and many other patients I worked with were able to remove their anxiety and channel it into service. Finding appropriate ways to express their needs and wants freed up this emotional energy for healing instead of wasting it on resentment or self-victimization. This opened the door to confronting fear of love and the fear of death, which are both activated when someone is diagnosed with a terminal disease.

When the floodgates of fear were released a reactivation of all basic fear patterns flowed out of the patient: fear of abandonment, which might have occurred as a child; fear of failing; fear of closed spaces; fear of the dark; fear of all the images of death. These fears had to be fully processed by the patient so she could make a conscious choice of love rather than fear. Working through these fears involved, once again, forgiveness. Only through the act of forgiving could meaning be created and life be reframed.

As Otis Lee Jefferson had shown me, forgiveness was basically for our own personal well-being. It was how we chose the direction of our life energy. This could be a powerful agent in the healing process: the realization that too much energy was wasted on resentment from the past. Though I was using this idea in treatment at that time, immunology is only now discovering that healing in one's emotional life can lead to healing of the physical and psychological.

We know that cancer puts the patient in a crisis situation, but is it completely devoid of positive outcomes? The Chinese word for crisis combines danger and opportunity. The danger of a disease is also an opportunity to shed one's old, empty identity and replace it with a full, clear identity. This is the soul identity which, when activated, is truly the higher power and the source of inner healing.

I also taught my mother silent meditation. I instructed her to reconnect with her essence, her soul, and through this reconnection she started to transform her experience and her shame toward the breast she was missing. This was a very painful experience for both of us. I told her that through reconnecting with her soul, she could rediscover the meaning and purpose in her life that I had found to be so miraculously healing in mine.

"How will I know when I have reached the proper state?" my mother asked as she sat cross-legged on the floor of the living room with me.

"In my travels and studies," I explained, "I've learned many techniques for reaching a state I call soul awareness. This type of meditation is just one. You'll know you've reached this state when you start observing the marks of soul awareness.

"One of the first signs is a sense of timelessness. When you are in a state of soul awareness, you focus on the now, the present, and it starts expanding, wiping out any preoccupations with the past or the future. You start losing your sense of time passing.

"Another mark of soul awareness is universal love. When you start to feel compassion and caring for all living beings, all animals, all plants, and even for the rocks, you've gone beyond the narrow bounds of your ego and expanded into the realm of the spirit.

"The longer you remain in that state of soul awareness, the more expansive your feeling of love for all things will become. This will result in a deep feeling of obligation to serve the world in some way, which is another signpost.

"As you remain in a state of soul awareness, ideas and concepts will reenter your mind. However, thoughts that seem at odds, contradictory thoughts will seem a very natural synthesis to you. Acceptance and comfortableness with paradox is another sign that you have reconnected with your soul," I said.

"What kind of paradoxes?" asked my mother.

"A common paradox that may float through your consciousness in this state will be the feeling of being alone, different and separate from the rest of humanity," I answered. "But you will also feel that it is this separateness, this uniqueness, that allows you to connect so deeply with the rest of humanity."

"So I'll have connected with what makes me different from every human being on earth, and not just my fingerprints," said my mother, nodding in understanding.

"Exactly," I said, "and the connection you eventually realize will be more than just a connection with humanity. Your feelings of love for all things and your desire to serve all things may expand yet further in this state. You will come to feel a part of all things. In soul awareness, you recognize that your love for and service toward other beings involves bridging some gap between who you are and who or what they are. Eventually, there will be no gap to cross.

"For the soul is not part of your body," I concluded. "It is part of the universe."

I taught my mother a meditation where she said, "I am not my body, I am not my mind, I am not my feelings. I have a body, I have a mind, I have feelings but I am that which I am."

Once my mother opened to this inner wisdom, the true healing began. This inner self is the ancient part of ourselves, the part that has evolved down through the ages. In all cultures—with the shamans, the Sufis, the Jews, the Christians, the Tibetans, you name it—this intuitive wisdom and love energy is accessed through meditation and through guided imagery. This technique is very important because it also reveals that the autonomic nervous system speaks in images. Our inner self does not speak in logical thought or words but in global images. It is through certain healing images that the immune system starts reactivating itself and allows us to love ourselves. Only by learning to love ourselves can we rise to the highest level of the healing pyramid: from the physical body to soul awareness.

One thing to keep in mind is that the healing model I used with my mother began with the physical. I was very much in agreement with whatever physical therapy needed to be done, be it radiation or chemotherapy. In her case she ended up having chemotherapy later, but she also had homeopathy and energy healing. The physical therapy enabled her to reach the level of taking responsibility, and then to move on to the level of self-love. More and more, she was able to live a life of loving herself, and she shared her newly discovered wisdom with others who were beginning to see disease and illness as a doorway to transformation. She was able to set goals, even small goals, which activated the heart of hearts. This heart of hearts allowed her to reach soul awareness.

Through this process there are a number of questions the patients can ask themselves, questions that the brain gets triggered to answer automatically. One such question is, "What am I the most happy about in my life now?" It's taken for granted that they are sick and depressed and have nothing to be happy about, but the truth is they all have something that makes them happy.

Patients must train themselves to ask the question "This thing I'm most happy about in my life, how does it make me feel?" The answer will be some variation on, "Well, I'm alive." Then the brain shifts its own mechanics, rejoicing in "aliveness."

I taught my mother to ask herself, "What about my life am I most proud of now? What about my life I most grateful for now?" My mother often said, "I am most grateful that my husband is alive." This shifted her attention to "Who do I love? Who loves me?" instead of "How are you feeling today?" a typical doctor's question.

When a doctor asks a patient, "How are you feeling today?" to someone who's already diagnosed, the patient doesn't have too much permission to feel well. But if the doctor asks the person, "What are you most grateful about in your life?" then the patient is not thinking of his or her illness. In the same sense a patient could start each day by asking the specific question, "What am I enjoying the most in my life? What have I achieved today?" Then maybe toward the end of the day she can learn to program for the nighttime by asking, "What have I given today? How have I made a contribution? What have I learned today? What has added to the quality of my life?" Those questions trigger or create a new frame of reference that definitely opens up a healing process.

Once my mother started to release some of her fear and shame about her illness, I took her to see an older woman whose name I had gotten from Don Eduardo. She was his teacher and a Machi (medicine woman), a shaman of the Mapuche Indians. Don Eduardo explained that she was a healer, counselor and judge for one of the Mapuche tribes just south of Santiago. The Mapuche Indians contact the spirits through their dreams and visions.

My mother and I arrived at the Machi's home on a ranch south of the city. The Machi, a dark-complected woman in her late sixties, was older than my mother with dark black hair streaked with gray. We entered the house, and she asked us to sit around her dining room table. She brought out a bundle of dried plants, lighting it with a match and smudging the room with smoke. Then she set the smudge stick in a bowl of water nearby and sat down at the table with us.

She seemed to enter a trance. After about five minutes she stated that she had made contact with the spirits, and they were not yet ready to receive my mother. "They give me instructions on what you must do. If you follow these instructions, you will live five more years. No, six more years." She paused. "More than six years. They do not say how long, but we know that life goes in cycles of seven years."

Over the next few weeks, I took my mother back to see the Machi several times. She gave me a list of herbs to give to my mother, and my mother agreed to take them instead of going through radiation treatments. She also gave my mother a new diet that relied heavily on wholesome meals, herb teas and juice drinks. The Machi led my mother through some rituals to help open her up. With dance and drumming and prayer, the Machi "opened up the tunnel of light," she said. I wondered what connection this had to the tunnel of light my grandfather had described to me in my childhood vision.

When my mother and I arrived home from visiting the Machi one night, my father took me aside and told me Maria, a friend of mine from medical school, had called from the hospital. He said it sounded urgent. I called Maria at the hospital.

"This is Dr. Carlos Warter," I told the hospital receptionist who answered the phone. "I'd like to speak to a physician working in the pathology department there. Her name is Maria Sanchez."

"Oh," the receptionist said, "I don't think Dr. Sanchez is in her office. I believe she's up in intensive care. I'll put you through to the nursing station on that floor."

When Maria finally answered the phone, somewhat breathless, she said quietly, "My mother tried to commit suicide again. Can you meet me here tonight?"

Without hesitation, I told her. "I'll be right over."

As I drove toward the hospital, I thought back to the various reports I had heard from Maria over the years about her elderly mother's three previous suicide attempts. Maria's father had already died, so Maria, the only daughter, felt a heavy burden to check daily on her mother's fragile emotional state.

When I got to the intensive care ward of the hospital, I asked the nurse at the desk to get Maria for me. Maria gave me a hug when she arrived. Her eyes were red with tears. "Come down here to the lounge for a few minutes," Maria said.

"My mother took an overdose of barbiturates," Maria explained as we sat on a couch in the visitors' lounge. "She was in a coma when I found her this afternoon. I'd just stopped by on my way home from the hospital like I do every day. My mother has back spasms, and it looks like she horded the pills her doctor prescribed, for a couple months at least. From the look of the empty bottles, she must have taken almost a hundred of them."

Maria broke down crying again. Through gasps of air she said, "We've always fought. Now I'm afraid she'll die thinking I hated her."

I volunteered to stay there with Maria that night. I talked to her about what I believed happened to a person's soul during a coma and then during death. The Machi I had visited that night told me about using a drum to call back the soul of an old man she said would not wake up. The old man was wandering the spirit world lost, she said, and the drumming helped lead him back to his body. I shared the story with Maria, and she asked if she thought we might be able to bring her mother out of her coma through drumming.

I went home and brought back a drum the Machi gave my mother to use in her meditations. Maria and I entered the room where her mother lay unconscious. She was hooked up to an oxygen tube and an EKG monitor beeped slowly with her heartbeat. I told Maria to take hold of her mother's hand. I sat in the bedside chair and placed the drum in my lap. I beat the drum slowly and began humming, and that turned spontaneously into the mantra I had just learned in Israel, "Ribbono Shel Olam," or Master of the Universe. I got into an emotional/spiritual trance state. I motioned for Maria to join me in the chant, and she did.

After about 45 minutes of this, Maria noticed her mother gripping her hand tighter. "Look!" she said.

The old woman's eyelids fluttering much as Carmen, the young catatonic woman, had years before when she came back to consciousness. "Try talking to her," I suggested.

"Mama," Maria whispered, "can you hear me?"

Her mother's eyelids fluttered again in response.

"Mama, it's Maria. You're here at the hospital. You took some pills. Do you remember?"

No response from her mother.

"Tell her you want her to talk to you," I whispered to Maria.

"I want to talk to you, Mama," Maria said. "Can you say something so I know you're hearing me?"

The old woman's mouth fell open slightly, and barely audible over the hiss of the oxygen coming into her nose through a tube, I could hear her say, "I hear."

It was at this point that I used everything that Otis Lee Jefferson taught me. Maria told her mother of all her regrets and fears. She apologized for not being more available to her mother, and she apologized for disagreeing with her mother's wishes. "I want you to know that I love you," she concluded, "and I don't want you to die."

A tear formed in the corner of one of her mother's eyes. She opened her eyes and looked at her daughter for the first time that night. "I love you, too, daughter," she said. "But it's my time to go now."

I left mother and daughter there to finish their reconciliation. I waved to Maria as I left the room and told her I'd check on her in the morning.

I got a call from Maria around ten the next morning. Her mother had passed away earlier that morning but she was content because they had one last chance to talk. She said some cousins were helping her organize a memorial service in four days, and she asked me if I would speak at it. I said I would be honored to speak at the service.

At the memorial service I spoke about the immortality of the soul and how I believed it was reborn elsewhere when one body dies. I later shared the story of another patient I had treated in Chile with those gathered at the service. The woman was named Lourdes and came to see me suffering anxiety attacks because doctors had discovered her eight-year-old son Rudy had a brain tumor. He was being treated in the neurosurgery department of the same hospital where I was seeing Lourdes. I knew this was a real case of anxiety because it was a natural response brought on by her bankruptcy and the neurosurgeon's admission that there was little hope for her son.

One day Lourdes' son Rudy asked for a piece of paper and a pen. When these things were brought to him, he went to work writing on the paper. When he finished, Lourdes looked to see what he had written and saw that he had been signing the signature of his great-grandfather, her grandfather, Don Jose Joaquin Varela. The signature was written in a handwriting with a lot of flourishes—one from the last century, a kind of calligraphic handwriting.

The boy was very sick and went into and out of a coma state when he fell asleep. He was kept in the hospital and not allowed to go home. One day he came out of the coma, sat up and said, "You must go to the notary public in Vina Del Mar where I left some papers signed there. These papers will give you back the land I owned."

Lourdes did not know what to do when she heard this so she asked me to examine her son. I interviewed the boy and observed his behavior. The child went into trance-states, which according to the neurosurgeon were hallucinations or delusions caused by his brain condition. Lourdes did not believe these were hallucinations and, after observing the boy, neither did I. Instead of accepting the neurosurgeon's evaluation, we followed the instructions the boy had given his mother. We went to Vina Del Mar, a city on the Chilean coast, and saw an old notary public who had papers from the beginning of the century, specifically from the twenties when her grandfather was alive. The papers showed there was a piece of land that the family had not lost. Shortly after she gained backed her piece of land, her child Rudy died.

We were left to wonder, what exactly had happened? Was it the grandfather being channelled and speaking through the boy? Was the boy the reincarnation of the grandfather? Or was it what the neuro-surgeon claimed, hallucination and delusion? We never found out, but there was no question that the information given by the boy was accurate and it saved Lourdes from even more grief and despair.

Evidently the audience, quite a number of whom were friends from my days in medical school and residency, were inspired by the talk. They came up to me afterward and asked what had happened to bring me such peace and tranquility in the seven years since I had seen them last.

The crowd of about a dozen friends and acquaintances stood around me waiting for my reply. I thought about briefly telling them of my travels as I had so many times before, but instead I remembered the call I felt toward service and said to them, "I just got back from 18 days in Israel a few months ago. I'm about to go on a little vacation to the south of Chile next week. Put together a group of 18 people and when I return I'll teach you what I have learned that brings me tranquility."

Epilogue

The vacation was taken at my mother and father's insistence. As a break from my caregiving responsibilities, I went down to Lake Puyehue, a lake in the Andes just east of Osorno, Chile. I stayed at an inn on the south side of the lake. Looking across the water, I had a breathtaking view of a huge volcano. I took a few sheets of paper from my bag and, little by little over the next few days, wrote down an outline of what I would teach when I returned to Santiago.

While I was at Lake Puyehue, I told the story of my encounter with Jesus to another tourist at the inn. The woman was a charismatic Catholic and she took me to a mass of people speaking in tongues. This mass invoked for me the trance-like situation I had experienced during my trip in Israel when I was wearing the robes and I felt that I had lived 2,000 years ago. I could see the synthesis of Judaism, Christianity and Islam in the same room, and also the other spiritual traditions that pointed to this radical unity and of the process of life and death. It was giving birth to a new cycle. Death was a part of life and life was a part of death, though our culture had forgotten that, remembering the Bardo process of the Tibetans.

The program I devised at Lake Puyehue and gave for a group of 18 the weekend after coming back, became the basis for teachings and workshops I shared with tens of thousands all over the world during the next seven years.

The healing process I engaged in with my mother allowed her to live another seven years. Love was the most fundamental quality in her healing. It was genuine love given of my own free will and not something that could be taken for granted. It was not assigned as a task because, like learning, it is boring and insignificant if one is forced to love. Loving has to be chosen deliberately. The possibility of choosing to love is what makes our free will worth the risk. When we use our freedom properly and choose to love, then love becomes tremendously meaningful. When it comes from our deepest essence, the source of all our freedom, then we can feel true love. This love was similar to the love therapy I awakened to in my first years as a physician. There is a physiology of love. It is not just an emotional experience, but a whole soul experience. Love is the golden thread that unites all the forms of healing. This can be a very abstract concept, so we need to see it in a very practical way.

It is really affection, expression and helping people to get back on the path of their own lives. Each of us seems to be born with a blueprint that turns us into a specific person: intellectual, spiritual, psychological. When we have the opportunity to serve those with illnesses, we allow them to care for themselves once again. The inner resources of love are awakened when you facilitate them to live their own message and when you tell them the inspiration of other courageous patients. The therapeutic process becomes very important when patients realize that they're mortal. The awareness brings with it the desire to make the most out of life in the present moment, to reconnect it with the original now meditation and experience the completeness of life at each particular stage.

Serving my mother in those years allowed me the privilege of integrating my spiritual learning into the healing process. The healing that took place was empowerment: not overpowering the illness but empowering the soul. I gave my power away freely in order to bring my mother back from cancer; and in the process she was able to bring forth her own soul awareness and was educated by the self-knowledge of her soul.

Wholeness or health is our natural state: the nature of my mother's healing involved moving the obstructions that psychologically or spiritually reduced this natural state, allowing her to come back into her world. The life force came back and the whole system of life allowed her to live these last years with an improved quality of living that was guided by self-discovery and the recovery of the sacredness in her own life. Thus illness in her case, and death in the case of Maria's mother, was an opportunity for healing.

These events took place many years back on the spiritual path I have followed. I call it a path and not a career because it is not leading to any goal I have placed at the end, but wandering where it will and presenting many wonderful and beautiful surprises along the way. The opportunity to heal my mother depended more on the quality of the relationship than on the time spent or the technique: this transformed the process from curing to healing. From the joining of hearts and minds comes the realization that both son and mother, doctor and patient, are one in our suffering. When embracing the essence of this relationship both healer and patient explore the depths of their experiences and their resources. It is through this unity that both can be healed.

A positive, dedicated, life-affirming attitude is the key to the healing process. A healing attitude, therefore, is not superficial. It involves, "physician, heal thyself." A deep inner knowledge that we're not victims of the world, nor of karma, nor circumstances. We have the authority to respond to adversity any way we choose. By taking responsibility for our source, for our health and for our entire life we gain a mastery in any circumstance.

Healing goes far beyond the confines of the physical body. It occurs as we tap into our own inner resources instead of looking for external intervention. Meditation and a quiet mind; prayer and a hopeful mind: these change human physiology. With intention, attention and practice we can learn to control our minds. With this control we can find the deepest kind of healing, which is victory over suffering. By opening the intuitive heart to soul awareness humankind can recover the sacred and go beyond the search for the meaning of disease or healing, to the search for meaning and purpose in life.

My life has already gone on for many years since the events described in this book, and I have experienced further developments on the path to soul awareness. Because of this, and to prevent you the reader from being left with an incomplete feeling of resolution, I will fill in what happened to the various characters in this book as time passed.

For several years after she moved back to Europe, I didn't have much contact with Françoise , the woman who started me on my quest for greater soul awareness. After 12 years, I was in Santiago, Chile again and a telephone book fell off a table near me. Remembering Clarisse's advice about such circumstances, I stepped back and observed. The book fell open to a page on which I noticed the name of one of Françoise's cousins who was still living in town. I gave her a call and she told me that Françoise had divorced and remarried and moved to New York City. When I was in New York for a conference about seven months later, I looked her up and met with her, and we have kept in close contact as friends for many years since then.

I did not encounter Don Eduardo again. After he gave me the referral to the Machi that helped me care for my mother, I heard he had moved to the rain forests of Brazil to work with native peoples who used ayahuasca in their visionary rituals.

I ran into Horst, the leader of the Sufi tariqa group, several times over the years. He seemed quite contented to serve as an initiator of new spiritual seekers from then on and did not continue his own studies.

In 1984 I was in Mexico City for an international health congress and called Don Hector again. Under his direction, I went through a second initiation at Teotihuacan and at Machu Picchu even more amazing than the first.

The sheik who supported the zawya Habibya community in Meknes, Morocco died several years later. After 17 years away, I returned to Meknes to pay my respects to the sheik's tomb in a corner of the zawya. The blind man was still there, now the caretaker of the tomb, and recognized me by smell—nearly two decades after we'd first met—before I could reintroduce myself. He helped put me in touch with a secret religious order dating back to Richard the Lion-Heart and the Middle Ages.

Mr. Idries Shah and I parted company without any plans to meet again, except that he promised to check up on me in seven years. I had already been touring the world giving workshops and receiving international awards for the humanitarian agencies I founded, when one day I received a letter postmarked from England. It had been seven years to the day after I left Langton House. Shah was sending me Sufi stories to analyze and report on again, just as he had at the beginning of my initiation.

I met with Jonah on my second trip to Israel seven years later. This time I went with my mother and together we went back to that alley in Nazareth where I had seen the white-robed figure. The woman who had ordered me away remembered me from seven years before and this time welcomed me and my mother into her home. She also took us to some caverns beneath her home and showed us a secret she and her family had kept for nearly 2,000 years.

The workshop I developed while at Lake Puyehue became the basis of workshops and lectures I gave mostly in Chile, Colombia, Venezuela, Uruguay, Argentina, India and Spain. For over seven years I traveled between these seven countries teaching 40 weeks out of the year. I also completed several more books, started study groups, worked with police, governments, orphanages and artists on bringing more soul awareness into their work, and taught medical students the importance and the intricacies of the doctor-patient relationship.

I developed a network of programs that extended to seven countries called "A Drop of Honey." When a disaster occurred, there was often an outpouring of generosity toward the victims but there was generally no agency in place to get the right supplies to the people who needed them. The volunteers in "A Drop of Honey" found ways to get these material goods to orphanages, nursing homes, hospitals and prisons by accepting donations from individuals and businesses and trading our surplus for other supplies that were needed. But our work did not stop there.

When we arrived at these places we did more than just drop off supplies. So often victims of circumstance become attached to what has happened to them. They identify with the events of their Small Story and cannot see themselves in any other way. Through interaction with these individuals, we activated their soul knowledge and allowed them to gain a new perspective on themselves: they stopped identifying with their current position and its third dimensional expression. We were able to reach people we would not have otherwise had contact with, and help them align with their soul identity. I remember a particular boy who said to me, "I am a spiritual human being, not an orphan. One day I will have a family, but today and every day I have God with me. He will guide me and protect me."

This program was an example of responsible living. We were able to apply our words of intent and see them manifest. We may have been but a pebble of love dropped in a lake of suffering, but we caused a ripple effect to happen: a shift of light. Each "Drop of Honey" facilitated a pearl of light that imploded and detonated into soul awareness producing the growth of self-confidence, self-love and service to others.

The moments in your life are leading you on a journey. Your life is not made up of random events with no connection to each other. You are on a path, and even if you currently find the path unfulfilling because it was dictated by your family or by cultural messages before you were aware of other choices, you must know that ultimately it is your essence that determines where your path leads.

When I teach people how to discover the meaning in their lives, how to find out why they came into existence at this time and place, I try to show the difference between what I call "the Small Story" and "the Big Story." The Small Story is what too many people think of as their lives. It includes personal likes and dislikes, jobs, possessions, vacations, births, deaths and even the lucky and unlucky events of one's life.

The Small Story is the tale told by your ego, the part of you that identifies with your physical body, your name, your age, your citizenship, your profession, your personality. We often invest more of ourselves in the Small Story because its subjects—other people and things—are finite objects we can examine and observe again and again. They are measurable, factual and make us feel secure. The Small Story is that part of existence which is rooted in the third dimension, including the events that happen each day.

The Small Story is an illusion. It is impermanent and limited. It creates artificial boundaries through perception of the material world.

Because it is based on appearance more than anything it is the source of self-deception. It is also the source of suffering: when we identify with who and what we are in third dimensional reality we separate ourselves from the soul.

Sometimes we as humans search for some sense of purpose or connection through fantasies and intrigues. If the meaning or direction of our life seems missing, we tend to create a mental framework on which the events and actions of our lives fit. But in the Small Story, events or thoughts occur that don't seem to fit the original framework we created. We are forced to ignore the piece of the puzzle that doesn't fit or start building a new picture of ourselves and our lives into which it will fit. Either way, this is no casual undertaking. The ego sees the crises involving these pieces that don't fit, sometimes called cognitive dissonance, as a sort of death—the death of the old personality or life-concept. Because the ego sees them as threatening we tend to opt for ignoring the pieces that don't fit.

The Big Story is completely different from this Small Story: it's the tale told by your soul. Many people find it difficult to trust in the Big Story because each person must verify their own role within it. There is no one else to point the way for us, to tell us what our purpose is. Without this personal verification, people are uncomfortable and inexperienced with their soul and have little idea how to progress. The clues to the meaning of their Big Story seem vague or ambiguous. In Western culture we depend too heavily on our five senses because they aid in survival. By doing so we neglect our intuition, the sense that leads us toward fulfillment, joy and completion in our lives.

Each of us has a divine mission or function. Each of us has a role to play in the Big Story, our natural role, the one we were born for. It is our part in the unity of consciousness, in all beingness. But we can only discover what our mission is by embracing the "I am", by reconnecting with our souls.

The Small Story allows only glimpses of the divine presence through physical experience. When we embrace the Big Story, when we follow our sacred paths, every moment is filled with the full radiant expression of the divine. The antidote for the suffering we encounter in the Small Story is forgiveness, love, compassion and grace to ourselves and others. I learned this through Otis, through the Esalen Institute, through my many teachers. But the important thing to remember is that the technique employed does not matter as much as the attention to the soul. The different techniques I explore in this book are ways to move from third dimensional reality to true reality based on the sacred, but they are not the only ways. The focus must never be on the process, but instead must be concentrated on unlocking the mystery that exists in each of us.

This book does not cover the entire Small Story of my life, nor is my story finished. I have continued to live my Small Story, and I have continued to learn about The Big Story we all share. There are many amazing events and meetings that made my life purpose clearer: working for social issues worldwide and establishing the World Health Foundation for Development and Peace; finding my soulmate; the death of my parents and birth of my children; encounters with higher beings; working as a therapist with multiple situations and learning about other dimensional beings who are influencing earthly lives; meeting world political and religious leaders, including Jimmy Carter, Mikhail Gorbachev, Pope John Paul II and the Dalai Lama; playing a role in the expansion of peace on our planet; and coincidences and introductions to people in all areas of public life. I was present in Jerusalem as peace began creeping into the Middle East with the first historic meeting of Golda Meir and Anwar Sadat, the nations of Israel and Egypt. I was invited to Jimmy Carter's inauguration and felt the energy of his role in establishing lasting peace between these countries. I was present in Poland and the Soviet Union as these two countries that had known decades of oppression struggled to be free.

I have seen things I never could have imagined. I've gone through secret initiations in Egypt and India; journeyed to secret sites in Peru and Bolivia, received ancient messages on Mt. Shasta; come in contact with the White Brotherhood and the guidance of angels: participated in sacred retreats in the desert; treated alien abductees in therapy; been a consultant for the White House Institue of Peace; and mediated as part of Central American conflict resolution.

But these events and the insights revealed will have to wait for my next book.

The Big Story behind the events of this book showed me the commonalities of man's religions. The ideology and the forms of the rituals may change, but the essence is the same, and that is the soul. Sickness has an open door when an individual or society loses awareness of his or her essential essence: the soul is the key to the functioning of the entire human system. Even if the body has decayed or been damaged to such an extent that it can not be repaired, the soul can still heal, reconnecting the individual to his own essence which is where true healing lies. Disease and social chaos present themselves as an opportunities for transformation once an individual returns to his essence. The soul has a wisdom that at times we cannot fathom with our conscious minds, and yet its wisdom is somehow known to us. We are meant to keep growing well into adulthood through the expansion and realization of our essential selves, and service to others and knowledge of oneself is the surest route to this personal evolution.

We live in a time of great change, a time of a political and social paradigm shift. We live in a critical period of human history. The outcome of our thoughts and actions will determine the fate of life on our planet. As more and more people experience their own personal evolution, the planet is entering a time of spiritual sovereignty. Not only will we acknowledge and follow our individual soul, we will move to a state where we acknowledge that our soul is a global soul, that it is a galactic soul, that it extends and connects us to all other life in our universe. We are not just citizens of our community, we are citizens of our universe.

This unity of soul will allow us to turn and face the radiance of the sacred. We will go beyond human potential and attain our divine potential. When we realize this we can fulfill our true purpose and fulfill the destiny of our planet. We will become the true custodians of our world and not barbarian invaders that need to destroy all that they see. The world will awaken to the power of love and will realize that love is truly the path to all understanding. This is what each of us as individuals needs, and it is what the planet as a whole must have to survive.

This book is part one of the story of my spiritual adventure. It is the story of a man who pursued his essence in order to find the path he was destined to travel. As Otis helped me to reconnect with my guardian angel, I hope in some small measure I have helped you reconnect with the spirit and with your own essence. Humankind is rising to a new level of freedom: we are entering a time of angelic ethics when individuals will not rely solely on themselves but will seek and receive the guidance of angels and other higher beings. I hope my journey will act as an invitation to you: it will open you to the existence we share and be an example of the possibilities that await us all.

Traditionally, each individual in a culture was responsible for his own soul. The shaman could help to heal the individual—he helped men and women find their way back to their essence—but his real responsibility was for the soul of the community: it was his vocation to establish a relationship between the soul of each individual and the community, and to establish a connection between the community and the entire planet. I have pursued this role with my life, and will continue to pursue it until we live in a world where the sacred has been recovered and we all share the blessing of soul awareness and a completely spiritual culture on earth.

About the Author

Dr. Carlos Warter, M.D., specialized in psychiatry, has a Ph.D. in psychology and is licensed to practice medicine in Chile and the United States. He is a psychotherapist, author and public speaker. He has been the president of the World Health Foundation for Development and Peace since 1985, and is the vice president of the External Degree Program at the International University at Hawaii.

Among other awards, Dr. Warter has been distinguished with the United Nations Peace Messenger in 1987, the Pax Mundi Award by the Dag Hammarskjold Diplomatic Academy in 1989, and Knight Commander and Grand Cross to the Knights of the Sovereign Order of Saint John of Jerusalem in 1992. He has written over fifteen books in English and Spanish, including *The Ebb and Flow of Living*, *Despertar* (Awakening), and *Soul Remembers*. He has served as a keynote speaker at a large number of consciousness, academic and scientific meetings in recent years.

Born in 1947 in Chile of Austrian parents, Dr. Warter is married to Carolina Penna de Warter who is a sculptress of Italian-Argentinean origin. They live with their three children—Alexandra, Charles and David-Gabriel—in Sedona, Arizona.

Dr. Warter travels extensively to promote public service and the preservation of human development through focusing on essential values. The source of his approach to Inner Work is similar to all genuine schools of work throughout history. His unique integration of ancient knowledge and personal essence is developed in the context of contemporary psychological and spiritual teaching. This unique synthesis, under the coined name psychosynergy—synergy of the mind and soul—is presented around the country and the world in retreats, seminars, lectures and ongoing study groups which integrate the major aspects of psychological and spiritual work.

Dr. Warter believes global planetary synergy can be accomplished through a transpersonal culture of democracy and peace. He has developed a new approach for the awakening of human potential based on the essential values of ethics, creativity and a sense of belonging to a global community. He has conducted research on consciousness, and through the use of essential values has developed a method of individual and social healing in which he trains groups within a community who then reach the larger community. He has trained over seventy thousand individuals from all walks of life during the past two decades. Results have ranged from enhanced personal awareness and increased immunity, to emotional well-being and improved relations within families, businesses and administration.

Dr. Warter is interested in your reactions and responses to this book and in assisting you in your own development. The author is available to lecture, initiate study groups and develop retreats in which his unique focus is presented. Frequently his study groups participate in retreats at sacred places around the planet with specific attention given to initiations and healings indigenous to the locale. University credits for life experience and inner development work are available for participants in Dr. Warter's groups.

Proposals, scheduling inquiries, event information and letters can be sent to:

Dr. Carlos Warter
c/o Health Communications, Inc.
3201 SW 15th Street
Deerfield Beach, FL 33442-8190